How to Do *Everything* with Your

iPAQ Pocket PC

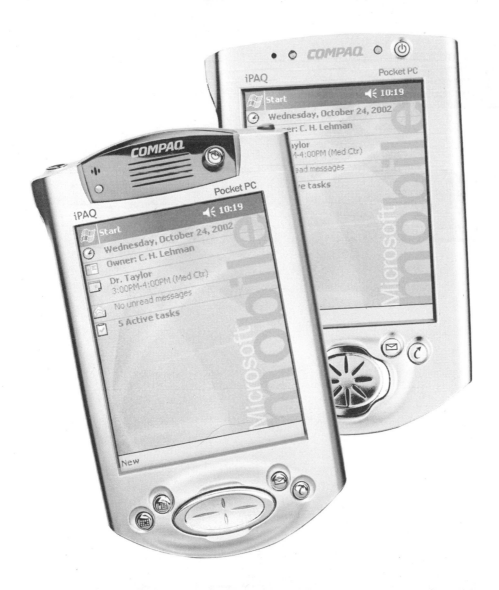

How to Do *Everything* with Your

iPAQ Pocket PC

Derek Ball
Barry Shilmover

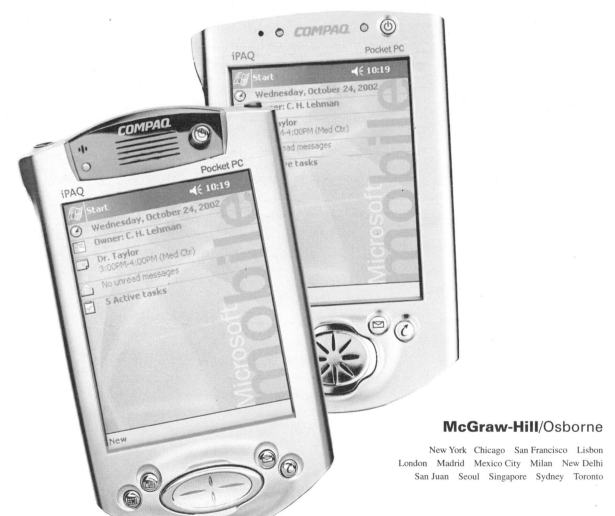

McGraw-Hill/Osborne

New York   Chicago   San Francisco   Lisbon
London   Madrid   Mexico City   Milan   New Delhi
San Juan   Seoul   Singapore   Sydney   Toronto

McGraw-Hill/Osborne
2600 Tenth Street
Berkeley, California 94710
U.S.A.

To arrange bulk purchase discounts for sales promotions, premiums, or fund-raisers, please contact
McGraw-Hill/Osborne at the above address. For information on translations or book distributors
outside the U.S.A., please see the International Contact Information page immediately following the
index of this book.

How to Do Everything with Your iPAQ Pocket PC

4567890 CUS CUS 0198765432

ISBN 0-07-222333-2

Publisher	**Freelance Project Manager**	**Indexer**
Brandon A. Nordin	Laurie Stewart	Jack Lewis
Vice President & Associate Publisher	**Acquisitions Coordinator**	**Computer Designer**
Scott Rogers	Tana Diminyatz	Kate Kaminski, Happenstance Type-O-Rama
	Technical Reviewer	
Acquisitions Editor	Jason Dunn	**Series Design**
Megg Morin		Mickey Galicia
	Copy Editor	
Project Manager	Erin Milnes	**Cover Design**
Jenn Tust		Dodie Shoemaker
	Proofreader	
	Kelly Marshall	

This book was composed with Quark XPress 4.11 on a Macintosh G4.

Dedication

For "my girls" who support and encourage me
through every crazy project I pursue. Thanks for
riding the roller coaster with me!

—Derek

To my family. Thanks for everything.
Thanks for understanding when I had deadlines.
For giving up your weekends with "Daddy" so that
I could try to meet my deadlines. For putting up
with the late nights. Thanks. I could not have
done it without your support!

—Barry

About the Authors

Derek Ball is President and CEO of Sonic Mobility, Inc. (**www.sonicmobility.com**), a company focused on delivering solutions for handheld wireless devices such as the Compaq iPAQ. Derek has published seven other books on technology topics and has traveled the world speaking at conferences and seminars on emerging technology. In between trips, Derek lives in Calgary with his wife, Lesley, daughters Jamie and Carly, and golden retriever, Casey.

Barry Shilmover is the Chief Technical Evangelist for Sonic Mobility, Inc. Barry has published many books on system administration, network management, security, and mobile computing topics. Barry is an MCSE and has worked for many well-known technology companies including Microsoft. When not traveling throughout North America speaking and training, Barry lives in Calgary with his wife, Shawna, and two boys, Jory and Conor.

About the Technical Reviewer

Jason Dunn is the Executive Editor of Pocket PC Thoughts, one of the most popular sources of information on the Internet for the Pocket PC community. He's also been a Mobile Devices Microsoft MVP since 1997, volunteering his time to help others with their Pocket PCs. When he's not using his Pocket PC, he runs a technology company (**www.kensai.com**) that specializes in new media communications.

Contents at a Glance

Contents

Acknowledgments

Writers are a strange lot. Technical writers perhaps even more so. We have had the tremendous opportunity (curse?) to embark upon several book projects in the past. However, as is typical with "selective memory," we often forget what a monumental effort it actually takes to complete a book, not only on the part of the authors, but of all the other people who are involved in the project and without whom no book would ever see the light of the sun through the book store window.

There are a great many people we would like to thank, but thanks hardly seem to be enough. Megg Morin at McGraw-Hill/Osborne has been amazing. From the initial book proposal through the writing, editing, and delivering of all the elements of the book, Megg had to deal with the ins and outs and ups and downs of these two crazy authors. She relentlessly pursued every detail. For all of your support, encouragement, and on occasion "stronger" motivation, we want to pass along our deepest gratitude.

A few other people directly involved in the editing and production of the book are Tana Diminyatz, Laurie Stewart, Erin Milnes, Kate Kaminski, and Kelly Marshall. Between the two of us, we have written many books in the past, and never have we had the pleasure of working with an editorial and production team of the caliber that we had on this book. Thank you all!

Our technical reviewer, Jason Dunn, has helped us to make sure our information is as accurate and up-to-date as possible. He was invaluable in validating and correcting our information. Thank you, Jason, for helping to ensure the quality of this book, and for pitching in to help with the product information.

Special thanks are due to several folks at Compaq Computer, Inc., who helped secure the images and permissions for the product images for this book's cover. Specifically, thanks go out to Mary Callahan, Alicia Green, Michelle Waybright, and Rhonda Hetman.

There are many other individuals behind the scenes involved in the production of the book whose names we may not know, but whose contribution to delivering this book into your hands is no less significant. Your efforts are also appreciated.

And finally to our families, who have put up with late nights and family activities where Dad couldn't go, for encouraging and supporting us through this process. Your love and support made all of this possible. Our deepest gratitude and love.

Introduction

When Compaq introduced the iPAQ Pocket PC to the world, it began a revolution that saw the pendulum of the existing PDA market begin to swing from the heavily Palm-oriented world to that of the Microsoft Pocket PC. To date, more than 1.4 million iPAQ Pocket PCs have been shipped, and they are selling more every day.

This remarkable device contains so much power that mobile individuals could now do things never before possible with a PDA. Beyond simple contact and calendar management, now people could send and receive e-mail, write MS Word documents, build spreadsheets, make presentations, surf the Internet, and so much more, all from a device that you could slip into a pocket.

The iPAQ Pocket PC has gone through several iterations of development, becoming more powerful and flexible with each release. The recent merger of Hewlett Packard with Compaq is rumored to be producing the next generation of the iPAQ Pocket PC as a converged iPAQ/Jornada device (maybe they will call it the iNada?). The future of the iPAQ will be very interesting as more and more people are adopting this device and integrating it into their mobile lifestyles.

Who Should Read This Book

This book is intended for all iPAQ Pocket PC owners. We specify "iPAQ Pocket PCs" here because Compaq makes an entire line of computers and devices that are called "iPAQs" (the entire family is described in Part I of this book).

This book specifically covers the iPAQ Pocket PCs. If you're a new iPAQ Pocket PC owner, this book will help you understand how to get started using your new iPAQ Pocket PC properly. For the owner who has had an iPAQ Pocket PC for a while, this book will help you understand how to get more out of your investment.

Whatever your level of experience with the iPAQ Pocket PC, you will find relevant information in this book to do things with your iPAQ Pocket PC that you haven't done before.

You can follow along with the information in this book as it walks you through using built-in applications such as Pocket Word and Pocket Excel. In other sections of the book you will find opportunities to read about the potential of the iPAQ Pocket PC and future devices, and perhaps you will choose to integrate GPS or wireless connectivity into your mobility.

How This Book Is Organized

We have organized this book in sections to enable you to jump right into the area that is most relevant to you. Part I, "Meet Your iPAQ Pocket PC and Software That Comes with It," introduces you to the basic setup of your iPAQ and also explains how to use the powerful built-in software that comes with it. You will learn how to use office productivity tools such as Pocket Word, Pocket Excel and Pocket Outlook.

Part II, "Optimize Your iPAQ Pocket PC for Maximum Productivity," switches the focus to more advanced topics such as device security, performing mobile presentations, connecting to wireless networks, and using Global Positioning Systems for personal navigation. Part III, "Select Hardware and Accessories for Your iPAQ Pocket PC," shows you what kind of external devices you can use to expand the functionality of your iPAQ and how to use the myriad third-party products designed to increase the storage of your iPAQ Pocket PC, turn your iPAQ Pocket PC into a digital camera, enable your iPAQ Pocket PC to function as a mobile medical tool, and more. The appendices of the book are there to help you troubleshoot some common problems with the iPAQ Pocket PC, as well as point you to other resources that you might want to investigate for more information on your device.

As you read through the text, you'll see we've included sidebars for points of specific interest, so watch for the sections labeled How To, Did You Know?, Caution, Note, and Tip for special information about the section you are currently reading.

We hope that you will find this book helpful as you learn to live the mobile iPAQ Pocket PC lifestyle! We use our iPAQ Pocket PCs on a daily basis, and they have almost become an extension of our arm. Our most critical information is never more than a moment away, and we can consolidate many disparate information sources into one location. Your iPAQ Pocket PC can become as important a productivity tool as it is for us. We use them to find our way around foreign cities when we travel, give presentations while on the road, wirelessly stay connected to the office to manage our infrastructure and data, send and receive e-mail, and so much more!

If you would like to contact the authors, or have other questions about your iPAQ Pocket PC, please contact us through our website at **www.pocketpctools.com**. On this website we will address any questions that we receive from our readers as well as post updated information on new iPAQ Pocket PC accessories, software, tips, and news.

Part I

Meet Your iPAQ Pocket PC and the Software that Comes with It

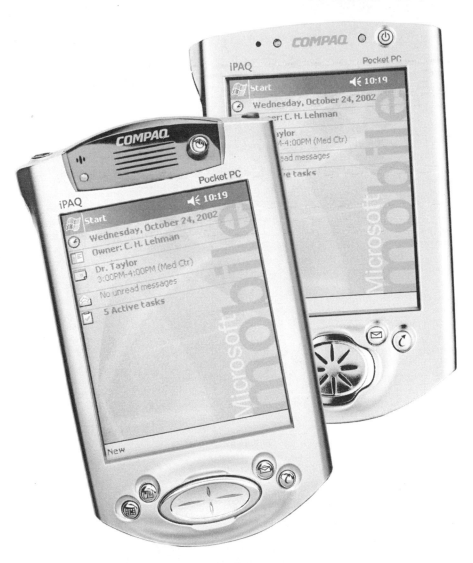

Chapter 1

Meet Your Pocket PC

How to...

- ■ Tell one iPAQ from another
- ■ Live the mobile lifestyle

Ever since we human beings learned to store information somewhere other than in our heads, we have been working on ways to not only make permanent records of our information, but also ways to take those records with us, wherever we go. Over many millennia, this pursuit has taken us from crude paintings on cave walls, to hieroglyphics on stone tablets, to papyrus, to the printing press, to the day planner, and now to the personal digital assistant (PDA).

Now we are no longer satisfied to simply carry our information with us. We are pushing for a new era of portable information. We want our PDAs to do even more than was even hinted at by early science fiction writers and television shows like "Star Trek." More than ever we want our devices to become an extension of ourselves, to function as a personal secretary, travel agent, guide, doctor, communicator, and entertainment device.

Leaping into the raging river of this opportunity is the Compaq iPAQ family of devices, and the overwhelmingly popular Compaq iPAQ Pocket PC. With its sleek retro styling, powerful Intel StrongARM processor, abundant memory, and ultra bright and clear touch screen, this device sports an adoption rate second to none. In its early days it was hard to find an iPAQ on store shelves, although increased production has made them much easier to come by today.

It used to be that carrying a PDA was more of a status symbol than a truly practical tool, but that is changing as they become as ubiquitous as cellular phones. With the recent release of Pocket PC 2002, we see that we are getting closer and closer to the handheld PDA as an extension of ourselves.

The History of Pocket PC and Windows CE

Many years ago, Microsoft realized they would need to develop a lightweight operating system for non-PC devices. Without a clear picture of the kind of device that would use the new OS, it was difficult for Microsoft to move forward. At the time, there was a great deal of prognosticating by futurists as to the impact of multimedia on our culture. This resulted in one group at Microsoft wanting to push Windows CE to become heavily multimedia oriented for use in television set–top boxes. A different group wanted to strip NT down to its bare bones and use that as the new Windows CE operating system.

In an attempt to bring some unity of vision to this space, Microsoft brought all these groups together in 1994 under the direction of senior vice president Brad Silverberg. This team realized that what was really needed was a new operating system, one that would be compatible with the existing and future Windows operating systems, but would not necessarily just be a subset of them. This resulted in the development of Windows CE version 1.0, which appeared on the market in late 1996.

The team knew that if they were going to be successful in building a new operating system, it was critical that users not "feel" they were using a new OS. This meant that the user interface had to mirror the already popular Windows 95 and use a similar desktop of icons as well as the start menu toolbar at the bottom of the screen.

The devices of this time were called handheld personal computers, or HPCs for short. They were extremely limited in capacity with very little memory (usually 4MB or less), a small, grayscale screen, and a very limited processor that ran between 33 to 44 MHz.

The limited power and storage capacity led to very limited adoption of the initial Windows CE device, except among the most hardy computer enthusiasts. The average business user instead tended to adopt the more portable competitor to the Windows CE platform, the Palm OS devices, such as the well-known Palm Pilot from 3Com and the Visor from Handspring.

The next generation of the CE platform was version 2.0, which came out in 1998. The devices that ran this operating system generally had double the CPU power and RAM of the earlier devices, and on top of that, many of these featured color screens!

Microsoft hoped that this new version would provide greater competition to the very successful Palm Pilot line of PDAs. Unfortunately, this wasn't to be, as sales of the Windows CE 2.0 operating system were also very slow. Microsoft had also anticipated a much more accelerated adoption of portable computer systems in cars. The company had hyped its Windows CE 2.0 operating system as its answer to the expected surge of "Auto PCs" (a handheld computer installed in any car in place of an existing stereo). Through a voice interface a driver could request directions to any address in their Pocket Outlook contact list. The adoption of the Auto PC never happened.

Microsoft followed up Windows CE 2.0 with version 2.1, which was primarily aimed at embedded developers. These developers were building applications that run on specialized devices with the operating system embedded directly within their hardware. Examples of places where developers would use an embedded version of Windows CE would be customized gas monitors, handheld inventory tablets, or point of sale (POS) systems.

While all this development on Windows CE was going on, Palm OS–based devices continued to gain market share. Things were not looking good for Microsoft's vision of a handheld version of Windows.

Then in January of 2000, Microsoft released Windows CE version 3.0. This product was dubbed the Pocket PC operating system. It overcame many of the limitations of the previous versions and also had the good fortune to come into existence when a new line of powerful processors was poised to come out of the gate. Intel's StrongARM processor would give the new devices running the Pocket PC OS several times the CPU power of the most powerful Palm device at the time. Many of these devices were also equipped with at least twice, and sometimes as much as eight times, the memory of the most well-endowed Palms.

Sales of these Pocket PC–equipped devices began to pick up steam. The HP Jornada took an early lead in the race, but the release of the Compaq iPAQ handheld set a new bar that all new devices had to hurdle. Sales of the iPAQ have soared and show no sign of slowing at the time of writing of this book.

The next, and most recent, chapter in the Pocket PC saga occurred in October of 2001. Microsoft released the latest version of their Windows CE operating system, dubbed Pocket PC 2002. The Pocket PC 2002 operating system features an improved user interface, better character recognition options, enhanced Pocket Outlook features, expanded Pocket Word and

Pocket Excel features, Pocket Internet Explorer enhancements, terminal server client, and more. A Pocket PC user can now expect more functionality than anyone has ever experienced on such a compact device.

This book will focus only on the most recent version of Compaq iPAQs that run the Pocket PC 2002 operating system.

Pocket PC vs. Palm OS

Now that you are a proud owner of a shiny Compaq iPAQ, you might find yourself being approached by owners of Palm OS–based devices who will try to engage you in debate about your device vs. their own. To compare Pocket PC and Palm OS is to tread into the arena of religion for many PDA users and can be dangerous territory for any author. That being said, we offer a brief comparison here of the two platforms.

The Processor

First consider the processor. The top-end processor available right now for the iPAQ is the Intel StrongARM processor, which runs at 206 MHz, whereas the top-end Palm runs with a 40 MHz Motorola Dragonball processor. It is important to note that the Pocket PC OS was designed for a more generic processor and hardware combination and uses substantially more of the processor for basic overhead. The extra power available for the Pocket PC also correlates to faster battery drain on the Pocket PC devices. In general, your Pocket PC processor can do much more than a Palm OS processor, but at the cost of battery life.

Memory

The Pocket PC operating system is also designed to handle much larger memory allocations than the Palm. What this means to you is that you can work with larger files and more sophisticated programs that take more memory.

Early versions of the iPAQ came with 16MB or 32MB of RAM, but the later 36xx, 37xx, and 38xx series come with 64MB of RAM standard and can be upgraded (by a third party) to up to 256MB of RAM. In comparison, the most powerful Palm devices come with 16MB of RAM.

The same comment can be made in the area of memory efficiency as was made about the processor. The Palm makes very effective use of its memory as far as applications go, whereas the Pocket PC and Pocket PC applications are often larger. However, when it comes to raw data, the memory usage is essentially the same.

Multitasking

The ability for the processor to work on more than one task at a time is an important feature of the Pocket PC environment. For many day-to-day activities, this can be a mixed blessing. On your iPAQ, every time you launch a new application, the other application keeps running in the background, just as on your Windows desktop. However, because you don't see the other applications, this can get a little confusing. Suddenly, you have several applications all open and running at the same time. With a little practice, this isn't hard to manage. The Palm OS, on the other hand, does not support multitasking, which means that every time you start a new application, that action effectively closes the previous application. This is a simple, tidy way to work and is very effective on a handheld device but can be limiting in more complex work environments.

Multitasking can become an extremely valuable feature as you learn to expand your PDA experience beyond the basic built-in applications. For example, with multitasking, you can connect to your wireless provider and download your e-mail in the background while surfing the Web and pasting information from a website into your Pocket Word document. This complex activity isn't possible on a Palm.

Applications

There are two categories to consider when looking at applications: those that come with the operating system and those that are provided by third parties. A number of applications come bundled with your iPAQ, including contact management, e-mail, notes, to-do lists, and calendaring software. Whether you prefer these built-in applications or third-party products will usually depend on what you used before you turned to your handheld device. Users of Microsoft Outlook will likely appreciate the similarity between the Pocket Outlook features and those on their desktop.

Pocket PC also comes standard with many other applications, including Pocket Excel, Pocket Word, and Pocket Money. Each of the applications that come with Pocket PC will be addressed in detail in subsequent chapters. At a minimum, these applications allow easy access to your existing files, or to file attachments that arrive in your e-mail Inbox.

Unlike Pocket PC 2000, the current version of Pocket PC does not include Pocket Money preinstalled. Pocket Money can be downloaded for free at the Microsoft website: **http://www.microsoft.com/MOBILE/pocketpc/downloads/ money.asp**.

The Palm comes with basic contact management, calendaring, e-mail, and to-do list software as well. In addition, you can purchase third-party applications separately for the Palm that will also allow you to do some rudimentary work with Microsoft Word documents and Microsoft Excel spreadsheets, but these come at an additional cost and with limited functionality. Where the Palm really shines is in the variety of software designed for it; more than 10,000 third-party applications are currently available for the Palm. In contrast, approximately 1500 applications are currently available for the Pocket PC platform. The large number of Palm applications is a direct result of Palm's early ability to grab market share and, concomitantly, Windows CE's previous inability to achieve significant market penetration. This ratio is coming down dramatically as consumers and businesses are buying more and more Pocket PCs. The quantity of third-party applications available for the Pocket PC platform is growing so quickly that it is getting very difficult to keep track of them all. In other chapters of this book we will examine some of the best third-party applications that you can take advantage of to extend your iPAQ's functionality.

Another important element to consider is that several companies are currently working on Palm emulators for the Pocket PC that will allow you to run any Palm application on your Pocket PC device. Although there will likely be little need to run Palm applications on a Pocket PC, should you locate a particular Palm app that you must have, with an emulator, you will be able to run it directly on your Pocket PC.

Expandability

The Pocket PC can be expanded through one of four standards (or any combination) depending on your hardware options. The most common expansion technique is through CompactFlash (CF) cards. Some of the Pocket PC devices include built-in CF expansion ports. The iPAQ handhelds use an expansion sleeve to support CompactFlash. CompactFlash has a similar form factor as the Secure Digital format and also has a very wide range of accessories available for it.

The second option for expanding your Pocket PC is through PCMCIA. This is the PC card standard that has been used in laptop computers for many years. This means that if you have a PCMCIA slot or expansion sleeve on your Pocket PC device you can use almost any card that your notebook computer uses. You can share your modems, network cards, wireless accessories, VGA display adaptors, and a plethora of other tools.

The third option is to use Secure Digital (SD) cards. This expansion format allows for a postage stamp–sized card to be inserted into your iPAQ to provide a wide range of functionality such as external storage, GPS capabilities, and more. This feature is not available on the older iPAQ versions. The first versions featuring a SD slot are the 38xx series iPAQs.

The fourth option is only available on the top end 38xx series iPAQs. The 3870 model also provides internal support of the new Bluetooth standard. Bluetooth is a short-range, low-power, wireless networking and connectivity protocol that allows your iPAQ to communicate with any other Bluetooth-enabled device. For example, if you have a Bluetooth-compatible phone, your iPAQ could automatically look up and dial numbers of contacts in your address book on your cellular phone. This feature also allows you to synchronize your iPAQ without having to plug it into a sync cable (as long as the host PC is Bluetooth enabled). The use of Bluetooth is spreading rapidly, which will result in many other ways for you to use your iPAQ without wires, such as printing to any printer, surfing the Internet from a public Bluetooth node, sharing notes or Microsoft PowerPoint presentations with other Bluetooth iPAQs and devices, and much more.

The combination of CompactFlash, PCMCIA, Secure Digital, and Bluetooth means that you will have a tremendous range of expansion and connectivity options on your iPAQ.

When comparing this with the Palm, we see that early versions of the Palm device had little expandability, but third-party licensees of the Palm technology, such as Handspring and Symbol, added to the expandability of the hardware. Handspring was one of the first to introduce hardware expansion through their proprietary Springboard module. You could plug in third-party manufactured modems, pagers, GPS units, and more. Later versions of the Palm have adopted the Secure Digital format to allow for expandability. The SD format has limited support at present, in contrast to the widely supported CompactFlash format.

The Bottom Line

The Pocket PC platform is in a state of mass adoption. The devices are flying off the shelves at an unprecedented rate. It will not take long for the Pocket PC to erode the substantial user base that Palm has garnered, and this process is already well underway.

The variety and power of the hardware platforms that are available for the Pocket PC is impressive. On this handheld device you can now perform processing that was literally the realm of "Star Trek" until recently, such as speech recognition and 3D modeling. Many of the devices are very well adapted to the wireless world, which will be the next major wave driving the handheld device space. The number of applications available for the Pocket PC is growing daily and includes many of the titles that you are already accustomed to using on your desktop.

This doesn't mean that the Pocket PC platform is perfect. The hardware tends to suck battery power quickly, can be bulkier than the Palm, and definitely presents a more complex environment than a Palm. The Palm was an early riser in the PDA market and secured a very significant market share. It is well liked by users for its simplicity of operation, lightweight, long battery life, and voluminous catalog of third-party applications. However, the Palm faces declining popularity, limited hardware expandability, limited wireless support, and limited processor power.

The Pocket PC, in formats like your iPAQ, offers the best opportunities for the future of handheld computing.

The iPAQ Family

The term "iPAQ" has come to be used by the mass media and ourselves to refer to the sporty handheld unit with the familiar PDA style running the Pocket PC software. That unit is the focus of this book too. However, it is important to point out that iPAQ is much more. Compaq has produced an entire line of consumer devices and Internet appliances all bearing the iPAQ moniker. This section will explain what these other devices are and how they fit into the Compaq universe, but the rest of this book will be dedicated to only the handheld device.

Internet Appliance

Compaq has aimed their iPAQ Internet appliance offering at the home market. These devices are essentially stripped down PCs running MSN Companion, which allows you to access the Internet and receive e-mail. At last check, these devices were seeing very limited acceptance in the marketplace, and they may be a very short-lived offering.

The Internet appliance comes in two configurations; the IA-1, with a 10-inch display and a wireless keyboard, and the IA-2, with a 15-inch display but fewer gizmos to play with. Both come with six months of free Internet access from MSN.

Audio Players

Compaq has released two audio players under the iPAQ name, one a portable unit and the other a home unit to hook into your stereo.

The portable unit is very much like other MP3 players on the market. It uses a 64MB MultiMediaCard (MMC) to provide up to two hours of music. It supports both the MP3 and WMA music formats.

The home unit is designed to plug into your home stereo system and provide digital music playback for your MP3 and other digital format music files. It comes with a CD tray and will convert your audio CDs to MP3 files and store them on its internal 20GB hard drive. Approximately 400 audio CDs can be stored on the unit. Through a network connection it can connect to Internet radio stations as well as online sources to decode the artist and song names of any audio CDs you insert (this saves a lot of typing). Through your PC you can customize the play lists of your iPAQ music center.

Blackberry

The Compaq iPAQ Blackberry is a Compaq branded version of the popular Blackberry two-way pager from Research In Motion (RIM). The intention behind launching this device was to allow for a less expensive option to the iPAQ handheld with an expansion sleeve and CDPD card. The Blackberry is first and foremost a two-way pager that handles e-mail through a direct e-mail link, or through a Microsoft Exchange gateway. This device has some limited capability to run third-party software, but generally is only used as an e-mail device with a calendar and contact database.

This device comes in two versions; the pager-sized W1000 (aka the RIM 950), and the larger H1100 (aka the RIM 957).

Compaq Residential Gateway Products

The iPAQ networking components are designed to allow home users to build shared networks in their homes that can communicate through and share a single Internet connection. This includes a variety of wireless base stations, wireless cards, Ethernet cards, HomePNA (phone line–based networks) access points, and hubs. The cost for components varies. This technology competes with a host of other home networking technologies that are currently on the market, including solutions from 3Com, Linksys, and others.

Home PCs

If that isn't confusing enough, Compaq has also released a line of desktop PCs being called the iPAQ. This line of products is aimed at the home user and is tagged as being low cost and easy to install. Interestingly, they are priced only slightly higher than the Internet appliance.

Handheld Pocket PC

Finally we come to the line of handheld PCs for which the iPAQ label has become a one-word description. There are a half dozen different models currently on the market or about to come out, including the following:

Model	Description
H3135	A grayscale screen iPAQ with 16MB of RAM and a 206 MHz StrongARM processor.
H3635/3650	The color version of the H3135 with 32MB of RAM.
H3670	The 3650 with 64MB of RAM.
H3760	The 3670, but with 32MB of ROM so it supports complete installation of Pocket PC 2002.
H3850	With 32MB of ROM, this unit supports Pocket PC 2002. Features the same 206 MHz processor and 64MB of RAM. Also features voice command and control software and a reflective screen that supports 65,536 colors (16-bit).
H3870	The H3850 with Bluetooth support.

Adopting the Mobile Lifestyle with Your Pocket PC

As PDAs have become more popular, many people seem to be carrying them around in their briefcases or pockets. However, it is amazing that many people also still carry around paper-based day planners and files of business cards or keep that trusty paper phone book by the telephone (although it always seems to have been moved by someone when you need it most).

In order to get the most out of your handheld device, it is important to adopt habits that will centralize all of your information in your device. You will never make effective use of your handheld if you keep some of your appointments in a paper calendar and some in your Pocket PC.

Tips for Adopting the Mobile Lifestyle

Here are some suggestions to help you integrate your handheld device into your life:

- Pick one point in the day, usually at the very beginning or very end of the day, where you will enter any business cards that you have picked up into your Outlook Contacts folder. This will keep your Pocket PC business contacts completely up to date. Then you can discard the business cards, or, if you feel compelled to keep them, you can place them in a binder to be kept in your office.

- Whenever someone gives you personal contact information such as a phone number, resist the urge to scribble it on a piece of paper and stuff it in your pocket or briefcase. We all have drawers of unidentifiable scribbled phone numbers that aren't of much use. These scraps of paper also don't tend to be in your hand when you need to call that person back. Instead, take the extra 45 seconds to put that person's information into your Pocket PC. Now it is permanently preserved and will be available to you any time you need it.

- When you book an appointment or plan an event, even in the distant future, always immediately enter the event into your handheld calendar. If you are consistent with this behavior you will learn to trust the calendar in your Pocket PC. If you aren't consistent, you will find yourself missing appointments or double booking as you try to organize yourself with both a paper system (or worse, your memory) and a Pocket PC.

- If you use your Pocket PC for expense management, use the same diligent technique of once a day entering all your receipts or financial information into your system.

- Whenever you think of something that you need to do, personal or professional, instead of "making a mental note," put it into your task list. You can categorize it, prioritize it, and assign a date to it.

- Every morning when you get up, look at your calendar and to do list. If there is something that you know is happening that day that isn't in your calendar, enter it. If there is something you need to get done that day, put it on your task list. Not only does this help to keep track of your tasks and appointments it helps you to feel that you've accomplished something when you look back on your day. Instead of that "where did the day go, and did I actually get anything done?" feeling that sometimes comes at the end of the day, you will be able to look at your list and see at a glance all the activities and tasks that you knocked off.

- When a special event occurs such as a birthday or anniversary, record it in your calendar as a recurring event (the technique for doing this is described in detail in Chapter 5). That way your Pocket PC will become a true personal assistant by reminding you to make a dinner appointment or pick up a gift well in advance of the date!

Keeping Your iPAQ with You

Making the best use of your iPAQ also means that you need to keep it with you as you live out your mobile life. The iPAQ, although small and lightweight, isn't quite small enough to slip into your shirt pocket or the back pocket of your pants like a wallet, especially if you are using an expansion sleeve and a wireless card.

As future versions of the product are released, hopefully the form factor will continue to get smaller, and the overall weight to get lighter. Right now the best method is to carry it in a briefcase or purse when you move around. But what about those times when you don't want to carry your briefcase or purse?

Your iPAQ doesn't weigh any more than a conventional portable CD player, and is as easy to carry with you. In fact, you will probably find your iPAQ works as well or better than your CD player while you run, work out, or perform any such activities. What's more, with MP3, you will never again experience that annoying skipping that even the very best "skip-free" CD players are prone to.

For casual walking around, cargo pants with the side pockets can be very useful places for storing your iPAQ. For more of a business casual appearance, Dockers has released a line of casual pants called "Mobile Pants," which contain a special pocket for holding your iPAQ. This idea is a good one; unfortunately, Dockers' execution wasn't great. The pocket (specifically identified in advertising as being good for an iPAQ) is too small. It is possible to squeeze in the iPAQ with no expansion sleeves or accessories, but it is extremely tight. Unless you are standing at just the right angle, the bulge of the iPAQ is still obvious, and don't you dare sit down! This pocket seems better suited to something of the form factor of a Palm V. Dockers has the right idea; hopefully other clothing manufacturers will actually try putting an iPAQ (with an expansion sleeve) into the pocket and using it before they tout their clothing as "Mobile" wear!

NOTE   *For those people that are constantly on the move, finding the right cases and bags to hold all their gear is critical. RoadWired (**www.roadwired.com**) has produced the most durable and lightweight range of bags, portfolios, and cases for your iPAQ and accessories. We have been using them for several months now. The portfolio pockets aren't quite big enough for the iPAQ, but the briefcases are excellent. For a thorough review of the various bags, cases, and accessories, refer to Chapter 15 or the website for this book: **www.pocketpctools.com**.*

One popular method for carrying the iPAQ is to get a third-party case with a belt clip. The cases that come with the iPAQ are generally of poor quality, don't fit the expansion pack, and do not feature a belt clip. As a result, they are mostly unusable. If you want a case you will need to search through third-party offerings. In Chapter 15 we will review many of the cases available from third-party manufacturers and give you the pros and cons of each one.

There are other carrying methods as well such as the secret agent–style under-the-jacket holster, or the multipocketed vest. One of the vests specifically targeted to the PDA owner is the SCOTT eVest (**www.scottevest.com**). It is a lightweight water-repellent vest that appears rather like a safari vest. It is loaded with pockets for all your wireless toys and has a unique feature: Velcro-enclosed conduits to hold all the wires that connect your devices together and keep the cords tucked safely away. They call this a personal area network, or PAN. The vest isn't something that you could wear to a business function, and for personal recreational wear, the $160 price tag is rather steep. There are also a variety of other vests and PDA-oriented clothing that will be discussed in Chapter 15.

Chapter 2

Get Started with Your iPAQ Pocket PC

How to...

- Unpack your iPAQ
- Use your iPAQ for the first time
- Use the iPAQ controls
- Set up owner information
- Use and customize the Start and New menus
- Use the companion CD
- Enter data by hand
- Connect your iPAQ to your PC
- Set up ActiveSync
- Beam data between devices

We know how it is—you've got the box in your hands, and you can't wait to get home or to the office so you can open it up and start using your new tool. But before you can jump into scheduling appointments with Pocket Outlook or analyzing data with Pocket Excel, you'll need to get to know your iPAQ and set it up to work best for you. This chapter is to help you understand the basics of getting your iPAQ set up and ready for use, as well as what software you should add to the iPAQ from the companion CD that comes along with it.

Unpacking Your iPAQ

Different versions of the iPAQ come packaged differently, however, what is packed inside the box varies only slightly from model to model. Your iPAQ should come with the following:

- Your iPAQ (of course!).
- A case. The case that comes with the iPAQ is sufficient for protecting the "naked" iPAQ (without any expansion sleeves), but is really inadequate for day-to-day use. There are many third-party cases worth considering. A full review of these cases can be found in Chapter 15. (Note that if you purchased the black-and-white screen iPAQ, you likely didn't receive any case at all, but this is no great loss!)
- A cradle (or sync cable if you purchased the black-and-white iPAQ).
- An AC adapter for charging your iPAQ.
- iPAQ companion CD-ROM.
- Spare stylus. (Note that not all models ship with a spare stylus.)

Some iPAQs, at various times, shipped with either CompactFlash expansion sleeves or PCMCIA expansion sleeves. These sleeves are addressed in detail in Chapter 13.

 *When you first pull the iPAQ out of the box, there will be a thin film covering the screen. This is to protect the screen during shipping, and you should peel this off before using your iPAQ.*

Before you get too carried away in your excitement, make sure ActiveSync is fully installed before plugging your sync cable or cradle into your USB port. Set up of ActiveSync is covered later in this chapter.

Hardware Orientation

All the iPAQ modules feature basically the same external hardware configuration with the exception of the 38*xx* series, which features a slightly different look and the Secure Digital slot.
As shown in Figure 2-1, the front of the iPAQ contains most of the items that you will use

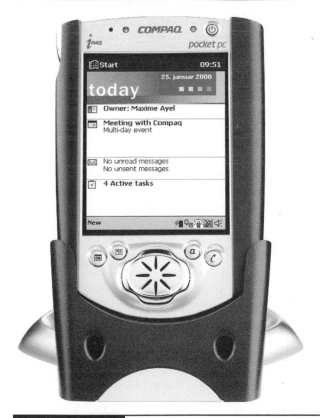

FIGURE 2-1   The front of the iPAQ is your primary interface, through the touch screen and hardware buttons.

as you work with the iPAQ. From left to right, top to bottom, the features are:

Microphone   The built-in microphone is useful for voice dictation and voice control software.

Light sensor   This sensor will automatically activate or deactivate the side lighting based upon the light in the room.

Power indicator/Charging/Alert light   This light glows a solid amber if your iPAQ is connected to AC power and fully charged. It is off if your iPAQ is running on battery power, flashes amber if your iPAQ is charging, and flashes green if you have an alert or reminder.

Power button   This button turns your iPAQ on and off. It also turns the side light off and on when held down for one second.

Screen   320×240 pixel touch-sensitive screen.

Button One (Calendar button)   This programmable button is by default set to open the Calendar, but can be modified to perform a number of functions.

Button Two (Contacts button)   This programmable button is by default set to open Contacts.

Button Three (Inbox button)   This programmable button is by default set to open the Inbox on the 37*xx* and 38*xx* series iPAQs, or the Quick Menu on older iPAQs.

Button Four (iTask button)   This programmable button is by default set to open the Compaq iPAQ iTask program. On older iPAQ models, this button opened the Compaq task switcher.

Speaker/Navigation disc   This control serves two purposes. First, it is the built-in speaker for any sound coming out of your iPAQ. Second, it is a multiposition disc for navigating through applications and data. Note that if you have a 38*xx* series of iPAQ, your speaker is not in the disc, but at the top of your iPAQ.

Looking down on the top of the iPAQ there are three controls to be aware of (from left to right):

Headphone jack   Use this jack to plug in stereo headphones and listen to any of the sounds the iPAQ produces (incidentally, it makes a good MP3 player).

Top microphone hole   This is a small hole that is linked to the internal microphone like the hole on the front of the iPAQ. It lets you record a sound by pointing your iPAQ at the sound source.

Infrared port   This port is used for sending and receiving information from other infrared devices. More information on this is in the "Beam Data for Easy Transfer" section later in this chapter.

Stylus   The stylus is conveniently stored inside the body of the iPAQ. Press the silver button to pop the stylus out of its slot if you have a 36*xx* or 37*xx* series of iPAQ. If you have a 38*xx* series, the stylus is released by pushing it down so it pops out.

2

On the bottom of the iPAQ you will find four items (from left to right):

Adapter jack   Use this jack to plug in an external charger.

Hard reset switch (36xx and 37xx series iPAQs only)   Use this switch for hard resetting the device (this will wipe out the memory of the device). Hard resetting is not something you want to do by accident, so the switch to cut and restore power is covered by a sliding door.

Sync port   This port is used for plugging in an external sync cable.

Soft reset switch   Use this switch for soft resetting the system (no data is lost). This is like rebooting your computer. This is a recessed switch and must be pressed with the tip of your stylus or other pointed object.

On the left side of the iPAQ you will find a single button. This button is intended for voice memos. When you press it, you will be taken to the Notes application, where a new note will be started with a voice recording.

Turning Your iPAQ On for the First Time

When your iPAQ ships, the master power switch is turned off. To turn it on, you must open the hard reset port on the bottom of the iPAQ. Use the tip of the stylus to slide the cover to the left. Underneath the cover, you slide the switch to the left to turn on the power. Be sure to slide the switch cover back after turning on the power to prevent its being accidentally switched off.

 *Note that the 38xx series iPAQ does not have a hard reset switch, only a soft reset switch, so there is no need to locate and slide the switch on your first use of the unit.*

The iPAQ will initialize and ask you to run through some initial calibrations. You must tap on the screen in various positions indicated to configure the touch screen. If you ever find that the places you tap on the screen register inaccurately, you can rerun this setup from the Settings area.

The initial setup will also get you to select your time zone. Once you have worked through these initial screens, your iPAQ is ready to use.

Setting Up the Owner Information

From the time when your iPAQ is first turned on until you complete this task, your Today page (which is the page that will appear first) has a line reading, "Tap here to set owner information."

Tapping this line will open up the Owner Information dialog box, as shown in Figure 2-2. This is very important to set up, as it will ensure that if someone finds your iPAQ, they can get it back to you.

FIGURE 2-2 Set up the Owner Information dialog box to make sure that if your iPAQ is lost, the person who finds it knows where to find you.

On this screen you will enter your name, company, address, telephone number, and e-mail address. You can also set an option that causes your information to be displayed every time the device is turned on. That way anyone turning it on will immediately know who it belongs to.

 *The option to show your owner information on startup is very important if you decide to set a power-on password for your device (discussed in Chapter 8) because it is the only way someone finding your device will know who it belongs to.*

Using the Start Menu

As in the desktop versions of Windows, in Pocket PC you launch applications from the Start menu. Tapping the Start menu at any time will open the list shown in Figure 2-3. Note that when an application is launched, the Start menu is replaced by the name of the program that you are currently running, but tapping on the program name will always cause the Start menu to appear.

The top bar of the menu shown in Figure 2-3 shows the icons of the last six applications that you ran. Tapping any of these icons will launch you back into that program. Note that this only works for programs, not for shortcuts or documents.

Below that bar are the most commonly used programs that you can launch. This list can be customized (discussed in the "Customizing the Start and New Menus" section later), but initially provides links to the Today page, ActiveSync, Pocket Outlook applications, Pocket Internet Explorer, and the Pocket PC Media Player.

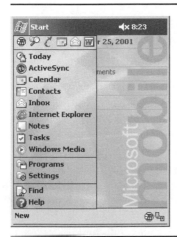

FIGURE 2-3 The Start menu is the primary launching point for applications on the Pocket PC.

The next section of the Start menu contains two shortcuts: Programs and Settings. Programs will take you to the folder where shortcuts to all programs loaded on the Pocket PC should be stored. This folder contains the full set of applications installed on your iPAQ, not just those featured in the short list above.

The final section contains a Find tool to search for any data contained in your iPAQ. It also has the Help utility. The Help utility is context sensitive. If you are in Pocket Word and you tap the Start menu, and then tap Help, you will receive Help for the section of Word that you are in. This aspect of Help makes it particularly handy while you're getting to know the Pocket PC applications.

Using the New Menu

The New menu is located in the lower left of the Today page. It is also available in other Pocket Outlook applications. When you tap the New menu in the Today page, a pop-up menu will appear, listing the types of documents that you can create, as shown here:

From this list you can create new appointments, contacts, e-mail messages, workbooks, documents, notes, and tasks. A tap on any of the commands in the list will launch the application that creates that document and open a blank entry in that format.

Customizing the Start and New Menus

Both the Start and New menus can be modified to meet your specific needs. Select Settings from the Start menu, and a window will open that displays the icons of different settings that you can modify. Tapping the Menu icon will open a dialog box where you can customize the Start and New menus.

The Start Menu tab of the Menus dialog box is focused on the Start menu. You will see a list of all known applications and subfolders on the Pocket PC that you can include on the menu. Adding a folder means that tapping it on the Start menu will open it. Modifying the menu is simply a matter of selecting the check boxes of the applications and folders you wish to appear in the Start menu, and deselecting the check boxes of those that you don't want, as shown in Figure 2-4.

FIGURE 2-4   You can customize the Start menu by selecting which applications you want to appear on the menu.

The New Menu tab in the Menus dialog box is focused on the New menu, as shown in Figure 2-5. You cannot add new items to this list, but you can remove documents that you do not want to be able to launch directly by deselecting those documents in the list. The more important option on this tab is Turn On New Button Menu. When this check box is selected, the New menu will show a pop-up arrow beside it. This doesn't impact how the menu works in the Today page, but in other applications with a New menu, normally New will only create a new document within that application. With the pop-up menu, you can create a new document of any type from almost anywhere at any time. For example, while editing a Word document, you could open the New menu and begin creating a new e-mail message or Excel workbook.

FIGURE 2-5   Documents listed in the New menu can be removed in the Menus dialog box.

What's On the Companion CD?

With every iPAQ you receive a CD-ROM from Compaq that contains some tools to help you make the most of your iPAQ.

To make sure that you can synchronize e-mail, the CD includes a copy of Outlook 2002, which you can install. If you are going to upgrade your Outlook installation, you should do this before you install ActiveSync.

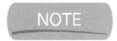

*Note that if you are upgrading an older iPAQ to Pocket PC 2002, you will not receive Pocket Outlook as part of the bundle. Check the Microsoft Pocket PC website at **www.pocketpc.com** to find the download.*

If you need to install ActiveSync, do not plug in your sync cable or cradle until after ActiveSync is installed.

After these basic essentials, the CD contains a set of applications (or links to downloadable applications) that can enhance the use of your iPAQ. These tools are divided into four categories: Productivity, Mobility, Entertainment, and Tools.

Productivity

The following applications are either included or downloadable through links on the CD:

Pocket Money 2002   This application was released after Pocket PC 2002, so it is not included as part of the standard install. You can link to the Microsoft site and download it through this link. This application allows you to synchronize with your desktop version of Money as well manage your accounts, portfolio, and expenses. This application is covered in more detail in Chapter 6.

Microsoft Reader   This application is usually pre-installed on your Pocket PC 2002–equipped iPAQ. If it is not, or if you are running an iPAQ upgraded from an earlier version of Pocket PC, then you can load it from this CD. This application allows you to read eBooks on your iPAQ. A large number of these books are available from a variety of sources including the Microsoft site. This software is covered in more detail in Chapter 11.

Handango   This isn't an application, but rather a link to the Handango.com website, which contains a tremendously large library of applications for the Pocket PC that you can purchase and trial. You can find more information on Handango in Appendix B.

iPresentation Mobile Converter LE   This application, included on the CD, converts Microsoft PowerPoint presentations so that they can be viewed on your iPAQ. This is a free application that the manufacturer hopes will encourage you to upgrade to their full application suite. This software and subject is covered in more detail in Chapter 10.

Compaq Dashboard   This dashboard operates as a replacement for the Today page. It has enhanced features and customizations that may make it more convenient for you than the built-in Today page. You can try it and decide for yourself.

Mobility

The following mobility applications are either included or downloadable through links on the CD:

AvantGo   AvantGo is already installed on your iPAQ and is accessed through Pocket Internet Explorer. AvantGo downloads information based upon a content profile that you create online and stores that information on your Pocket PC for you to browse while on the go.

MS Pocket Streets   The link to download MS Pocket Streets allows you to take content from MS Streets and Trips 2002, MS Autoroute 2002, and Microsoft Mappoint 2002 (note that these products must be purchased first) and put it onto your Pocket PC. With this ability, you can pinpoint addresses, restaurants, attractions, automatic banking machines, and more while on the move.

MSN Mobile   This application offers mobile access to your MSN Hotmail mailbox.

Compaq wireless LAN PC card drivers   These drivers enable you to use Compaq 802.11b wireless LAN cards in your iPAQ.

Callex   This software allows you to record voice messages and send them to an e-mail address. The recipient can reply with a text e-mail. This is the entry-level free product. If you upgrade, you can send these messages to any telephone number and enable the recipient to speak a response back.

Entertainment

The following entertainment applications are either included or downloadable through links on the CD:

Microsoft Pocket PC   The Pocket PC site from Microsoft has links to many games, including favorites such as Minesweeper, Reversi, and Hearts.

Audible Player   This application enables you to listen to a wide variety of audio content online including news, comedy, education, and much more. This Web-based service offers significant free content, and, of course, premium content for an additional charge.

Tools

The following utility and tool applications are either included or downloadable through links on the CD:

Transcriber   One of the most useful tools on the CD is Transcriber, which interprets your handwriting, wherever you scribble on the screen, and inserts it where the cursor is. This one is definitely worth installing (note that on all Pocket PC 2002 devices, Transcriber is already loaded in the ROM).

StarTap   This limited version software gives you a desktop like the one you are accustomed to in the Windows desktop.

Afaria   This sample software is used for deploying business information to handheld devices.

Entering Data By Hand

The iPAQ is designed to have data entered in a variety of formats. The most common ways of inputting data are writing characters with the stylus and typing text on a keyboard (either virtual or external).

Mastering Handwriting Recognition

The most common way of entering data into a handheld device is to use the stylus to write characters that are interpreted into text. Pocket PC 2002, which is loaded on the 37*xx* and 38*xx* series iPAQs, comes loaded with three handwriting recognition modes for text entry: Letter Recognizer, Block Recognizer, and Transcriber.

Only one method of character recognition can be used at a time. The icon at the bottom-right corner of the screen indicates the current method of recognition that you are using. Tapping on the up arrow beside the icon will open a pop-up menu you can use to change your input method, as shown here:

Using the Letter Recognizer

The Letter Recognizer uses the area at the bottom of the screen called the soft input panel (SIP). This area is divided into three sections where you will draw your characters, as shown in Figure 2-6. The left third of the SIP is reserved for drawing uppercase characters. The middle section is for lowercase letters, and the right third is for numbers. The far right of the SIP contains buttons for Backspace, Cursor Left, Cursor Right, Space, Return, Help, and Special Characters.

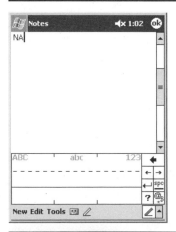

FIGURE 2-6   The Letter Recognizer divides the soft input panel into three sections.

The Letter Recognizer will interpret any characters that you write in the SIP area and put the translated character into the currently running program wherever the cursor is, just as if you are typing on a keyboard. The dashed line through the middle of the SIP is intended to be used so letters can be correctly interpreted. For example, because the uppercase and lowercase forms of some letters look the same when handwritten, to write a lowercase *o* or *c* you should write them below the dashed line, as shown here:

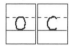

Characters that descend below the normal printed line are called *descenders*. Letters such as lowercase *p* and *q* are examples. You should draw them below the dashed line, with the descending part extending below the solid line, as shown here:

Similarly, letters with parts that extend above the dashed line, like *b* and *d,* are called *ascenders*. These should be drawn with the body below the dashed line and the ascender above the line, as shown here:

Punctuation can also be entered anywhere in the SIP Letter Recognizer, but it seems to be more effective to use the Special Characters button on the right of the SIP. This button shows three symbols as its icon: @, *, and $. When you tap this button, the SIP changes to show a number of special characters, as shown in the next illustration. You can select the character you want to insert by tapping it with the stylus. As soon as you have selected your character, the panel returns to normal Letter Recognizer mode.

The odd thing that you will need to get used to is that when you are using the Letter Recognizer, you always enter letters as lowercase, even if you want an uppercase letter. To get an uppercase *A,* you enter a lowercase *a* in the leftmost section of the SIP. This is a little counter-intuitive and can make the Letter Recognizer a little difficult for new users. It is not our preferred method of input.

You can configure some settings to change the way Letter Recognizer behaves and tweak it for your own uses. These settings can be accessed by tapping Options in the input method pop-up menu. (To open this menu, tap the up arrow in the lower-right corner.) The first option is Quick Stroke. Turning this on allows you to write letters with a single stroke of the stylus. This is different from the Grafitti language that is used on the Palm and requires you to learn new ways of writing letters.

The second option is Right To Left Crossbar. You will turn this option on if you are in the habit of putting the horizontal line in letters like *t* and *f* from right to left instead of left to right.

The third option is Allow Accented Characters. This will allow you to enter characters that use accents such as *è* (*e* with a grave accent) in French.

Using the Block Recognizer

The Block Recognizer is similar to the Letter Recognizer in that you write letters on the SIP one character at a time. This method, however, uses the Graffiti language that is standard with Palm handheld devices. If you are migrating to your iPAQ from a Palm, this option makes it easy to use the same input method that you are used to on the Palm. The SIP is divided into two entry sections. The left section is for letters (both upper- and lowercase). The right section is set up for numerical entry, as shown in Figure 2-7.

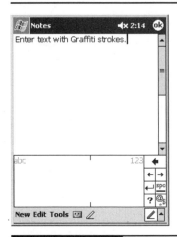

FIGURE 2-7   The Block Recognizer allows you to use Palm Graffiti to enter text into your iPAQ.

The keys on the right side of the SIP do the same as they do in the Letter Recognizer. If at any time you need help figuring out what strokes to use to make a character, tap the ? button on the right. It will enable you to launch a Demo that will show you how to draw any strokes you require.

Using Transcriber

Transcriber is our favorite way of entering text into the iPAQ, particularly when writing e-mail messages or documents. Transcriber allows you to write anywhere on the screen and then, when you pause, have your written text interpreted into words and phrases. You can print, use cursive writing, or mix it up, and Transcriber can still interpret what you are doing. Figure 2-8 shows an example of writing with Transcriber.

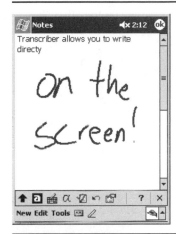

FIGURE 2-8   Transcriber allows you to write words anywhere on the screen and have them translated into text.

TIP   *When using Transcriber, don't write too small. The larger your text, the easier it is to interpret. On the other extreme, don't write so large that you can't fit your text on the screen. Also, remember that you can write anywhere, so use the full screen. Don't worry about writing over whatever is currently displayed; what is shown on the screen will not impact your Transcriber input. Try not to rest your palm on, or allow anything else to come into contact with the screen.*

Another advantage to Transcriber is that it works with any Pocket PC application, but doesn't take up screen space, giving you the maximum view of your application.

Training Transcriber to Recognize Your Handwriting   The way that Transcriber recognizes your handwriting can be adapted to your unique way of forming letters. For example, if you find that Transcriber regularly misinterprets a particular letter, you can train it using the Letter Shapes Selector. You open the Letter Shapes Selector by tapping the icon in the toolbar that looks like a cursive letter *a* (fourth icon from the left). This window is shown in Figure 2-9.

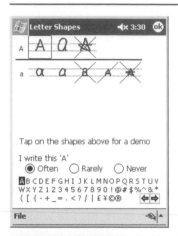

FIGURE 2-9 The Letter Shapes Selector allows you to train Transcriber to recognize the way that you write letters.

The Letter Shapes Selector window gives you all the characters of the alphabet as well as the most commonly used punctuation and special characters at the bottom of the screen. To select the character you want to train, tap it in the list (the arrows at the bottom right will move you to the next or previous character). In the top portion of the screen, you will see a series of characters displaying the different ways that Transcriber will expect to see the upper- and lowercase versions of the letter. You can select each variation and tag it as being one that is often, rarely, or never used by you. Any letter you select as rarely used will appear with one slash through the letter, and any that you mark as never used will appear with an × marked through the letter. Doing this serves two purposes. By eliminating letters that you never write, Transcriber has fewer letters to search through each time in order to find a match and can thus recognize text more quickly. The second purpose is that letters that look similar to other characters can be difficult to interpret. For example, a cursive Q looks very much like the number 2. If you never use the cursive Q style, then you can increase the chances of the number 2 being correctly interpreted.

While in the Letter Shapes Selector, you can see a demo of how any of the shapes is drawn by tapping it. This will cause it to draw itself for your observation.

If you are concerned that by tweaking your Transcriber letter shape settings, you might make your iPAQ not usable for someone that you share the device with, you don't need to worry. The Letter Shapes Selector also allows you to set one of two profiles: Master or Guest. By default, it assumes you are editing the Master profile, however, if you lend your iPAQ to someone, you can set it to the Guest profile, so they can use standard recognition or customize the settings for their own handwriting without affecting your settings. You can select the profile in the File menu, as shown in the illustration that follows. If many people are using the same iPAQ, you can save and load profiles from this menu as well. At any point, you can revert to the default setting by selecting Use Original Settings from this menu.

Selecting Text with Transcriber   Selecting text that you have already written is a bit tricky with Transcriber. When you move the stylus on the screen to select a letter or word, Transcriber will assume that you are now entering a word and begin drawing a line. There are three ways to select text. In the first method, you tap and hold the desired text until the text is selected (usually about two seconds). The text will appear highlighted to show that it is selected. The tap and hold method doesn't work very well if the application you are in has a tap and hold shortcut menu. For example, in Notes, if you tap and hold a word, a shortcut menu appears in which you are given options to insert a date, paste, or look for alternate words.

The second method to select text is to tap your stylus to the left of the text and drag it (drawing a line) across all the text that you want to select. Then, without lifting the stylus from the screen, hold the stylus in place at the end of the selection.

The third method for selecting text is to suspend Transcriber temporarily by tapping the hand icon in the bottom right of the screen. The box and white background around the hand will disappear. This means you can now use the stylus to interact with the screen without Transcriber. To return to Transcriber, simply tap the hand icon again. Suspending Transcriber enables you to drag and drop, select, and carry out other stylus activity that can be difficult with Transcriber active.

Using Drawn Gestures for Special Characters and Commands   To use Transcriber effectively, you will need to know how to use your stylus to input letter spaces, hit Enter, access commands, and perform other tasks by drawing. The sign you draw on the SIP is called a *gesture*.

Enter   (Equivalent of pressing ENTER on a keyboard) Draw a line straight down and then turn 90 degrees to the left. Make sure the horizontal line is at least twice as long as the vertical line.

Space   (Equivalent of pressing the SPACEBAR on a keyboard) Draw a line straight down and then turn 90 degrees to the right. Make sure the horizontal line is at least twice as long as the vertical line.

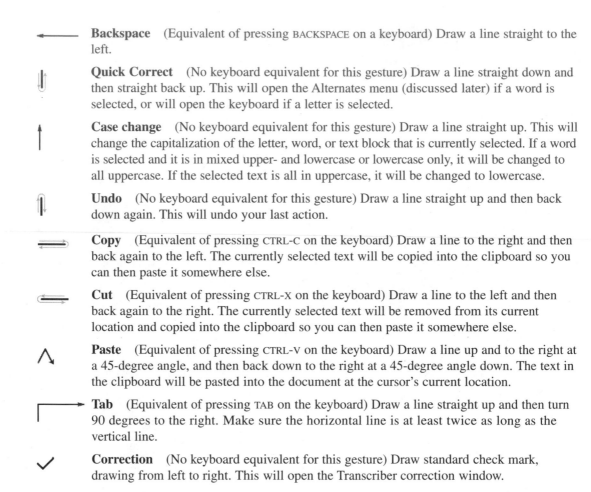

Backspace   (Equivalent of pressing BACKSPACE on a keyboard) Draw a line straight to the left.

Quick Correct   (No keyboard equivalent for this gesture) Draw a line straight down and then straight back up. This will open the Alternates menu (discussed later) if a word is selected, or will open the keyboard if a letter is selected.

Case change   (No keyboard equivalent for this gesture) Draw a line straight up. This will change the capitalization of the letter, word, or text block that is currently selected. If a word is selected and it is in mixed upper- and lowercase or lowercase only, it will be changed to all uppercase. If the selected text is all in uppercase, it will be changed to lowercase.

Undo   (No keyboard equivalent for this gesture) Draw a line straight up and then back down again. This will undo your last action.

Copy   (Equivalent of pressing CTRL-C on the keyboard) Draw a line to the right and then back again to the left. The currently selected text will be copied into the clipboard so you can then paste it somewhere else.

Cut   (Equivalent of pressing CTRL-X on the keyboard) Draw a line to the left and then back again to the right. The currently selected text will be removed from its current location and copied into the clipboard so you can then paste it somewhere else.

Paste   (Equivalent of pressing CTRL-V on the keyboard) Draw a line up and to the right at a 45-degree angle, and then back down to the right at a 45-degree angle down. The text in the clipboard will be pasted into the document at the cursor's current location.

Tab   (Equivalent of pressing TAB on the keyboard) Draw a line straight up and then turn 90 degrees to the right. Make sure the horizontal line is at least twice as long as the vertical line.

Correction   (No keyboard equivalent for this gesture) Draw standard check mark, drawing from left to right. This will open the Transcriber correction window.

Transcriber's Correction Window   If a word has been entered poorly or was recognized incorrectly by Transcriber, you can go to the Transcriber correction window to fix the problem. First, select the word that was incorrectly recognized. Then open the correction window by drawing the Correction gesture, as shown previously; by drawing the Quick Correct gesture and then selecting Go To Corrector from the menu; or by tapping the correction icon on the Transcriber toolbar (which appears as a red check mark over a page of writing).

The correction window will display a larger version of the word that you selected, as shown in Figure 2-10. You can correct an incorrect word by inputting directly over the letter or letters to change them. Alternatively, you can select an entire word and tap the alternates icon (appears as an uppercase *A* with a bar underneath it) in the new toolbar that is at the top of the screen.

2

FIGURE 2-10   In the correction window, you can correct erroneous words and add words to Transcriber's dictionary.

The Alternates menu that pops up when you double-tap the word is shown in the following illustration. In this menu you can select a replacement for the wrong word from a list of dictionary words, add this word to the dictionary, change the case of the selected letter, add a space, or cancel to close the menu.

The fourth icon from the left on the top toolbar allows you to switch the correction window from full screen mode to partial screen, as shown in Figure 2-11. In partial screen you can still see your whole document while the correction window floats in the front.

Other Transcriber Features   At any point you can tap the ? icon on the toolbar to go to the help area and learn more about the options on the toolbar. Tapping the OK button will close the correction window, returning you to the document with your modifications in place. Tapping the X button will close the window without making your modifications to the document.

FIGURE 2-11   You can set the correction window to operate in either full screen or floating partial screen mode, which is shown in this figure.

Transcriber has a built-in calculator that will solve simple equations simply by writing them on the screen. For example, if you need to know the answer to 4×3, simply write **4 x 3 =** on the screen, leaving the answer blank. Transcriber will fill in the answer in the results that is transcribes into the application, as shown here:

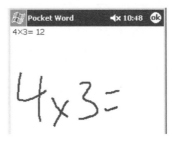

Configuring Transcriber Options   You can configure Transcriber to your particular preferences by tapping the Options button on the bottom toolbar. The Options button is located third from the right and looks like this:

The Transcriber: Options dialog box has two tabs: General and Recognizer. On the General tab are four options you can set, as shown in Figure 2-12:

Sound On   Tapping this check box turns Transcriber sound effects on and off.

2

Show Into Screen   Selecting this check box causes the Transcriber introduction screen to be shown each time Transcriber is started. This screen gives basic instructions and also shows how to draw gestures that aren't intuitively obvious like Enter and Backspace.

Show Iconbar   Tapping this check box toggles the Transcriber toolbar on and off.

Inking   In this section of the dialog box, you select a color and width for the ink that appears when you are writing on the screen.

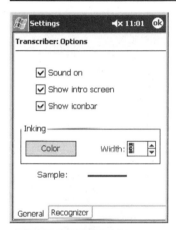

FIGURE 2-12   On the General tab of the Transcriber: Options dialog box, you can configure Transcriber.

The Recognizer tab of the dialog box, shown in Figure 2-13, enables you to set options for how Transcriber recognizes information. The top box shows you the version number of Transcriber that you are running. Selecting the Add Space After check box will cause a space to be inserted automatically after each recognized word. Selecting Separate Letters Mode tells Transcriber that you never write with your letters connected together (that is, you print instead of use cursive). If you print all your letters, then selecting this option will speed up the character recognition process. Use the Speed Of Recognition Vs. Quality slider to choose whether you want faster recognition and less accuracy or slower recognition and increased accuracy. The final option is Recognition Start Time, which is how long Transcriber will wait before deciding that you have finished writing and it should interpret the text. The default setting is about one second (with the slider in the middle). If you find that Transcriber starts interpreting your text before you finish writing, you can drag the slider to the right to increase the time. On the other end, if you find yourself impatiently waiting for Transcriber to hurry up and recognize what you have written so you can write more, drag the slider to the left to decrease the wait time.

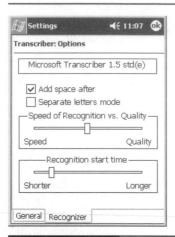

FIGURE 2-13   Use the Recognizer tab of the Transcriber: Options dialog box to set the speed and quality of Transcriber's character recognition.

Using a Keyboard to Enter Data

Another way to enter input into your iPAQ is through a keyboard. You can use either the built-in virtual keyboard or an external keyboard.

Using the Virtual Keyboard

The virtual keyboard is accessed by changing the input method as we did for the handwriting recognition options. Instead of choosing one of the handwriting options from the pop-up menu, you choose Keyboard. This will turn the soft input panel at the bottom of your screen into a standard QWERTY keyboard, as shown here:

You can tap any key in the keyboard, just as you would with a real keyboard, to have that character inserted where the cursor is. The 123 key at the top left of the keyboard will bring up a numerical keypad along with some special character keys, as shown in the illustration on the following page. Tapping 123 again will return you to the regular keyboard.

2

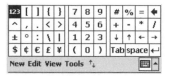

Tapping the button on the lower left with the two accented characters will open a keyboard of special foreign characters, as shown next. Tapping this key again will return you to the regular keyboard.

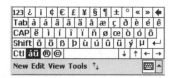

The arrow keys on the bottom right will move the cursor in the direction indicated by the arrow.

Changing Virtual Keyboard Options

You can modify the settings for the virtual keyboard. First, select Options from the input method selection pop-up menu (opened by tapping the arrow next to the current input icon on the bottom right of the window) to open the Input dialog box with the Input Method tab active, as shown in Figure 2-14. When Keyboard is selected in the Input Method box, you can opt to use small or large keys. If you select the Large Keys option, this by necessity means that some of the less frequently used keys will disappear off the keyboard. You can also turn on an option to use gestures in the keyboard area to represent certain keys, such as BACKSPACE and ENTER.

FIGURE 2-14   You can choose large keys or small keys for your virtual keyboard.

Using an External Keyboard

If you find yourself doing a lot of typing on your iPAQ—for taking notes in meetings or typing long e-mail messages, for example—you might find an external keyboard to be a very valuable accessory. As adept as you might become with the other handwriting and input mechanisms, you will never reach the speed of a touch typist on a full keyboard. The leader in the portable keyboard world is the Targus Stowaway folding keyboard. It is easy to carry with you. Folded up in its black case it is about the same size as an iPAQ and weighs only 7.9 ounces.

When attached to the keyboard, the iPAQ is propped up efficiently by a small stand at the back of the keyboard. The keyboard draws its minimal power requirements from the iPAQ.

In order to make the keyboard work, you must install a keyboard driver onto the iPAQ. This driver can be found on the CD that is supplied with the keyboard. More information on external keyboards is available in Chapter 15.

Setting Options for Word Completion and Recording

Two tabs in the Input dialog box are generally applicable to all input methods: Word Completion and Options. To open this dialog box, select Options from the Input Method pop-up menu.

The Word Completion tab, shown in Figure 2-15, enables you to turn on the automatic word completion option to have the iPAQ suggest words to you that it thinks you might be trying to enter. After you enter the specified number of characters, the iPAQ will prompt you with a list of words that contain the characters you entered. If your word appears in the suggestion list, tap it, and the word will appear in your text without further entry by you. You can select the number of letters you want to enter before word completion starts to recommend matches, as well as the number of words that should appear in the suggestion list (we prefer three words). Selecting the last check box will cause the iPAQ to insert a space automatically after the word if you make a selection from the word completion list.

Use the Options tab to set five other options:

Voice Recording Format   You can set the default quality level for any voice recording done on the iPAQ. You can choose from a variety of quality levels. The amount of storage per second of recorded audio is shown next to the option so you can see how quickly you will run out of storage space.

Default Zoom Level For Writing   This option defaults screen zoom to the percentage you specify (initially 200%) when you enter Writing mode for any Pocket PC applications that support Writing mode.

Default Zoom Level For Typing   This option defaults screen zoom to the percentage you specify (initially 100%) when you enter Typing mode for any Pocket PC applications that support this mode.

Capitalize First Letter Of Sentence If you select this option, your iPAQ will automatically capitalize the first letter of any sentence whether or not you enter an uppercase letter.

Scroll Upon Reaching The Last Line Selecting this option will cause the screen to scroll up automatically so that the next line comes into view when you have reached the last line visible onscreen while you are entering text.

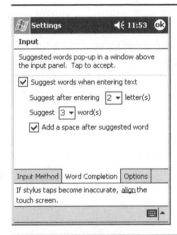

FIGURE 2-15　Word completion will suggest words you might be trying to enter as you type.

Connecting Your iPAQ to Your PC

There are a variety of ways to connect your iPAQ to your PC for synchronization and connectivity:

- USB (universal serial bus) cable
- Serial cable
- LAN connection (wired or wireless)
- Infrared port

The most common method is to connect with a USB connection. Your iPAQ will have arrived with either a cradle with a USB or serial connector that plugs into your PC or a sync cable that plugs into the bottom of the iPAQ and into your PC. It is important that you not connect your cables to your PC until after you have installed ActiveSync (described in the next section).

Also included in your iPAQ kit will be an AC adapter for charging your batteries. This adapter will plug into the back of your cradle, or can plug directly into the bottom of your iPAQ if you only want to charge and not sync. You can also buy sync cables from third parties. We highly recommend the Belkin iPAQ sync/charger cable (**www.belkin.com**). It enables you to charge your iPAQ from your USB port using a single cable. If you travel, it saves having to take your adapter with you on the road. In addition, it comes with a cigarette lighter adapter allowing you to charge your iPAQ in your vehicle, which for road warriors is invaluable. As a final bonus, this cable costs less than one-third the price of the same cable from Compaq.

Most people will sync their iPAQs with a USB cable, but if you don't have a USB port on your computer (older computers may not have a USB port), then you can sync with a serial cable that can be obtained at a significant additional expense from Compaq. It is probably cheaper to buy a USB card for your PC than to buy the cable. Serial syncing is also very slow, so it is not recommended.

You can also sync your iPAQ with your infrared port. Many laptop computers have infrared ports that allow you to sync with your iPAQ if the ports are aligned and the port on your laptop is active. Desktop PCs rarely have infrared ports. This is also a slow sync method and is rarely used. However, it is useful to know that it can be done if you are on the road with your laptop and have forgotten your cable at home.

The fastest way to sync your iPAQ is through a network connection. In order to obtain a network connection you must use an expansion sleeve (discussed in detail in Chapter 13) to insert either a CompactFlash (CF) or PCMCIA networking card. One of the ways of networking your iPAQ that is rapidly growing in popularity is to use a wireless 802.11b wireless local area network (WLAN) card to connect your iPAQ to your network. That way, as you roam around your office, your iPAQ is always connected in real time to your network. The whole concept of how to connect your iPAQ to your network (both wired and wireless) is covered in detail in Chapter 9.

Setting Up ActiveSync

Once you have determined how you will connect your iPAQ to your PC, you must configure the software so you can synchronize information and load new software onto the iPAQ. This is accomplished using software provided by Microsoft called ActiveSync. You can install ActiveSync from the CD that came with your iPAQ. The program installs very easily and doesn't need any information from you to get it installed.

 *Do not connect your iPAQ to your PC with the sync cable until AFTER you have installed ActiveSync on your computer. If you do, the install may not work properly.*

2

Setting Up an ActiveSync Partnership

Once ActiveSync is installed, you can physically connect your iPAQ to your PC. This will initiate a conversation between your iPAQ and the PC as they attempt to establish communication. The first time you connect a new iPAQ to your system, a wizard will open, asking whether you want to set up a *partnership* with the device, as shown in Figure 2-16. A partnership is required if you want to allow your iPAQ to synchronize calendar, contacts, notes, e-mail, and other Pocket Outlook data with your PC. If you only want to use the cable to load software or files onto your iPAQ, then you do not need to set up a partnership. Without a partnership, a device will be connected as a guest. Select Yes or No and tap Next to go on to the next screen of the New Partnership Wizard.

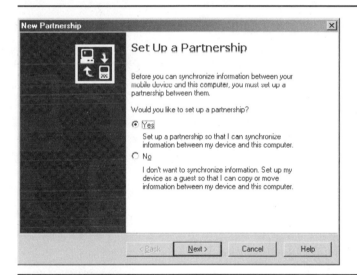

FIGURE 2-16   You must establish a partnership between your iPAQ and your PC to synchronize Pocket Outlook data.

In the second screen, you will be asked whether you want to synchronize this device with more than one computer, as shown in Figure 2-17. If you only ever synchronize with one system, then choose Yes to set up the relationship. If you choose No, then you will not be given the option to synchronize e-mail. However, if you have a computer at work and another at home and want to connect to both of them, you can configure your settings to accommodate this. Set up the computer where your primary e-mail account resides as a Yes (exclusive) relationship, but set up the other machine as a No relationship. This will synchronize your calendar and contact lists on both systems, but your e-mail will only synchronize with the machine that has the Yes relationship. Tap Next after you have made your selection.

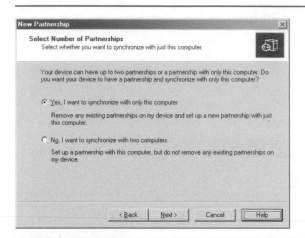

FIGURE 2-17   Select how many systems you will be synchronizing information with on this screen.

 *If you want an e-mail account to stay synchronized instead of relying on ActiveSync to keep the e-mail on your iPAQ, use a new e-mail service with IMAP4, which will always keep your Inbox in sync, no matter which computer you are syncing with.*

The next screen of the wizard will ask you which programs you want to synchronize with your iPAQ, as shown in Figure 2-18. Each of the programs has separate settings that you can configure to modify how it synchronizes. The programs to synchronize are AvantGo, Calendar, Contacts, Favorite, Files, Inbox, Notes, Pocket Access, and Tasks.

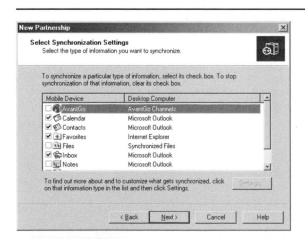

FIGURE 2-18   Choose the programs that you want to synchronize with your iPAQ.

Sync AvantGo

AvantGo is a third-party service (**www.avantgo.com**) that provides, free of charge, informational content that can be delivered to your iPAQ whenever you synchronize. You must set up a *channel* with AvantGo in order to use the service. You set up a channel through your iPAQ by launching Internet Explorer from the Start menu. The Pocket IE home page appears, as shown in the following illustration. Select the AvantGo link at the bottom of the page to begin setting up your channels.

The first time you use this link it will give you instructions on setting up your channels. In order for this to work, your desktop computer must have Internet access. If you have completed the ActiveSync New Partnership Wizard, selecting the AvantGo link will bring you to the AvantGo setup pages. The first of these pages asks you to select a language, as shown here:

Once you choose your language, you will be taken to a default page where you will see the channels that are going to be synchronized with your device. Now you can customize those channels by using the options on the page. Because these web pages might change at any time, we won't show illustrations of the options here. But the AvantGo site operates like any other website, so you can easily follow the links to set up your channels (channels are content that you have elected to bring down and store on your iPAQ such as the latest news, sports scores, and so on).

Once the link is set up, you can go to AvantGo in Pocket IE at any time and read the latest news or other information from the last time that you synced your iPAQ. There is also a new wireless version of AvantGo that will allow you to get real-time updates while you are on the move between syncs. Wireless AvantGo will be discussed in detail in Chapter 9.

Don't select too many channels in AvantGo. Remember that everything you select is stored on your iPAQ and will take up valuable memory space.

It's worth noting for people that already have an AvantGo account that they can select Properties in AvantGo and change their username and password to sync against their current account. This method is a huge time saver as compared to re-configuring everything.

Sync Calendar

If you double-click on the Calendar detail line in ActiveSync on your PC, you will be presented with the sync options for the Calendar, as shown in Figure 2-19.

The Calendar Synchronization Settings dialog box offers three options:

Synchronize All Appointments This means that all appointments both in the past and in the future will be synchronized between the device and your desktop. This is useful if you find that you often make changes to appointments that occurred in the past and you want that information also kept on your iPAQ. This kind of syncing can take some time to complete if you have a lot of historical information on your iPAQ and desktop.

Synchronize Only The With this option you specify how far into the past and future you want ActiveSync to look when synchronizing appointments. You can select a specific number of weeks for the past (the default is two) and for the future, but given that your future data is usually the most important, we do not recommend that you change the latter from the default of All.

Synchronize appointments in selected categories You can choose specific categories of appointments that you want to synchronize. This is useful if you have certain types of appointments on your desktop (or iPAQ) that you don't want kept in sync between the two.

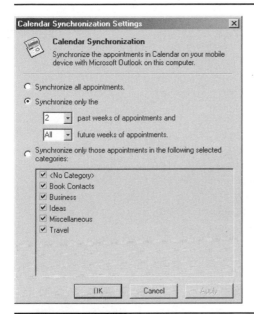

FIGURE 2-19   Specify your sync options for the Calendar in this window.

After you select the options you want, click the OK button to save the changes. The changes you select will only affect this device's profile. ´

Sync Contacts

By double-clicking Contacts in the details of ActiveSync on your PC you will open the Contact Synchronization Settings dialog box shown in Figure 2-20, allowing you to set the sync options for the Contacts application.

You have the following choices for syncing contacts:

Synchronize All Contacts   This is the default option and will keep all of your contacts on your iPAQ and desktop PC synchronized.

Synchronize selected contacts   This option enables you to select specific contacts that you want to synchronize. We don't recommend this option, because any new contacts you add to a specific device will have to be set up independently in ActiveSync if you want to keep them synchronized.

Synchronize contacts in selected categories   This option enables you to select specific categories of contacts that you want to be synchronized with your iPAQ. This setting is useful if you have contacts that you do not want shared between your iPAQ and your desktop.

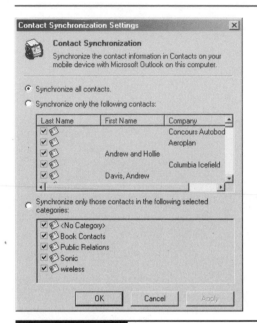

The Contact Synchronization Settings dialog box allows you to set the synchronization options for your Outlook contacts data.

As with the Calendar, once you have selected your options, click OK to have them applied and return to ActiveSync.

Sync Favorites

The Favorites sync options are accessed by double-clicking Favorites in the detail area of ActiveSync. In the Favorite Synchronization Options dialog box, shown in Figure 2-21, you can set which of your Internet Explorer Mobile Favorites settings (web page addresses that you have stored in Mobile Favorites or added to Favorites on your iPAQ) you want to synchronize between your handheld and your desktop.

On the General tab you will see all the pages and folders in the Mobile Favorites folder. Each folder and page can be individually flagged to synchronize to the iPAQ. The Customize tab, shown in Figure 2-22, enables you to choose to synchronize offline content if any of your Favorites are flagged to store offline content in Internet Explorer. Because of the amount of memory images and sound files use, you can choose to exclude those from your offline content.

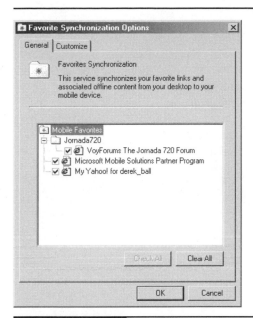

FIGURE 2-21   Use the Favorite Synchronization Options dialog box to set up how you want to sync your favorite web links with your iPAQ.

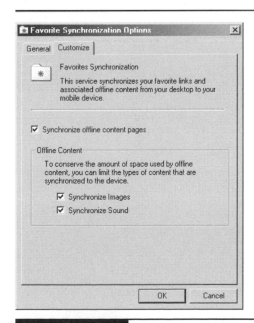

FIGURE 2-22   If you have offline content in your desktop web browser, you can sync that content with your iPAQ.

Sync Files

When you choose to synchronize files between your desktop and your handheld, a special folder will be created in your My Documents folder. It will be named the same as the partnership that you set up for this device (for example, Pocket_PC My Documents). Any documents in this folder will be synchronized automatically with the My Documents folder on your iPAQ when you synchronize. In the File Synchronization Settings dialog box, shown in Figure 2-23, you can choose to not synchronize specific files that are in these folders by removing them from the list using the Remove button. You can add additional files to the list by using the Add button and selecting the file in the File selection dialog box.

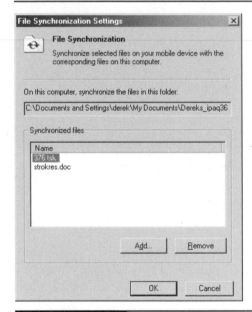

| FIGURE 2-23 | You can keep files synchronized between your desktop and your iPAQ with the File Synchronization Settings dialog box. |

Sync Notes

There are no options for you to set when you have selected to sync Notes in ActiveSync. All notes will be synchronized, and there is no way to exclude any of them.

Sync Tasks

By double-clicking the Tasks line in the details of ActiveSync on your PC, you will open the Task Synchronization Settings dialog box, shown in Figure 2-24, where you can set the sync options for the Tasks application.

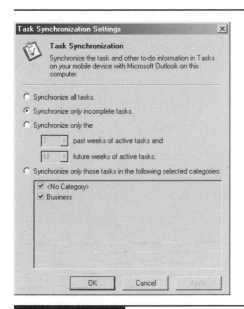

FIGURE 2-24   Set which tasks should be synced between your iPAQ and your desktop with the Task Synchronization Settings dialog box.

Your choices for syncing the tasks are the following:

Synchronize All Tasks   This option will keep all tasks fully synchronized on your desktop and your iPAQ. This isn't the default, because keeping all of your historically completed tasks on your iPAQ is generally not an efficient use of memory.

Synchronize Only Incomplete Tasks   This is the default option. If it is selected, ActiveSync will only synchronize tasks that aren't complete yet. This way you will keep the minimum task information on your iPAQ. This works effectively as long as you don't need to refer to any notes or other items that you might have stored in relation to the task, after the task is completed.

Synchronize Only The   If you schedule a lot of tasks for specific dates in the future, you might not want to have all of those tasks taking up memory on your iPAQ. Instead, you can set a specific range of weeks that you want to keep current in the iPAQ with this option.

Synchronize tasks in selected categories   This option enables you to select specific categories of tasks to synchronize.

Sync Pocket Access

A very useful feature if you want to put information from a local or corporate database onto your iPAQ is the ability to create a Pocket Access database and have it synchronize with the corporate or PC database. You can synchronize any Access database, or any database to which you have an ODBC connection. This includes Microsoft SQL Server, Oracle, Informix, Sybase, and many other popular enterprise databases. There isn't actually a Pocket Access program available for the Pocket PC, so don't go looking for it on your Pocket PC. In order to make use of the Pocket Access database, you will need to use a database viewer program, SQL CE, or write your own program!

After double-clicking Pocket Access in the detail list in the main ActiveSync window, you will be prompted to add or remove a database from the list of databases, as shown in Figure 2-25.

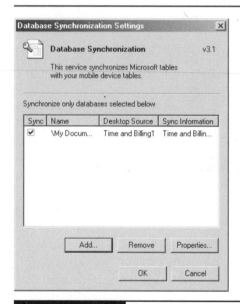

FIGURE 2-25   You can synchronize data in desktop databases using the Pocket Access sync options.

The first time you synchronize, the system will need to create a Pocket Access (.cdb) file on your iPAQ and copy the data to it. You will select the tables and fields that you want copied using the dialog box shown in Figure 2-26.

Another way to synchronize a Microsoft Access file is to drag the .mdb file on your desktop PC to your mobile device icon in the Mobile Devices window.

Sync Inbox

Double-clicking Inbox in the details area of the ActiveSync program on your desktop PC will give you the opportunity to select which folders you want to synchronize with the Inbox application on the iPAQ, as shown in Figure 2-27.

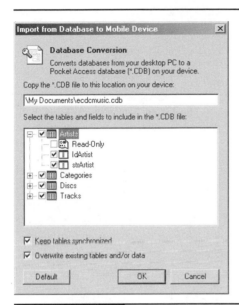

FIGURE 2-26   The Import From Database To Mobile Device dialog box lets you select which tables and fields will be copied onto your iPAQ database.

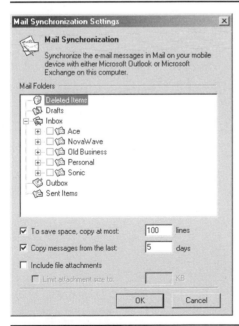

FIGURE 2-27   The Inbox sync options let you control what messages are synced to your iPAQ.

The other options you can set will let you maximize your usage of memory by enabling you to:

- Limit the number of lines downloaded to the Pocket PC Inbox
- Restrict the number of days of messages that will be downloaded to the Pocket PC Inbox
- Choose to include or exclude file attachments, and if including them, limit them to attachments under a certain size

ActiveSync Sync Mode

The Sync Mode tab of the ActiveSync Options dialog box, shown in Figure 2-28, enables you to alter how frequently the data from your iPAQ is synchronized with your desktop. By default, your iPAQ will synchronize with your desktop on a continuous basis. Every time a piece of information is changed in a desktop or Pocket PC application, the relevant record is synchronized on the other device. If this is not the behavior you desire, you can set ActiveSync to only replicate when your device is first connected to your PC, or you can set it to be manual, and only synchronize when you click the Sync button in ActiveSync.

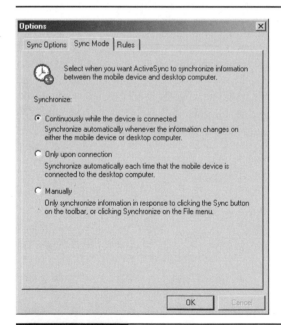

FIGURE 2-28 Setting the sync mode will alter when your iPAQ is synced to your desktop.

ActiveSync Rules

The Rules tab of the ActiveSync Options dialog box allows you to set three critical elements: how to resolve sync conflicts, how to do file conversions, and how to access the Internet, as shown in Figure 2-29.

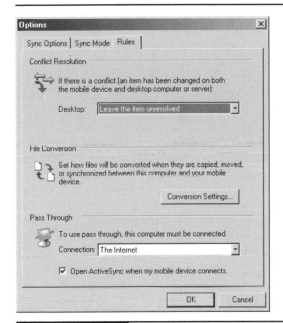

FIGURE 2-29   The Rules are important for determining how to resolve sync conflicts, perform file conversions, and access the Internet while connected to a desktop.

For conflicts in synchronization, you can choose to have a manual resolution (in which case you are prompted about what to do with the information), or you can set it to always favor the desktop over the iPAQ, or the iPAQ over the desktop.

The Conversion Settings button will enable you to specify whether files are to be converted when moved between the Pocket PC and the desktop. You can choose to not convert files such as Word documents (or any other file type). This feature enables your Pocket PC to act as a mobile hard drive as you move around between different computers, but to access the file on your Pocket PC itself, it will need to be converted by the relevant program.

The Pass Through setting specifies how this device will be able to connect to synchronize IMAP4 e-mail services and browse the Web. The selection you make in the Connection box is generally some type of Internet connection.

Syncing with a Server

Here's an interesting challenge. You are often out of the office, and your office manager will use your Calendar in Outlook to schedule appointments for you while you are away. At the same time, you are setting up new appointments in your iPAQ. This leads to scheduling and sync conflicts. To get around this, you have the option of setting up your iPAQ to sync with your server over your wireless connection. To do this, you need to have added Microsoft Mobile Information Server to your server. It will allow you to dial in with your wireless modem and synchronize your Inbox, Calendar, and Contacts.

 If you are syncing data with a server through MS Mobile Information Server, you cannot also sync it with a desktop PC. You can only use one or the other.

To enable syncing with a server, select Options in the Tools menu in ActiveSync to open the Options dialog box. From here, select the Enable Synchronization With Server check box, and click the Configure button to go to a dialog box where you will enter the information for the server you will be synchronizing with.

 *If you are running ActiveSync 3.5, you will not see the Enable Synchronization With Server check box. It will be available in the next version of ActiveSync, which will ship with MS Mobile Information Server 2002.*

Beaming Data for Easy Transfer

There is a very convenient way for people who have Pocket PC devices to share data: beaming information back and forth through the infrared ports that are standard on most Pocket PCs and all iPAQs.

Beaming Between Two Pocket PCs

To beam between two Pocket PCs you simply align the two infrared ports, and then on the device that is sending information, you choose the information you want to beam. You can choose to beam contacts, appointments, notes, tasks, or files. To initiate the sending of information, you select the item that you want to send by tapping and holding the stylus on that item. For example, if you wanted to beam a particular contact, on your iPAQ, you would select the contact and then tap and hold the stylus to produce the shortcut menu shown on the following page.

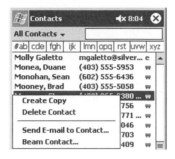

The sending iPAQ will immediately begin searching for another Pocket PC to send the information to. If you have a Pocket PC 2002 system to receive the information, it will automatically detect the beamed information and allow you to begin receiving the information. If you are running Pocket PC 2000, you will need to explicitly set your iPAQ into receive mode by running the Infrared Receive program found in the Programs folder.

Beaming Between Your iPAQ and a Palm

Out of the box, Pocket PCs loaded with the original Pocket PC 2000 software do not talk to Palm devices. Pocket PC 2002 includes OBEX support, which allows you to beam to a Palm or a Nokia cell phone. If you want to use Pocket PC 2000 and beam contact and other information to and from Palm devices you will need to use a third-party product. One of these is Peacemaker from Conduits Software. Peacemaker has both a free version and a more sophisticated full version. The free version allows you to beam contacts to and from Palm devices one contact at a time. The paid version allows you to select multiple data sets (multiple contacts, appointments, files, and so on) of information and transfer them all at the same time. You can get more information from Conduits directly at **www.conduits.com**.

Chapter 3

Use Pocket Word to Read and Write Documents

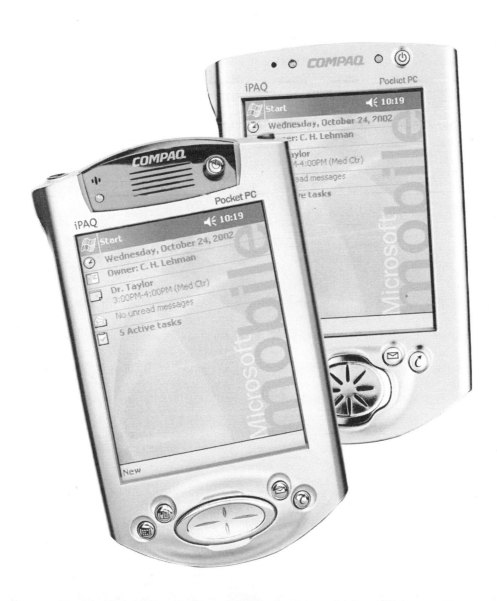

How to...

- Read a Word document on your iPAQ
- Create a Word document on your iPAQ
- Move documents between your iPAQ and your desktop
- Create sketches and drawings
- Capture audio in your documents
- Format a document
- Beam or e-mail a document

One of the most useful features of having a handheld computer running the Pocket PC operating system is access to scaled-down versions of the popular Microsoft Office software. The most commonly used program in the world for documents is Microsoft Word. Your Pocket PC comes with Pocket Word, which allows you to read, compose, and edit documents on your handheld that are compatible with your desktop version of Word.

In this chapter we will examine how to use Pocket Word to not only read, but also to write and edit documents. In order for any of this to be of value, you will need to be able to move documents between your iPAQ and your desktop, so we will also discuss that topic. To make sure that you don't get yourself into any trouble, we will cover exactly which parts of the document you can work with in Pocket Word and which you can't, and what that means for you as a document reader or author.

What Pocket Word Can Do

Pocket Word is a scaled-down version of the full desktop Microsoft Word product. As you would expect, it has only a limited set of features, but this doesn't mean it isn't powerful enough to do almost all of what you need while away from your desk.

It is important to understand that Pocket Word doesn't actually work directly with the .doc files that are created by your desktop Word program. When you move the files over to your Pocket PC (either by copying them with Windows Explorer, syncing, or downloading an e-mail attachment), they are automatically converted from the .doc format you are familiar with to the .psw format, which Pocket Word works with. This reduced format supports the most important features of Word, but some information is stripped out. If you are moving your files back and forth between your iPAQ and your desktop, this could become a problem. To help you understand the details of what is and isn't supported, we've produced lists of the different features and characteristics.

NOTE   *A downloaded e-mail attachment isn't actually converted to the Pocket Word format until it is opened. This is an important distinction because otherwise you would be unable to forward the original .doc file to someone via e-mail.*

The set of fully supported document characteristics includes the following:

Standard text formatting   Consists of bold, italics, underlining, strikethrough, highlight, font type, and font size.

TrueType fonts   Any TrueType fonts you want to use must be installed on your iPAQ (by placing them in the /windows/fonts folder). By default, Courier New and Tahoma are installed with Pocket PC, and you also get Bookdings and Frutiger Linotype with Pocket PC 2002.

Bullets   Any bulleting of text will be supported on the iPAQ.

Paragraph spacing and aligning   Your paragraph spacing and aligning will be retained on the iPAQ.

There are a number of other characteristics that are supported, but not fully, or are altered in their implementation:

Indentation   This is altered to make a document more readable on the iPAQ's smaller screen.

Images   The color depth of images is reduced to 256 colors.

Tables   Table data is brought over and inserted as text, and any formatting information is not retained. If you move a document containing a table back to a desktop Word format, the table will appear as simple text aligned with tab stops.

Table of contents and index data   This information is retained, but as with tables, any formatting is lost.

OLE objects   These objects are not brought over, but are replaced by a bitmap placeholder.

When a document is transferred onto your mobile device, some document characteristics are preserved but ignored for the purposes of Pocket Word. This means that if you restore the document to a desktop environment, those settings reappear. These characteristics include:

- Margins and gutter settings
- Paper size settings
- Header and footer vertical locations

It is very important to understand the characteristics that are completely ignored when you move from the desktop Word environment to the Pocket Word environment, as these settings will return to the default if you ever move the document from Pocket Word back to the desktop. These characteristics include:

- Borders and shading
- Columns
- Numbered lists
- Headers and footers

- Footnotes
- Annotations and comments
- Revision marks
- Frames and style sheets
- Page setup information
- Password protection

 *If you have password protection on a document, you will not be able to convert it to a Pocket Word format. You will need to remove the password protection first.*

Even with these limitations, Pocket Word is an excellent way to view attachments to e-mails that are sent to you, edit short documents while you are on the go, or reference important memos without having to carry briefcases full of paper. With applications like Transcriber (described in Chapter 2), Pocket Word becomes a great place to keep your notes while you are on the move if you want to pull them over to your desktop and edit them later. Or if you are a salesperson on the road, you can edit documents such as contracts while sitting with a client, rather than having to wait until you are back in the office to do it.

Opening an Existing Document or Creating a New Document

When you tap on the icon to launch Pocket Word, you will be presented with a list of documents in the My Documents folder, as shown in Figure 3-1.

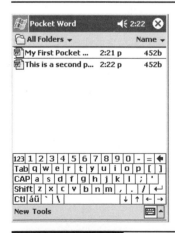

FIGURE 3-1   The document list window shows the Word documents stored on your iPAQ.

To open a specific document, simply tap on it, and it will open within Pocket Word.

If you are already in Pocket Word, you can open a document by tapping OK in the upper-right corner of the title bar. This will close the document you are in and return you to the document list of Figure 3-1.

At the top of the document selection window, you can see a list of the folders by tapping the folders drop-down arrow in the top left, as shown here:

If you have a large number of documents on your iPAQ, you can select to sort the document list by changing the Sort By setting by tapping on the drop-down arrow in the top right of the window, as shown in the illustration that follows. As with your desktop version of Windows, you can sort by file name, date, size, or type.

If you want to create a new document, you select the New option from the menu at the bottom of the document list window. If you are already in a document, you can always select New from the menu at any time to begin creating a new document.

Entering and Editing Text and Drawings

The essence of working in a document editor is to be able to enter text and information in your document. In Pocket Word you can do that in a few different ways. You can select the input mode that you want to use from the View menu. The four options are Writing mode, Drawing mode, Typing mode, and Recording mode. You select the mode that you want to use from the View menu, as shown here:

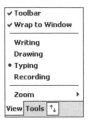

Entering Text in Typing Mode

Typing mode is the default entry mode for Pocket Word. You enter text through the soft input panel (SIP), which is the area at the bottom of the screen that appears as a keyboard or as a character recognition area. The soft input panel is covered in detail in Chapter 2.

All entries that you make in Typing mode end up as text in the document, just as they do with your standard desktop word processor. Wherever the cursor is, that is where your text will appear. You can move the cursor wherever you like in the text simply by tapping the appropriate spot with your stylus. Figure 3-2 shows text entered into a Pocket Word document in Typing mode with the soft keyboard selected.

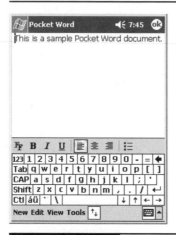

FIGURE 3-2   Typing mode with the soft keyboard visible

Also visible in Figure 3-2 is the toolbar, the group of buttons above the soft keyboard. (In Typing mode, the toolbar contains buttons for formatting text.) By default, this toolbar is off, but you can turn it on by selecting Toolbar from the View menu. It can also be made visible or hidden by clicking the up/down arrow button in the menu bar at the bottom of the window, as shown in Figure 3-3. The toolbar works much the same way as its counterpart in desktop Word. You select the text that you want, and then choose the relevant button to apply formatting to the text. The buttons on the toolbar allow you to select text formatting such as bold, italic, underline, left justified text, right justified text, and center justified text or to start a bulleted list. These formatting options are discussed later in this chapter.

Entering Text in Writing Mode

In Writing mode, the strokes you write with your stylus directly on the screen of the iPAQ are captured and saved in the document. Your handwriting is not converted to text in the document; instead, each word is saved as an image and embedded into the text.

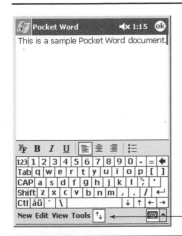

FIGURE 3-3   The formatting toolbar can be toggled on and off by selecting the up/down arrow in the main menu bar.

When you switch into Writing mode, lines are displayed on the screen to help you keep your handwriting in a straight line, as shown in Figure 3-4. The text is also enlarged to make the writing easier. If you are like me, your handwriting is terrible, so you might find that you use Writing mode very rarely.

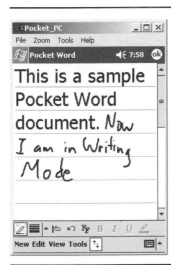

FIGURE 3-4   In Writing mode the strokes you make with the stylus are captured as images.

Each word that you enter is captured as a separate image allowing you to erase one word at a time by selecting the image and deleting it.

The toolbar changes when you are in Writing mode, as shown in Figure 3-4. The first icon in the toolbar allows you to toggle the pen on and off. When the pen is on, wherever you tap with the stylus becomes a word in your handwriting. If you want to move the cursor or select text, you will need to toggle the pen off first. Next to the Pen button is the Pen Weight button, which allows you to select a different weight (line width) for the text that you are writing. You can even change the weight after you have written. The following illustration shows the Pen Weight selections (Fine, Normal, Bold, and Thick) and the word *Writing* changed to a thick weight.

The third button from the left is the Insert/Remove Space button, which allows you to alter the space between words. The next button is for the undo functionality. Since you cannot simply backspace to correct an error when you are writing, Undo lets you erase the last word that you wrote (or the word before that, or more, depending on how many times you tap the button). The formatting buttons are still on the toolbar, and if you select written words, the program will do its best to make bold, underline, italicize, or strikethrough the written words you have created. The button on the far right of the toolbar is the Highlight button, which works the same as it does in the desktop version of Word, allowing you to put a colored background behind the selected text.

Creating Sketches and Diagrams in Drawing Mode

Writing mode is focused on letting you write words in straight lines across the page. If you would like to add sketches and drawings to your Pocket Word document, you will need to switch to Drawing mode. In this mode the system will not try to group your lines into words (which is what happens in Writing mode). Instead each line will be its own image, and you can select multiple lines to group them yourself. Figure 3-5 shows a Pocket Word document with a mixture of text entered in Typing mode, and a drawing entered in Drawing mode.

When in Drawing mode, any text that you have entered in Typing mode is grayed out to remind you that you are in Drawing mode. You will also see a grid appear on the screen to help you align your drawing. You can adjust the zoom factor by selecting Zoom on the menu.

Figure 3-5 is shown in 300% zoom. If you adjust the zoom to 100%, you will see smaller grid boxes and be able to draw a much larger, less grainy image, as shown in Figure 3-6.

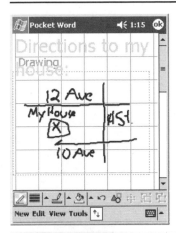

FIGURE 3-5   Drawing mode lets you add sketches to your Pocket Word document.

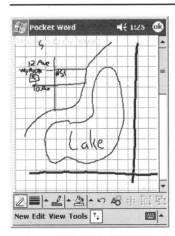

FIGURE 3-6   Changing the zoom factor can give you a larger drawing area.

The toolbar, as shown in Figure 3-6, contains some buttons that are similar to those in Writing mode, such as the Pen toggle and Pen Weight. Next to those you have a pop-up menu for selecting the colors you want for the lines you are drawing, and one for the fill (which will fill in any closed shape that you draw). Tapping on the arrow next to the button brings up a list of colors to choose from, as shown here:

For example, let's say you would like to color the lake in the drawing in Figure 3-6 aqua. First you select the Pen Toggle button to toggle from drawing to selecting. Then you select the lake by tapping on it. Next you tap on the Fill button to display the Fill pop-up menu and choose Aqua from the list. Now the lake is colored aqua, as shown in Figure 3-7.

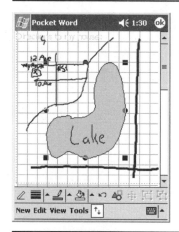

FIGURE 3-7   You can color in any closed shape by using the Fill button.

Every line that you draw in Drawing mode becomes its own discrete object. You can group these objects together by tapping and holding the stylus down and dragging a rectangle around the objects that you want to group. Once they have been selected, you can choose the Group button on the toolbar (second icon from the right showing two squares) to group them together. You can undo this action by selecting a group and choosing the Ungroup button (rightmost icon showing two squares with dark boxes in the corner of each square) on the toolbar.

An action similar to grouping can be done to align objects. Select the objects that you want to align, and then select the Align button (third icon from the right showing two small squares with arrows in each direction). This will give you a pop-up menu with the options to align all the selected objects to the left, right, top, bottom, vertical center, or horizontal center, as shown in Figure 3-8.

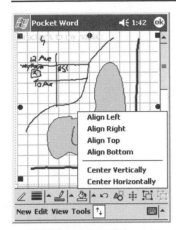

FIGURE 3-8   Clicking the Align button brings up a menu of alignment options.

Tapping and dragging one of the handles (dark boxes or circles that appear on an object's or a group's perimeter) lets you resize any selected object or group of objects.

Drawing mode is good for a quick sketch, but if you want to do any serious art on your Pocket PC, you should probably acquire a third-party graphics program, as discussed in Chapter 11.

Quick Shape Drawing Techniques

If you draw a shape, then tap and hold on it to make the pop-up menu appear. From the pop-up menu, select Shape. This allows you to specify one of four shapes: Rectangle, Circle, Triangle, or Line. You can also resize these shapes, so if you need to do a quick organizational chart, this method actually works.

Using the Recording Mode to Capture Audio

Recording mode is used if you want to attach a live audio recording to the Pocket Word document that you are currently working on. Recording mode places a new toolbar on the bottom of the screen that allows you to use the built-in microphone on your iPAQ to record a voice or live audio attachment for your document. If you have an audio attachment, an icon will be shown in the top-left corner of the document. The attachment icon and the recording toolbar are shown in Figure 3-9.

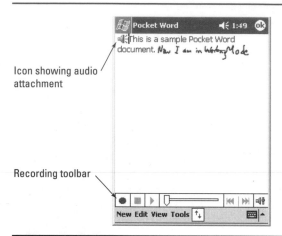

Icon showing audio attachment

Recording toolbar

FIGURE 3-9   The audio attachment icon and the recording toolbar show when your Word document has an attached audio file and allows you to work with that attachment.

The buttons on the recording toolbar are made to resemble those you would see on any tape recorder or VCR. The big red dot will start the recording when tapped. The square will stop the recording. The single right arrow will play a selected recording. The slider bar shows you where in the audio file you are and can be dragged to move to a specific position within the file. The double arrow buttons are to skip to the beginning or end of the recording. The last button lets you adjust the playback volume.

Formatting Your Document

The amount of formatting that you can accomplish in Pocket Word is limited. Any truly fancy formatting will have to wait until you have transferred the file to a full desktop version of Word. However, you can perform some formatting on the text and paragraphs right on your iPAQ.

Text Formatting

To format text in your Pocket Word document, first you must select the text you want to work with. To select a block of text, tap and hold your stylus just before the first letter that you want to affect. Drag your stylus until just after the last letter that you want to format. This will select all the text between your initial tap and your final release. Then select the Format button on the toolbar, as shown here, or choose Format from the Edit menu.

Performing either action will open the Format dialog box, shown in Figure 3-10.

FIGURE 3-10   The Format dialog box allows you to change the characteristics of the selected block of text.

In this dialog box you can use the drop-down lists to change the text font, size, weight, color, and fill color. You can also set the selected text to be bold, italicized, underlined, highlighted, or struck through. When you have finished setting the formatting options for the selected text, tapping the OK circle in the top right of the dialog box will return you to the document.

Paragraph Formatting

To change the formatting of the current paragraph of the document, you only need to place the cursor anywhere in the paragraph by tapping. If you want to affect more than one paragraph at a time, select the text in the paragraphs by tapping and dragging your stylus until all the desired paragraphs have been highlighted. To select the entire document, choose Select All from the Edit menu.

Once you have selected the desired paragraphs, from the Edit menu choose Paragraph to open the Paragraph dialog box, shown in Figure 3-11.

FIGURE 3-11   The Paragraph dialog box lets you change the characteristics of a paragraph.

In this dialog box you can set the alignment to be left, center, or right. You can also convert the selected paragraphs to a bulleted list by checking the check box. Set left, right, and special indentations in this dialog box by entering the desired amounts. Special indentations include extra indentation for the first line of a paragraph and hanging indentation.

Saving Your Document

Saving your current document works slightly differently in Pocket Word than it does in the desktop version. Your Pocket Word document will be saved automatically as soon as you tap the OK button in the top-right corner to exit the document. You do not need to explicitly save the document. It will be saved into the folder that you are currently working in, with the name that you last used. If this is a new document that hasn't been saved before, Pocket Word will use the first words in the document as the file name. If you want to use a specific file name, save in a different folder, save to an external storage device (such as a compact flash card), or save as a different file type, you will need to choose Save Document As from the Tools menu.

Selecting Save Document As will open the Save As dialog box, as shown in Figure 3-12. Tapping OK will carry out your instructions and make a copy of the document where you have requested.

Remember that if you are editing an existing document and tap the OK button in the top-right corner, your changes will be automatically saved. Pocket Word will *not* prompt you when you tap this button with a "Do you want to save?" message as the desktop version does; it will assume that you want to save, and the old version will be overwritten. If you have been making edits and decide you don't want to keep them, be careful not to exit the program with the OK button. Instead, use the Revert To Saved command on the Tools menu. You will be asked to confirm that you want to undo all the changes that you have made since opening the document. If you select Yes, the document will revert to its original state. If you select New after editing a document in Pocket Word, it will prompt you with a message asking whether you want to save, cancel, or save as prior to opening a new document.

FIGURE 3-12 In the Save As dialog box you can change the file name, type, folder, and storage location of your document.

Beaming and E-mailing Your Document

Pocket Word realizes that if you are writing documents on your iPAQ, there is a good chance they will be short, and you will probably want to be able to transmit them to someone else either by e-mail or by "beaming" them to another Pocket PC owner. To make this process as easy as possible, Pocket Word has added Send Document By E-mail and Beam Document commands to the Tools menu.

Selecting Send Document By E-mail from the Tools menu will create a new e-mail message in your Outbox with your document already attached. You will need to select to whom you wish to send the message as well as add a subject line and any text to the message. Tapping the Send button will queue it up to be sent the next time you have an active wireless connection or the next time you connect with ActiveSync.

Selecting the Beam Document command will automatically set up your iPAQ to beam or transmit the document from your infrared port at the top of your unit to a receiving unit that has a physically aligned infrared port. You will see the Pocket Word beaming window, shown in Figure 3-13, which shows the status of the beam. In Figure 3-13 the device hasn't yet located an aligned infrared port that is ready to receive. If you are running Pocket PC 2000, the receiving unit must be set to receive the file by selecting the Infrared Receive program in the Program Files folder. For Pocket PC 2002 users, the unit is always in a receive state unless you specifically turn this feature off. Once the document has been successfully transmitted, you will see the results window, as shown in Figure 3-14.

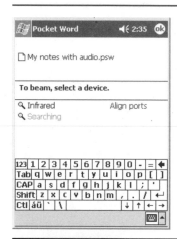

FIGURE 3-13   Setting up to beam a document to another Pocket PC through the infrared port

FIGURE 3-14   The results window appears after a document is successfully beamed to another Pocket PC device.

Zoom

The Zoom command on the View menu allows you to change the size of the document view. There are five preset zoom levels: 75%, 100%, 150%, 200%, and 300%. Figure 3-15 shows our sample document zoomed to 75%, the smallest setting, as well as the Zoom command fully expanded.

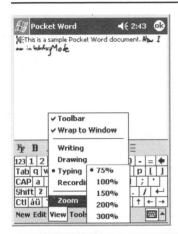

FIGURE 3-15   A document zoomed to 75% allows you to see more information on the screen at one time.

Undo/Redo

Undo and Redo commands are available on the Edit menu. Undo will undo the last action that you took, including formatting, zooming, typing, deleting, or other action. This command is also available on the standard toolbar. Tapping Undo multiple times will undo multiple previous actions. The Redo command will let you restore the change that you just undid. Redo can be useful if you tap the Undo button one too many times and accidentally undo more steps than you intended to.

Spell Check

Spell check is only available with Pocket PC 2002. If you are running an earlier version of Pocket PC or have upgraded an older iPAQ to Pocket PC 2002, you will not have this feature (although it can be installed separately).

You can start the spell checker by choosing it from the Tools menu.

Word Count

You can determine the length of your document by selecting Word Count from the Tools menu. A window will pop up that gives the count of words entered in the document, as shown next. Note that this does not include any words that you have entered in Writing mode.

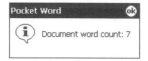

Setting Your Options

You can set global options for Pocket Word by selecting Options from the Tools menu. The Options dialog box will open, as shown in Figure 3-16.

FIGURE 3-16   You can set Pocket Word options in the Options dialog box.

Default Template

The Default Template drop-down list allows you to set the standard template that will be used every time a new document is opened using the New command. It is rare that you would want to change this selection from the default Blank Document, unless you find that the vast majority of new documents you create are based on another template. The standard set of templates that install with Pocket Word are:

Blank Document   The initial default template is a completely blank document.

Memorandum   This template contains a title and the standard fields To, CC, From, and Date.

Meeting Notes   This template contains a title, subject, date, attendees, and action items headings.

Phone Memo   This template contains a title, caller, company, phone, date and time, and message headings.

To Do   This template contains a title and a list of blank bullets for entering to do items.

Alternatively, to start a document with a specific template, you can select the Templates folder from the document list window discussed in the section "Opening an Existing Document" or "Creating a New Document" earlier in this chapter.

You can add new templates to this default set by creating a template you want and putting it in the Templates folder. For example, if you are a real estate inspector and find that you use your iPAQ for doing inspections in the field, you could set your default Word document template to be a blank inspection report. Just remember to use the Save Document As command to avoid overwriting your initial template. (We recommend keeping an extra copy of all your templates in a different folder because at some point you will accidentally overwrite your template.)

Save To

The Save To command allows you to save your documents by default to the main memory of your iPAQ or to an external storage location. External storage locations can include Secure Digital (SD) cards (if you have an iPAQ 38*xx* series with a Secure Digital slot), CompactFlash (CF) cards, external PCMCIA hard drives, or other storage devices. These devices are examined in detail in Chapter 15.

Display In List View

The Display In List View command allows you to select what types of files appear in the document list window that opens when you first launch Pocket Word. By default this list will show all known file types. You can restrict this list to show only Pocket Word documents or only Pocket Word documents and text documents.

Synchronizing with Your Desktop

Synchronizing your data with ActiveSync is covered in detail in Chapter 2, and if you are in need of detailed instructions you should refer to that chapter. Note that keeping a synchronized document on both your Pocket PC and desktop system can be a great convenience. Every time you make a change on your Pocket PC or desktop, the document will be synchronized with the other system. If you reference and update this document frequently, then this capability could save you a great deal of time.

Chapter 4

Use Pocket Excel

How to...

- Open and work with an Excel workbook on your iPAQ
- Create a Pocket Excel workbook on your iPAQ
- Move workbooks between your iPAQ and your desktop
- Format cells and workbooks
- Use formulas in a workbook
- Beam or e-mail a workbook

Like Pocket Word, Pocket Excel is part of the unique capabilities of the Pocket PC–based handhelds like the iPAQ. Pocket Excel allows you to view, create, and edit spreadsheets on your handheld that are compatible with your desktop version of Excel.

In this chapter we will examine how to use Pocket Excel to not only view, but also to compose and edit spreadsheets. As we did in Chapter 3, on Pocket Word, to make sure that you don't get yourself into any trouble, we will cover exactly which parts of the spreadsheet you can work with in Pocket Excel and which you can't and what that means for you as a spreadsheet reader or author.

What Pocket Excel Can Do

Pocket Excel is a scaled-down version of the full desktop Microsoft Excel product. As you would expect, it only has a limited set of features, but this doesn't mean it isn't powerful enough to do almost all of what you need while away from your desk.

Like Pocket Word, the files that Pocket Excel works with are converted versions of the .xls files that are on your desktop. The converted Pocket Excel workbook extensions are .pxl for workbooks and .pxt for templates. When you move the files over to your Pocket PC (either by copying them with Windows Explorer, syncing, or downloading an e-mail attachment) they are automatically converted to the correct format. This reduced format supports the most important features of Excel, but some information is lost. If you are moving your files back and forth between your iPAQ and your desktop, this could become a problem. You shouldn't notice any significant problems with basic spreadsheets, but some that utilize more sophisticated functions could operate differently in Pocket Excel. To help you understand the details of what is and isn't supported, we've produced lists of the different features and characteristics.

This is the set of fully supported spreadsheet characteristics:

Standard text formatting   Bold, italics, underlining, highlight, font type, font color, and font size formatting are fully supported.

True Type fonts   Note that any TrueType fonts you want to use must be installed on your iPAQ. By default, Courier New, Tahoma, Bookdings, and Frutiger Linotype are preinstalled.

Cell formatting   Standard and custom formats are supported for cells including General, Number, Currency, Accounting, Date, Time, Percentage, Fraction, Scientific, and Text.

Alignment   Horizontal and vertical alignment options are supported along with word wrap within a cell.

Row heights and column widths   Adjustment of row heights and columns widths are supported.

There are a number of other characteristics that are supported, but not fully, or are altered in their implementation:

Formulas with arrays   You cannot use arrays in your formulas. When you copy a spreadsheet that contains arrays from your desktop, the arrays in the formulas will be converted to values in Pocket Excel.

Formulas with unsupported functions   Many of the functions in Excel are supported in Pocket Excel, but not all. We won't list all the functions here, but to give an example, the Round() function is not available in Pocket Excel. You can see a full list of supported functions from the Insert Function comman on the Tools menu. When you copy a spreadsheet that includes unsupported functions from your desktop, those functions will be converted to values.

Pivot tables   Pivot tables are not supported in Pocket Excel, and, like the unsupported formulas, will be changed to values if brought over from desktop Excel.

Borders   Borders are supported, but not if you try to be fancy. You can only create borders with single lines. Any different borders that are brought over from desktop Excel will be converted to single line borders.

Vertical text   Vertical text is not supported and will be changed to horizontal text if brought over from a desktop file.

Hidden names   Any hidden names that are brought over from a desktop file will be displayed.

Passwords   You can set a general password for your spreadsheet in Pocket Excel, but you can't choose options like adding a password in order to modify the spreadsheet, or flagging it as read-only.

When a spreadsheet is brought onto your mobile device, there is one characteristic that is converted, but is ignored for the purposes of Pocket Excel: cell shading. This means that if you restore the spreadsheet to a desktop environment, the cell shading originally assigned to a cell reappears.

It is very important to note which characteristics are completely unsupported when you move from the desktop Excel environment to the Pocket Excel environment, as these settings will return to the default if you ever move the spreadsheet from Pocket Excel back to the desktop. These characteristics are:

- Graphics of any kind (images, object charts, picture controls, drawing objects, and so on)

- AutoFilter

- Add-ins

- Data validation
- Cell notes
- Cell patterns
- Cell and sheet protection
- Scenarios
- Text boxes
- Hyperlinks
- VBA scripting

Pocket Excel is a very handy way to whip together quick calculations, write up expense sheets while on the go, gather sports statistics at the park, calculate a tip at the restaurant, and more. The wonderful Transcriber application we've already mentioned also works well with Pocket Excel.

If you need some of the functions that are not provided in Pocket Excel, third-party applications may be the answer. For example, Developer One (www.developerone.com) makes a program called Pocket AutoGraph that allows you to work with Excel data in graphs. The ClearVue viewers from Westtek (www.westtek.com) allow you to view full Excel documents including charts and graphics, but do not allow for editing.

Opening an Existing Spreadsheet or Creating a New Spreadsheet

When you tap the icon to launch Pocket Excel, you will be presented with a list of workbooks in the default folder, as shown in Figure 4-1.

To open a specific workbook, simply tap it, and it will open within Pocket Excel.

If you are already in Pocket Excel, you can open a workbook by tapping OK in the upper-right corner of the title bar. This will close the workbook you are in and return you to the list shown in Figure 4-1.

At the top of the workbook selection window you can browse through the folders by tapping the show folders drop-down arrow in the top left, as shown here:

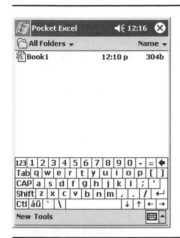

FIGURE 4-1   The workbook list window shows the Pocket Excel workbooks stored on your iPAQ.

If you have a large number of workbooks on your iPAQ, you can select to sort the list by changing the sort by rule. To change the sorting method, tap the drop-down arrow in the top right of the window, shown next, and make a selection from the list. As with your desktop version of Excel, you can sort by file name, date, size, or type.

If you want to create a new workbook, select New from the menu at the bottom of the workbook list window. If you are already in a workbook, you can always select New from the menu at any time to begin creating a new workbook.

Entering Data and Formulas into Cells

The benefit of spreadsheet software like Pocket Excel is that you can analyze groups of numbers or information by entering the data into the spreadsheet and then building formulas to calculate and manipulate the values automatically. Typical examples of this include tracking expenses, tallying up sales for a group of stores, keeping sports statistics, or any other numerical activity. For non-numerical activities it might contain items like your grocery list or Christmas gift list.

Selecting Cells

Before you can enter data into a cell, you must select the cell or group of cells that you want to work with. To select a single cell, tap the cell you desire with your stylus, as shown in Figure 4-2.

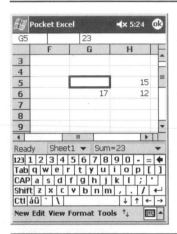

Before you can enter data into a workbook, you must select the cell or cells you want to work with.

If the cell you want is not visible, you can scroll using the scroll bars on the right and bottom or you may use the Go To command in the Tools menu. Selecting Go To will open the dialog box shown next, allowing you to specify a specific cell (which you can name by its cell address, H9, for example, or if you have named ranges in your workbook you can use the name).

The Go To Current Region command will select a rectangular cell range around the currently selected cell bordered by blank rows or columns, as shown in Figure 4-3.

You can select a range of cells by tapping with the stylus and dragging the rectangle so that all the cells you desire are contained within the shaded area.

FIGURE 4-3   The Go To Current Region command will select the set of all cells around the current cell that contain data.

Entering Data into a Cell

Once you have selected a cell or range of cells, you can enter data, labels, or formulas into the current cell. You can enter data in the standard ways, through the character recognizer, keyboard, or Transcriber.

When you start typing in characters, they will appear in the entry bar where the current cell value is displayed, as shown in Figure 4-4. To the left of this bar you will find the address of the current cell, a button to cancel your entry and a button to complete your entry (which is the same as pressing ENTER on the keyboard). There is also a button for creating formulas, which is addressed later in this chapter.

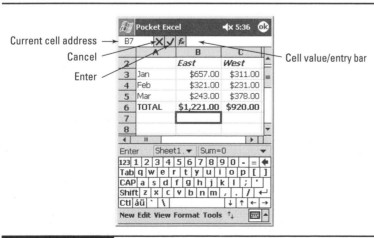

FIGURE 4-4   Data that you enter appears in the cell value box with buttons to cancel or accept your entry.

The difference between using the Enter button on the entry bar and ENTER on your keyboard is that tapping the Enter button will leave you in the current cell, whereas pressing ENTER on the keyboard will accept your entry and will make the cell below the current cell the new current cell. The latter action is convenient for entering a long list of data.

Entering a Formula

Being able to enter formulas to perform calculations on numbers is where the real power of a spreadsheet program like Excel becomes evident. Usually you are after more than just a list of numbers. You need to be able to add up those numbers, find an average, or perhaps perform a net present value calculation. All of this is possible with Pocket Excel formulas.

To enter a formula, first select the cell in which you want the result of your formula to be displayed. To tell Pocket Excel that you are creating a formula, enter an equals sign (=) in the cell value box. Next type in the formula that you desire along with any information that it needs in order to make its calculation, as shown next. (Note that the three buttons between the cell address and the cell value only appear when you are editing a specific cell.)

This illustration shows an example of one of the most commonly used formulas, the Sum formula. It is very likely, if you are a frequent user of Excel, that you will know the most common formulas such as Sum, Average, and Count, but you will not know all of the other functions that are available. To access these you can go to the Insert Function command under the Tools menu or tap the f_x button to the immediate left of the cell value area. Any of these actions opens the Insert Function dialog box, shown in Figure 4-5.

To select which subset of functions you want to look at, make a selection in the drop-down list in the Category box. The default setting is to show all functions, but you can choose to view subsets of Financial, Date and Time, Math and Trigonometry, Statistical, Lookup, Database, Text, Logical, and Informational.

The Function list shows all the available functions that match the category you selected. The arguments that the function expects are presented in parentheses. When you select a function in the list, a brief description of it will appear beneath the list. To list every function in detail is beyond the scope of this book, but if you have access to the desktop version of Excel, you can look up the details of each function; they work the same way in Pocket Excel as they do in the desktop version.

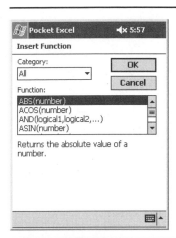

FIGURE 4-5   You can select from a list of all available functions in the Insert Function dialog box.

Once you have selected the function you desire, tap OK to return to the cell value box where the selected function will be pasted into place. Next, simply replace the argument placeholders with the values that you desire. In addition to typing in the cell addresses by hand, you can tap specific cells in order to enter them into your formulas or, to enter a range, tap and hold a cell and then drag the stylus over the range of cells you would like to select.

Tapping and Holding a Cell

If you tap your stylus and hold it on a cell without moving the stylus, you will be presented with a pop-up menu to help make it easier to perform common functions on a specific cell, as shown in the following illustration.

 *Tap-and-hold functionality is only available in Pocket PC 2002. If you are running an earlier version of Pocket PC, tapping and holding will do nothing.*

From this pop-up menu you can easily cut or copy the selected cell (or cells) into the clipboard, from which they can be pasted elsewhere in the spreadsheet. You also have commands to open the Insert Cells, shown next, or Delete Cells dialog boxes.

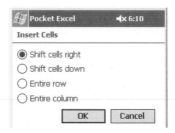

The Delete Cells dialog box works the same as the Insert Cells dialog box except that rows are shifted either left or up, or entire rows or columns are deleted.

Use the final command on the pop-up menu to edit the formatting of the selected cells.

Formatting Cells

The amount of formatting that you can accomplish in Pocket Excel is limited when compared with that available in the desktop version. Any truly fancy formatting will have to wait until you have transferred the file to a full desktop version of Excel. Nevertheless, there are still a number of items you can format in Pocket Excel.

When you select Format Cells from the tap-and-hold pop-up menu, or from the Cells command under the Format menu, the Format Cells dialog box will open. Along the bottom of this dialog box are five tabs to choose from: Size, Number, Align, Font, and Borders.

Size

You can format the row height and column width of the currently selected cell on the Size tab in the Format Cells dialog box, as shown in Figure 4-6. Only these two properties may be edited.

Row height is measured in points, and column width is measured in characters based upon the standard font. Row height can be set anywhere from 0 to 409. A value of 0 will make the row a hidden row. Column width can be set anywhere from 0 to 255 characters (decimal points are allowed) based upon the standard character font. Setting the column width to 0 will hide the column.

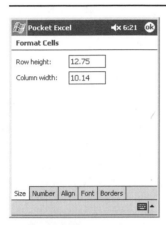

FIGURE 4 6	The physical size of the selected cell(s) can be adjusted by setting the Row Height and Column Width values on the Size tab of the Format Cells dialog box.

Number

You can change the data type of the number in a cell on the Number tab of the Format Cells dialog box. The Category list box contains a list of all the valid formats for Pocket Excel. You can scroll through this list and select the format that is appropriate for what you are doing. When you select a format, appropriate formatting options for that data type will appear below. For example, in Figure 4-7 the Currency data type has been selected; the options for this data type are the number of decimal places, how to display negative numbers, and whether you want the currency symbol to be shown. A sample of a number formatted as this data type is displayed below the options.

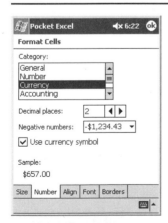

FIGURE 4-7	You can select the data type for a cell with the Number tab of the Format Cells dialog box.

The format types available are General, Number, Currency, Accounting, Date, Time, Percentage, Fraction, Scientific, Text, and Custom.

Align

The Align tab is used to set the alignment properties of the currently selected cell. From here you have the option to set the horizontal alignment to General, Left, Center, Right, or Center Across Selection. You can set the vertical alignment to Top, Center, or Bottom. There is also a check box that will allow to you wrap text onto multiple lines within a cell, as shown in Figure 4-8.

FIGURE 4-8   Use the Align tab to set options for horizontal and vertical alignment as well as word wrapping within a cell.

Font

On the Font tab you can select from the drop-down lists to change the selected cell's font, size, and color. You can also set the cell to be bold, italic, or underlined, as shown in Figure 4-9.

Borders

On the Borders tab you can select the options for a border around the currently selected cell or cells. You can only create one style of border—a single line—unlike desktop Excel, which has many line weights and types. You can set a line color and fill color for the cell from the drop-down lists. Given that most Pocket PCs available today have full-color screens, the use of colors in a spreadsheet can be very effective. You can also set which side of the cells you want to see a border on by checking the appropriate boxes for Outline, Left, Right, Top, and Bottom, as shown in Figure 4-10.

FIGURE 4-9   You can format the font settings for the selected cell on the Font tab.

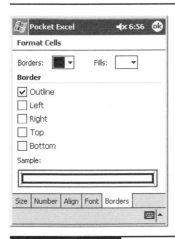

FIGURE 4-10   You can format the borders for your cells with the Borders tab.

Formatting Rows and Columns

Under the Format menu there are commands to set specific formatting for rows and columns. These do not deal with colors or fonts of the rows and columns, but rather allow you to either hide or show the selected rows/columns or set them to AutoFit. AutoFit means that the row height or column width is adjusted to automatically accommodate the widest or tallest data in the row/column.

Working with Sheets

Workbooks in Pocket Excel accommodate multiple sheets, just as the desktop version of Excel does. When you create a new workbook, it is automatically created with three sheets. You can see what sheet you are currently in by looking at the Sheet area of the status bar (immediately above the menu), as shown in Figure 4-11.

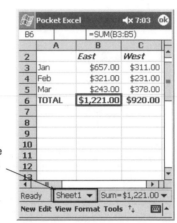

Displays the current sheet. To change sheet, select from the drop-down list.

FIGURE 4-11   See or change the current worksheet with the sheet box in the status bar.

You can add, remove, reorder, or rename sheets in your workbook by selecting Modify Sheets from the Format menu, which opens the dialog box shown here:

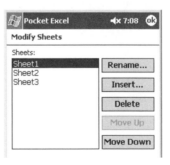

Using the AutoCalculate Feature

The status bar in Pocket Excel also contains a box for automatically showing calculated values on the currently selected range of cells. For example, if in the spreadsheet shown in Figure 4-12 we wanted to see the total of sales across both the East and West regions for January, we would select the relevant range of cells, and the AutoCalculate box in the status bar would show that the total sales are $968.00 as the figure shows.

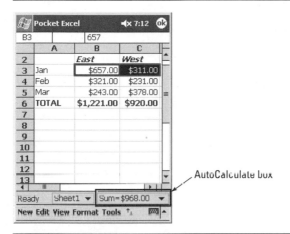

| FIGURE 4-12 | The AutoCalculate feature will perform automatic calculations on a selected range of cells. |

To change the kind of calculation being performed, tap the drop-down arrow in the box and make a selection from the list of calculations. The choices are Average, Count, Count Nums, Max, Min, and Sum, as shown here:

Using AutoFilter

Sometimes you have a large set of data, and you want to be able to easily jump between subsets of that data. For example, if you had a list of all your employees across the country, you might want to be able to quickly filter the list to only show those employees in a given city. You can do this using the AutoFilter command on the Tools menu. To use AutoFilter, select a cell in the title or header row of your spreadsheet, and then select AutoFilter.

Drop-down arrows will then appear in all the columns of your row, as shown in the following illustration:

Click the drop-down arrows in any column and select from the list to filter for a specific column value, get all the data, see the top ten items, or set a custom filter, as you can see next:

The following illustration shows the result of filtering an employee list for a specific city, in this case, Seattle.

The Custom command of AutoFilter is different from the others. Selecting Custom opens the Custom AutoFilter dialog box, as shown in Figure 4-13. This dialog box allows you to set custom filter criteria. You can select one or two conditions where the selected column is equal to, not equal to, greater than, less than, greater than or equal to, less than or equal to, or begins with a value that you enter in the second field. You can then set an AND or OR condition with a second criteria that you can choose.

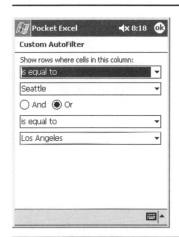

FIGURE 4-13   With the Custom filter command you can build a complex filter criteria with up to two elements that can be joined by an AND or OR condition.

Sorting

When you are working with lists of data and numbers, the ability to sort the information in a meaningful way is critical. To sort data in Pocket Excel, first select the range of cells that you want to sort, as shown in the following illustration. (You can include or exclude the header row; you have the option of excluding it later in the Sort dialog box.)

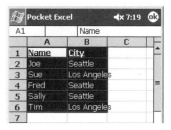

Once you have selected the cells you want, choose Sort from the Tools menu. The Sort dialog box will open, as shown in Figure 4-14. You have the option to sort by up to three columns. If the first column you select has two values that are the same, then the second column will be evaluated when choosing which row of data to place first, and so on with the third. The check box to the right of each column allows you to specify whether you want to sort in ascending or descending order.

FIGURE 4-14   The Sort dialog box allows you to select which columns to sort by.

The check box at the bottom of the dialog box allows you to exclude the header, or title, row if you included it in your selection. If this box is selected, the column title will appear in the drop-down lists that currently show Column A, Column B, and so forth.

Inserting Symbols

If you find that you need to insert special characters in your text, you can do that with the Insert Symbols command on the Tools menu. Typical examples of special characters include currency characters such as pound (£) or yen (¥) and letters with special accents and certain characters from the Latin alphabet as well as characters from the Hebrew, Arabic, Cyrillic, Greek, and other alphabets. When you choose Insert Symbols, the Insert Symbol dialog box opens, as shown in Figure 4-15.

From here you select the font that you want to work with from the drop-down list, as shown in the illustration on the following page.

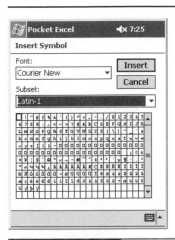

4

| FIGURE 4-15 | Use the Insert Symbol dialog box to insert special characters into your worksheet. |

Then you can select the subset of the font. For example, the subsets available for Courier New include a few Latin choices, some special formatting and spacing characters, Greek, Cyrillic, Hebrew, Arabic, Armenian, Devanagari, Gurmukhi, Gujarta, Oriya, Tamil, Telungu, Kannada, Malayalam, Thai, Lao, Basic and Extended Georgian, Hangul Jamo, and many more special sets of characters, drawing symbols, pictograms, and others.

The graph that displays all the characters is extremely small and difficult to read. It would be nice in future releases if they would provide a general zoom option on this window. In the mean time, you can see the character better by selecting it. This will show an enlarged version of the selected character, as shown here:

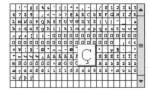

Now tap the Insert button, and that character will be inserted into your workbook at the point where your cursor is.

Defining Names

A seldom-used feature of Excel is the ability to assign a name to a cell or range of cells. This allows you to reference the cell by name when using it in formulas instead of having to remember the cell's address every time you want to use it. This technique can be very useful for large spreadsheets that contain a number of formulas. For example, if we take our list of sales by region, we can add names to the regions and then use those names in our formulas. To define the name for a region, we first select the region. In the following illustration, we have selected all the sales for the East region.

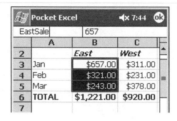

To give this range of cells a name, we select Define Name on the Tools menu to open the Define Name dialog box, shown in Figure 4-16. In this dialog box you can enter a name for the selected region. In our example, we call this region EastSales. Tapping Add adds the name that you enter to the list of defined names. The Refers To field below the list allows you to see which cell or range is included in the selected name.

FIGURE 4-16   In the Define Name dialog box you can give a name to your selected cell or range of cells.

Once a name is defined, you can substitute it for any cell reference (if it names a specific cell) or any cell range in any formula. In our example, we named a range of cells EastSales. In the formula in cell B6, as shown in the following illustration, we are summing the range of cells from B3 to B5. This is the same range we named EastSales, so we can substitute the range in the formula with EastSales, and Excel will perform the correct calculation.

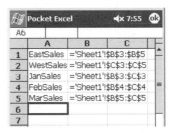

A final feature to mention in this section is the Paste List button shown in Figure 4-16. If you make extensive use of defined names, you may want to have a list somewhere in your workbook of all your defined ranges for reference. You can create such a list by placing your cursor where you want the list to be inserted and then opening the Define Name dialog box and selecting Paste List. A list of defined names that looks something like the one shown here will be pasted into your workbook.

Using the Fill Feature

The Fill feature of Excel allows you to fill a range of cells with data quickly and easily. Fill can be used for static copying of data from an existing set of cells or can include filling the range with a series or data that is different in each cell, such as an increasing number or date. To perform a copy type of fill, you must select the cells that you want to copy and then at the same time, select all the cells that you want to fill in with the copied data. The original data must be on one edge of the selection range. This can be any of the top, bottom, left, or right edges. Once the data and range are selected, you choose the Fill command from the Edit menu to open the Fill dialog box, as shown in Figure 4-17.

FIGURE 4-17   The Fill dialog box allows you to fill a selected range of cells with data.

To perform your copy, you simply indicate which row the original data is in by choosing your fill direction from the list of Down, Up, Left, or Right. The Fill Type in this case will be Copy. Once you've made your selections, tap OK to copy the original data into the range.

It's likely you will also use the Fill command to fill a range of cells with series data, such as a range of numbers or dates. When building a series, it helps to think in advance about what cells you need to select. For example, if you wanted to produce a list of days of the week on the left of your worksheet, you could enter the first day **Mon** on the first line. Then you would select the Mon cell along with the six cells beneath it, as shown here:

Select Edit | Fill, and in the Fill dialog box select a direction of Down, a Fill type of Series, and a Series type of AutoFill, as shown in Figure 4-18.

AutoFill instructs Excel to examine the data in the selected range and to extend the range. In our example, entering **Mon** on line 1 tells AutoFill to fill the lines in the range with the subsequent days of the week. Tapping OK will produce the results shown on the following page.

FIGURE 4-18   You can set the options in the Fill dialog box to produce an AutoFill of days of the week.

CAUTION   *We found a bug in the version of Pocket PC 2002 we are running. If you attempt to use AutoFill with numerical data, it will not enter a series, but will instead copy your data from the first cell into all the remaining cells. You can work around this bug by using the Series Type of Number instead of AutoFill.*

The other Series types that you can select are Date and Number. Selecting one of these means that the primer data that you have entered in the fill range only includes the starting point for the series (that is, the first day or number that you want). For the rest of the information you will indicate what you want to fill in (days or numbers). If you choose days you must choose the type of date information that you want to fill in, either Day, Month, or Year. Then with either option you must choose the increment or step value. This is the number that the Fill function will increase each subsequent line or column in the fill. For example, to fill a range with the first day of each week you would put your first date such as **Jan 1** on the first line in your range. Then in the Fill dialog box you would select a Fill type of Series, a Series type of Date, and a Step value of 7. Tapping OK would produce a worksheet like the one shown here:

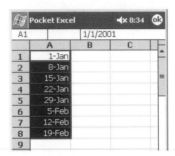

Zoom and Full Screen View

The Zoom command on the View menu allows you to change the view of your worksheet to make the work space larger or smaller. This useful feature allows you to see more of your worksheet at one time or focus on a small area of it, although you might sacrifice resolution and readability depending on the scale you select. There are five preset zoom levels you can select from—50%, 75%, 100%, 125%, and 150%—or you can choose Custom to set your own zoom percentage. Figure 4-19 shows our sample worksheet zoomed to 75%, and also the Zoom command fully expanded.

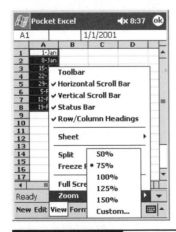

FIGURE 4-19　A worksheet zoomed to 75% allows you to see more information on the screen at once.

Panes/Splitting

If you want to view two different parts of the same worksheet at the same time, you can split your screen into panes. This can be done so you can look at two different sets of data or to keep certain information fixed at the top and left of your worksheet while you scroll around in the main part of the worksheet. Figure 4-20 presents an example of a divided screen where we have split our regional sales spreadsheet to allow us to scroll through the data section while keeping the column and row headers in place.

4

| FIGURE 4-20 | Windows can be split into panes to allow you to work with different sections of a worksheet at the same time. |

To break a spreadsheet into panes, select the cell where you want the split to occur. Then select Split from the View menu. To remove the split from any worksheet you are in, select Remove Split from the View menu.

The Freeze Panes command under the View menu works in a very similar way. The difference is that in a split, you have the ability to scroll anywhere on the spreadsheet within any of the panes. With a freeze, only the main "unfrozen" area freely scrolls in all directions. When you hit the boundary of a frozen pane, the cursor will automatically jump into the correct pane for editing purposes. Another difference is that frozen panes are displayed with a single, static line rather than the double, movable line used with a split screen. Choosing Unfreeze Panes from the View menu turns off the Freeze Panes command. An example of frozen panes is shown in Figure 4-21.

The Toolbar

By default, the toolbar for Excel is hidden, but you can make it appear by tapping the up/down arrow icon in the menu bar. This button toggles the toolbar on and off. From the toolbar, shown

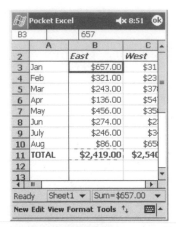

FIGURE 4-21   Frozen panes are displayed with a solid, static line.

next, you have quick access to cell formatting, alignment, common functions, number formatting, and a button to toggle through all the zoom settings.

Undo/Redo

Undo and Redo commands are available on the Edit menu. Undo will undo the last action that you took, including formatting, zooming, typing, deleting, or other action. Tapping Undo multiple times will undo multiple previous actions. The Redo command will let you restore the change that you just undid. This feature can be useful if you tap the Undo button one too many times and accidentally undo too many steps.

Find and Replace

To locate any specific text in your workbook, you can use the Find/Replace command on the Edit menu. Selecting this command opens the Find dialog box, shown in Figure 4-22.

You enter any text string that you are looking for in the Find What box. Then you can set options to require it to match case or to only match if the entire cell content matches your text. You must then select whether you would like to search in cells that contain formulas or cells that contain values. If you like, you can specify a value to replace the search text with by tapping the Replace button. In the new dialog box that opens, you specify your replacement string.

FIGURE 4-22   The Find dialog box allows you to search for and replace text strings in your workbook.

If you tap the Find button, Excel will find and make current the first cell after your current cell that contains the string. A new toolbar will also be displayed, as shown in Figure 4-23. This toolbar allows you to move on to find the next instance of your text string, replace the text (using the replacement text that you specified), or replace all instances (it will stop asking you to confirm each one). Or you may cancel your Find/Replace action by tapping the X button.

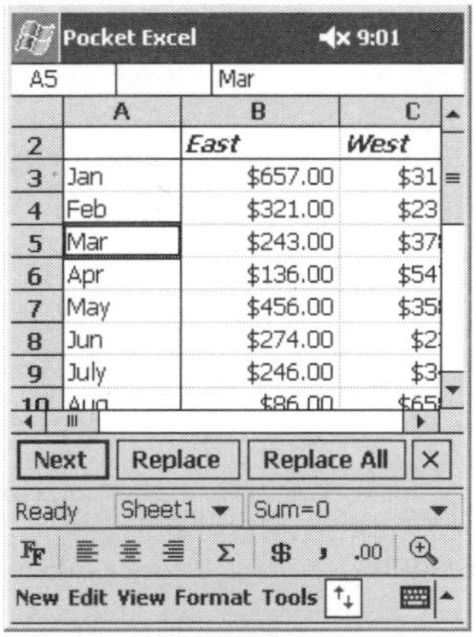

FIGURE 4-23   In the middle of a Find/Replace action, you will have an additional toolbar on your worksheet that includes Find and Replace commands.

Saving Your Workbook

Saving your current workbook is slightly different in Pocket Excel than in the desktop version. Your Pocket Excel workbook will be saved automatically as soon as you tap the OK button in the top-right corner to exit the workbook. You do not need to explicitly save the workbook. It will be saved into the current folder you are in, with the name that you last used. If this is a new workbook that hasn't been saved before, the file name of the workbook will be Book1, Book2, and so on, depending on how many workbooks you have in the directory that have already been named that way. If you want to use a specific file name, save in a different folder, save to an external storage device (such as a CompactFlash card), or save as a different file type, you will need to choose Save Workbook As from the Tools menu.

Selecting Save Workbook As opens the Save As dialog box, shown in Figure 4-24. Tap OK to carry out your instructions and make a copy of the workbook where you have requested.

FIGURE 4-24   In the Save As dialog box you can change the file name, type, folder, and storage location of your workbook.

Remember that if you are editing an existing workbook and you tap the OK button in the top-right corner, your changes will be saved automatically. Pocket Excel will *not* prompt you when you tap this button with a "Do you want to save?" message as with the desktop version. It will assume that you want to save, and the old version will be overwritten. If you have been making edits and decide you don't want to keep them, be careful not to simply exit the program with the OK button. Instead, use the Revert To Saved command on the Tools menu. You will be asked to confirm that you want to undo all the changes that you have made since opening the workbook. If you select Yes, the workbook will revert to its original state.

If you select New after editing a workbook in Pocket Excel, it will prompt you with a message asking whether you want to save, cancel, or save as, prior to starting a new workbook.

Beaming and E-mailing Your Workbook

Pocket Excel realizes that if you are writing workbooks on your iPAQ, that there is a good chance they will be short, and you will probably want to be able to transmit them to someone else either by e-mail or by "beaming" (beaming is transferring information through the infrared port of your iPAQ and is discussed in more detail in Chapter 5) them to another Pocket PC owner. To make this process as easy as possible, Pocket Excel has added Send Workbook By E-mail and Beam Workbook commands to the Tools menu.

Selecting Send Workbook By E-mail creates a new e-mail message in your Outbox with your workbook already attached. You will need to select to whom you wish to send the message as well as adding a subject line and any text. Tapping the Send button will queue it up to be sent next time you have an active wireless connection or next time you connect with ActiveSync.

Selecting Beam Workbook will automatically set up your iPAQ to beam the workbook from your infrared port at the top of your unit to a receiving unit that has a physically aligned infrared port. The Pocket Excel Beaming window, shown in Figure 4-25, will appear, showing the status of the beam. In Figure 4-25 the device hasn't yet located an aligned infrared port that is ready to receive. The receiving unit must be set to receive the file by selecting the Infrared Receive program in the Program Files, if you are running Pocket PC 2000. If you are running Pocket PC 2002, it is set to receive automatically.

| FIGURE 4-25 | Setting up to beam a workbook to another Pocket PC through the infrared port |

Once the workbook has been successfully transmitted, you will see the results message box, as shown in Figure 4-26.

FIGURE 4-26   The results message box appears after a workbook is successfully
beamed to another Pocket PC device.

Protecting Your Workbook with a Password

Unlike Pocket Word, Pocket Excel has limited support to password protect your workbook.
This is a single-level password, meaning that it either allows full access or denies access to
the workbook. There aren't commands for access to read-only or modify as there are in the
desktop version of Excel.

You can add or change a password on the Pocket Excel workbook by choosing the Password
command from the Edit menu. In the Password dialog box that opens, shown next, you can
add a password to your document or change the existing password.

Synchronizing with Your Desktop

Synchronizing your data with ActiveSync is covered in detail in Chapter 2, and if you are in
need of detailed instructions you should refer to that chapter. Note that keeping a synchronized
workbook on both your Pocket PC and desktop system can be a great convenience. Every time
you make a change on your Pocket PC or desktop, the workbook will be synchronized with the
other system. If you reference and update this document frequently, then this capability could
save you a great deal of time.

Chapter 5

Use Pocket Outlook to Take Control of Your Mobile Life

How to...

- Use and customize the Today page
- Manage appointments with the Calendar
- Create new appointments
- Set reminders and categories and invite meeting attendees
- Navigate and manage contacts
- Create new contacts
- Customize the Contact manager
- Read and compose e-mail
- Set up inboxes and connect to a mail server
- View attachments
- Attach files to an e-mail
- Read, edit, and compose tasks
- Read, edit, and compose notes
- Beam information
- Set up ActiveSync for all Outlook functions

The single most useful thing the average person does with an iPAQ is to keep track of personal information such as contacts/address book, appointment book, personal notes, to-do lists, and, of course, e-mail. These activities fall into a general category called personal information management (PIM). Microsoft Outlook has become the most widely used e-mail and PIM tool around today. On your iPAQ a Pocket version of this popular tool is pre-installed.

What Is Pocket Outlook?

Pocket Outlook isn't a single application. It is actually five applications that each perform a different part of the PIM job, but all interact together and synchronize with your desktop version of Outlook. Pocket Outlook doesn't have all the bells and whistles of the desktop version, but it has everything you need when you are on the move and is extremely effective. Speaking from personal experience, until we started using Pocket Outlook, we used to carry our Palm Pilot PDA and paper-based day planner. After using Pocket Outlook, for the first time, we went fully digital, and stopped using our paper day planner.

The five applications that make up Pocket Outlook are:

Calendar   Lets you schedule appointments and events to make sure you don't double-book and are in the right place at the right time.

Contacts   Keeps a database of all of your contacts and their relevant information. At your fingertips is complete contact information for anyone you know: phone numbers, e-mail address, notes, pictures, audio narratives, and more.

Notes   Allows you to take notes on your handheld instead of scratching them on little pieces of paper that you easily lose track of. We use it to keep track of an incredibly diverse range of miscellaneous information.

Tasks   Provides a convenient to-do list that lets you prioritize your tasks. It also includes check-off boxes so you can knock tasks off your list when they are completed.

Inbox   Allows you to receive your e-mail on your handheld and read your messages and respond to them while on the go. You can create new messages, attach files, and everything you would do from a full-sized PC. If you are wirelessly enabled, you can receive your e-mail from anywhere at any time (for details, see Chapter 10).

See What's Up with the Today Page

The Today page is the jumping off point to any of your personal information that is handled by Pocket Outlook. It allows you to see, at a glance, what appointments you have upcoming today, how many unread messages are in your Inbox, and how many unfinished tasks are on your to-do list, as shown in Figure 5-1.

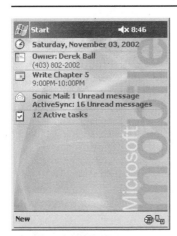

FIGURE 5-1   The Today page lets you see all of your important information.

Tapping any line item will take you to the appropriate application to view the item selected. You can modify the Today page in a number of ways.

Tapping the time line will bring you to the Settings window for the clock, where you can set the current time for your home time zone, or for the time zone you happen to be in if you are away from home, as shown in Figure 5-2.

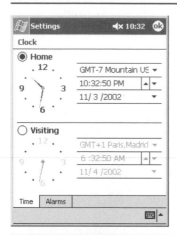

FIGURE 5-2   The Settings window for the clock lets you set both your current time, and also select a second time zone for when you are traveling.

You can customize the appearance and functionality of the Today page by going to the Settings command under the Start menu and choosing the Today icon. This opens the Settings window shown in Figure 5-3. From here you can select different themes for your Pocket PC. The theme changes the picture behind the Today page and the Start menu.

FIGURE 5-3   The Settings window for the Today page allows you to select different themes for your Pocket PC.

You can select any theme you like from the list of available themes. By default, only the default theme is loaded on your Pocket PC. You can download new themes from a variety of websites. There is one site, which you can access at no charge, that is solely devoted to Pocket PC themes: **www.pocketpcthemes.com**. To download a theme, you simply copy the theme file to your My Documents directory on your iPAQ. It will automatically appear in the list of available themes.

If you want to share a theme with a friend, you can select the theme and tap the Beam button to send it to another Pocket PC user via the infrared port. You can also select any picture to be your theme by selecting the Use This Picture As The Background check box and then browsing to your picture file.

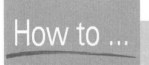

Customize Your Today Page

At the bottom of the Settings window, you will find another tab, the Items tab. From here you can select what items appear on the Today page, as shown in Figure 5-4.

The list of all the items that can appear on the Today page are shown with check boxes, allowing you to select which items you want to appear on the Today menu. You will notice the option for the Sierra Wireless AirCard that I use for wireless access from my iPAQ. You can also adjust the settings to cause the Today page to appear if the device is not used for a specific number of hours.

Some of the items in the list also have options you can configure, such as the Calendar. If you tap the Options button after selecting Calendar, you will see the options shown in this illustration:

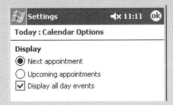

For the Calendar you can choose to see the next appointment only or all upcoming appointments. You can also choose to show or not show all day events.

FIGURE 5-4   Choose what items will appear on your Today page by selecting them on the Items tab of the Settings window.

Keeping Your Appointments with the Calendar

The Calendar application is an absolutely invaluable tool that can immediately make the purchase of your iPAQ worthwhile. I was always struggling with appointments, often double-booking myself or losing track of where I was supposed to be for a specific appointment. I found my paper day planner cumbersome, and I wasn't always diligent about updating it (not to mention it was large and heavy to carry around). Now, I always have my iPAQ in my pocket, and if someone asks me whether I am free for a meeting next week, I can pull it out, see my schedule, pick a mutually convenient time, and enter the meeting into my time table. When I am back in the office, my new appointment is automatically synced with my desktop Outlook calendar application, which is hooked into Microsoft Exchange. Everyone in my office shares calendars, so anyone who would like an appointment with me can see whether I am busy at that time. Over the past year, the number of appointments I have missed or double-booked has dropped to virtually zero, making me much more effective at work and also in my personal life.

Starting the Calendar Application

You can launch the Calendar application on your iPAQ in a number of ways. First, when looking at the Today page, you can tap the calendar icon to be taken directly to today's appointments. You can also get to the Calendar application by selecting Calendar from the Start menu. The iPAQ provides four small hardware buttons to launch specific applications. These buttons are configurable, but in their default out-of-the-box configuration, the leftmost button will launch the Calendar application, giving you a quick and easy way to access one of the most-used applications on your iPAQ.

Viewing the Calendar

After you open the Calendar application, what you will see will depend on the view that you last used. If this is your first time accessing the application, you will see the Agenda view. The Calendar has five different methods by which you can look at your data. It is always the same data, but shown in different levels of granularity. The five views are:

- Agenda view
- Day view
- Week view
- Month view
- Year view

The Agenda view, shown in Figure 5-5, contains a listing of all of today's appointments and their times. All of the views share most of the standard navigation icons and options shown in Figure 5-5.

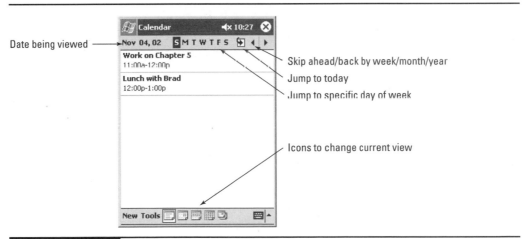

Date being viewed

Skip ahead/back by week/month/year

Jump to today

Jump to specific day of week

Icons to change current view

FIGURE 5-5   The Agenda view, featuring a list of today's appointments, contains many standard navigation items found in all views.

The top-left corner always shows the current day, date, month, or year being viewed. Immediately to the right of that are the days of the week, which can be tapped to jump to that specific day of the week. If a day other than the current date is being viewed, the current date will appear with a white square around the day letter. Tap the icon to the right of the day of the week letters (the one with a white square and a curved arrow) to jump immediately to today's date. The left/right arrows on the far right will scroll you ahead or back within the calendar. In the Agenda, Day, and Week views, it will scroll by one week. In the Month view it will scroll by a month, and in the Year view, it will scroll by a year.

The five view icons at the bottom of the window will allow you to jump to any of the views directly. You can also change the view you are currently looking at by pressing the hardware Calendar button. Each press changes the view down one level of granularity. The navigation dial on the hardware of the iPAQ is also useful with the calendar. It allows you to move from the current date being viewed to the next date by pressing the disc to the right or down. Pressing the disc to the left or up will move you to the previous day.

Tapping any item in the list in the Agenda view will open the details of that appointment, as shown in Figure 5-6. If you want to edit the appointment or add notes, tap the Edit menu. This will open the appointment in an editable window where you can change all the information such as subject, date, time, location, or notes.

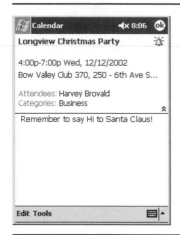

FIGURE 5-6   Tapping the Edit menu opens the current appointment in an editable window so you can change all the details such as date, time, and more.

The Day view looks more like a traditional day planner and like the desktop version of Outlook. It shows a single day divided into one-hour blocks with all of your appointments recorded in their relevant time slots, as shown in Figure 5-7.

All of the controls work the same as they do in the Agenda view, but here you will use the scroll bar on the right to scroll through the entire day. In all views, when looking at a specific appointment, you can tap and hold your stylus on the appointment to open a shortcut menu as shown in the next illustration. This enables you to move or copy an appointment to another point in your calendar.

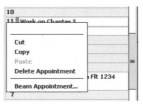

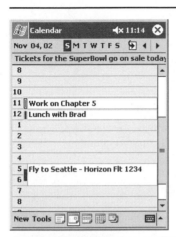

5

FIGURE 5-7   The Day view divides the entire day into one-hour slots where all of your appointments are shown.

Looking at Figure 5-7, if I wanted to make another appointment to work on Chapter 5 after my lunch with Brad, I would tap and hold to open the shortcut menu, and select Copy to copy the appointment to the clipboard. Then I would select another time slot, tap and hold to open the shortcut menu, and paste the appointment into the new time. The new schedule would look something like this:

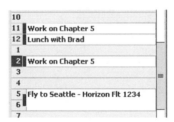

In the Day view, you will also see any relevant icons beside the appointment if this option has been turned on in the Options dialog box, as shown here:

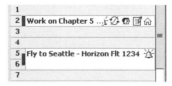

You might see the following icons:

Bell   Indicates that a reminder alarm has been set for this appointment

Circle with arrows   Indicates that this is a recurring event

Note page with pencil   Indicates that this event has notes

House   Indicates that this event has a specified location

Key   Indicates that this is a private event

Heads   Indicates that others are invited to this event

The Week view, shown in Figure 5-8, displays all of your appointments for a week. By default, the week is defined as seven days, but you can customize this setting to show a five-day or six-day week by selecting the Options command under the Tools menu.

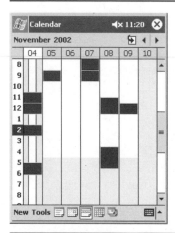

FIGURE 5-8   The Week view enables you to see your schedule for the entire week at a glance.

All of your appointments show up in the Week view as blue blocks in their appropriate date and time slots. You can easily see where you have free time and where you do not. To view the details of a specific appointment, tap on the blue block. This will open a small box at the top of the screen, which will display the details of the appointment, as shown in this illustration:

After ten seconds, the box will disappear, returning you to the default Week view. Tapping in the appointment box before it disappears will open the appointment details permanently in a window like the one shown in Figure 5-6.

The Month view, shown in Figure 5-9, enables you to see at a glance your entire month and what days you have appointments on. Each square in the view represents a day. If the current date is in the month you are viewing, that day will be outlined in red.

FIGURE 5-9   The Month view shows you an entire month's appointments in one window.

The Month view uses icons to give you a quick feel for how busy that day is. Each day will display one of the following icons to indicate the density of appointments:

No icon   Indicates there are no appointments for the day

Triangle (pointing to top left)   Indicates at least one appointment in the morning

Triangle (pointing to bottom right)   Indicates at least one appointment in the afternoon

Dark square   Indicates appointments in both the morning and afternoon

White square   Indicates an all-day event

NOTE   *I was unable to get the white square to appear for an all-day event, which might indicate a bug in Pocket PC 2002.*

Tapping on any specific date in the Month view will take you to the Day view for the day you selected.

The Year view will display the entire year calendar on your screen at once, as shown in Figure 5-10. You can tell the current date as it will appear in reversed-out type. (In Figure 5-10, the current date is November 4.) Tapping on a specific date will take you to the Day view for the selected day.

FIGURE 5-10   The Year view shows you an entire calendar year at a glance.

Entering a New Appointment

To begin entering a new appointment or event into your calendar, tap the New menu. Alternatively, you can tap and hold the stylus on a time in the Day or Week view, and when the shortcut menu appears, select New Appointment. Whichever of these options you choose will open the New Event dialog box.

Entering Details

You will enter the details of your new appointment or event in the New Event dialog box, shown in Figure 5-11.

FIGURE 5-11   The New Event dialog box is where you can enter the details for the new appointment.

You can fill in as many or as few details as you choose. The minimum information required to create a new event is a subject and a time. The subject line includes a drop-down arrow, enabling you to select from commonly used words for appointments such as *Meet with, Lunch, Dinner, Visit, Call, Birthday,* and *Complete.* You use the onscreen keyboard or other input mechanism to enter the text for the rest of the subject.

You can also enter a location, and a start and an end time for the appointment. On the Type line you can choose to make the appointment an all-day appointment. The Status line will change how this appointment appears to anyone who looks at your public calendar through Microsoft Exchange. You can set the time to appear as Free, Busy, Tentative, or Out Of Office. The Sensitivity line enables you to mark the appointment as private, which means that someone looking at your public calendar will not see the subject line of the event. Instead, they will simply see Private as the subject. Thus, you can keep your medical appointments and other personal information private from outside observers.

Setting Reminders

The Reminder line in a new event allows you to specify whether you would like an alarm and pop-up reminder to remind you about an event. You can set a reminder to occur anywhere from minutes in advance of an appointment to months. For example, I set my reminders for events such as birthdays a week in advance so I have time to buy a gift and card. I only set reminders for events such as internal meetings at five minutes.

On the Reminder line, you can select from one of two options in the drop-down list: None and Remind Me. If you select Remind Me, you will have to select the time before the event to remind you by first selecting whether you want to be reminded minutes, hours, days, or weeks in advance, as shown in the next illustration:

Once you have selected the units, you select the quantity by tapping the number to the left of the units. You can select from the drop-down list or type in your own quantity. Setting a reminder will cause an alarm bell icon to appear beside the event in the Day and Agenda views.

Setting Categories

You can also select a category for the appointment. This enables you to view only appointments related to a specific subject at one time. By default, the Calendar will display the appointments for all categories, but you can choose Categories from the Tools menu to open a dialog box similar to the one shown in Figure 5-12. From this dialog box you can check the categories that you would like to show.

You select a category by tapping on the Categories line in the event detail dialog box. You can choose multiple categories for a given appointment. If the category you want hasn't been created yet, you can add a category (or remove one) via the Add/Delete tab at the bottom of the category selection dialog box.

FIGURE 5-12   You can select the categories that you want to be visible in the Calendar to see subsets of your tasks.

Inviting Attendees

As in the desktop version of Outlook, you can invite individuals to meetings or other events in the Calendar. In Pocket Outlook you do this on the Attendees line in the event detail dialog box. Tap the Attendees line to open up a dialog box showing your list of contacts with check boxes beside their names, shown here:

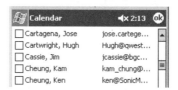

You can select as many attendees as you like by selecting their check boxes and tapping OK. A Microsoft Exchange event invitation will be mailed automatically to each of the selected individuals. In order to invite an individual to an event, he or she must have an entry in your Contacts list.

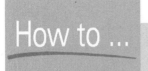

Set Up a Recurring Appointment

Many appointments that you schedule will occur on a regular basis, such as weekly status meetings and birthdays. You can set these appointments to recur automatically. Tapping on the Occurs line in the event detail dialog box opens a drop-down list of the most common recurrence options, shown in this illustration:

From this list, you can select the option to make this event repeat every week, on the same day every month, or annually. If your recurrence pattern for your event is not listed, choose Edit Pattern. Doing so will open the first of three windows that make up the Recurrence Wizard, shown here:

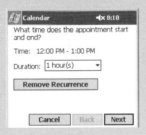

Here you set the duration of the appointment and have the option to remove the recurrence of the event. Once you have set the duration, tap the Next button to open the second window of the wizard, shown next:

5

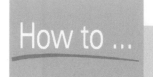

Set Up a Recurring Appointment (continued)

In the second window you can choose the following options:

Daily   You can set the recurrence as every *X* number of days or every weekday.

Weekly   You can set the recurrence as every *X* week(s) and also specify any combination of days of the week you want the event to occur on.

Monthly   You can select which day of the month to have the event recur on and then set it to recur every *X* month(s). Alternatively, you could have it occur on a specific day of the week in a month every *X* month(s), such as the third Tuesday of every month.

Yearly   You can select which day of the year you want the event to recur on. Alternatively, you can have it occur on a specific day of the week in a specific month. For example, Mother's Day occurs on the second Sunday of every May.

The third window in the wizard is where you will set the start and end date for the pattern, as shown next. You can choose to have the pattern not end, end on a specific date, or end after a certain number of occurrences of the event.

Adding Notes

You can add notes to any appointment by selecting the Notes tab at the bottom of the event detail dialog box. From here you can add any notes you want by typing in the input area, using a transcriber, or using a keyboard. You can also tap the pencil icon to add sketches and drawings, as shown in Figure 5-13.

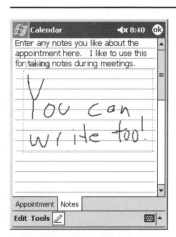

FIGURE 5-13   You can enter text as well as drawings in the notes area.

Beaming an Appointment

Imagine you are sitting with someone, trying to plan a meeting together. You can enter the details of the meeting into your Calendar. Then, by tapping and holding a specific appointment, you can choose Beam Appointment from the shortcut menu. This will start the process of searching for and transmitting the appointment to a Pocket PC with an aligned infrared port. The receiving Pocket PC device will be given the option of accepting the beamed appointment. Beaming to non-Pocket PC devices is possible with third-party add-in software. For details about beaming outside the Pocket PC universe, see Chapter 2.

ActiveSync Settings for the Calendar

There are three options you can set in ActiveSync on your desktop PC to change what information is shared in the Calendar application:

Sync All Appointments   This setting can lead to very memory-intensive and time-consuming syncing but will ensure that any modifications made to past appointments in either your iPAQ or your desktop are all up to date.

Sync Only The   This default setting will enable you to set the number of past weeks to synchronize (defaults to two weeks) and the number of future weeks (defaults to all).

Sync Only Selected Categories   This setting enables you to select only specific categories of appointments to synchronize. This can be useful if you synchronize with multiple desktop systems or if multiple people share the same iPAQ.

Managing Your Contacts

The other personal information management tool that is right at the top of the list with the Calendar is keeping track of all of your contacts. The Contacts application in Pocket PC is extremely useful and flexible. In addition, it seamlessly synchronizes with the contacts in your desktop version of Outlook, enabling you to access this crucial information both at your desk and when you are on the move.

Navigating Your Contacts

You can launch into the Contacts application by pressing the hardware button for opening Contacts (second from the left in the default configuration) or by selecting Contacts from the Start menu. Either action will open a window similar to the one shown in Figure 5-14.

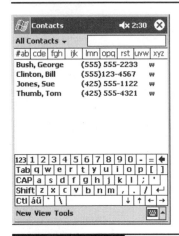

FIGURE 5-14   The Contacts window is your personal address book for your iPAQ.

By default, you will see a list of all of your contacts sorted in alphabetical order. If you are like me, you probably have hundreds of contacts. There are many ways to make it easier to sort through your reams of associates. On the top left you will see a drop-down arrow. Tap this arrow to display a list from which you can select a subset of your contacts to view. In the categories list, you can choose to see All Contacts (the default), Recent (the most recent contacts you have looked at), or choose to view a subset based on the pre-assigned category you have given each one. In order to do this, you will need to have assigned one or more of the static categories in Outlook to each of the contacts. In our sample data, I have four contacts, which have been divided into two groups: Government and Business, as shown in the next illustration. The drop-down list shows me all my categories and one No Categories option for any contact who does not have categories assigned. The More option in the drop-down list will take you to the full list of categories where you can select a specific category you would like to view. You select the category by tapping on a check box, or you can select multiple categories by tapping on multiple check boxes.

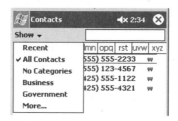

In the box to the right of the categories drop-down list, you can type specific text that you want to search for in your list. Any text that you enter will be matched against the first or last name of the contact. For example, with our set of data, entering **b** in the text search box will cause it to filter the list to show *Bush, George* (a last name match), as well as *Clinton, Bill* (a first name match), as shown here:

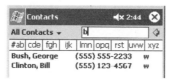

Immediately below the categories drop-down list and the search text box you will see a series of boxes, each containing three letters of the alphabet. Tapping any one of these boxes once will cause the view to scroll to the appropriate subsection of the contacts list. If you are currently viewing your contacts sorted by last name, then tapping the ijk box would cause the list to scroll to show those contacts with last names starting with *I*. If you are viewing your list sorted by company name, then it would scroll to show company names beginning with *I*. If you tap the box again, it will scroll to the second letter in the box, *J*. A third tap will scroll to *K*; the same method applies to the rest of the letter boxes.

You can use the three techniques above for narrowing your list of contacts alone, or together. For example, you could select Government from the drop-down list of categories, type a **b** into the text search box, and tap the cde box to get a list of all the contacts who are categorized as Government with first names starting with *B* and last names starting with *C*.

You can also navigate through your list of contacts with the scroll bar on the right side of the window if your list of contacts is more than will fit in one window (which they almost always are). You can also use the hardware navigation disc and press up to scroll up your list or down to scroll down your list. If you hold the button down, a large box will appear and cycle through all the letters of the alphabet, enabling you to scroll to the specified letter, as shown in Figure 5-15.

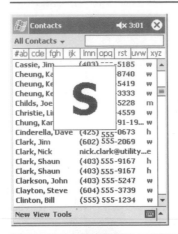

FIGURE 5-15   Holding down the hardware navigation disc will enable you to scroll through all the letters of the alphabet.

By default, when you enter the Contacts application, you are looking at a view of your contacts sorted by name. You can change this to see a list of companies instead, if this is your preferred method of navigation. Change your sort rule by selecting View | By Company. The resulting window will look something like this:

The number in parentheses after the company name is the number of contacts that you have in your list who work for that company.

In your list of contacts you will see a blue letter to the right of each entry's contact information. This letter tells you what type of contact information is being shown. For example, a small blue *e* indicates an e-mail address, a *w* is a work phone number, an *f* is a work fax number, an *h* is a home number, and so on. If you tap this letter, you will see a drop-down display of that individual's contact information. A black dot indicates which contact information is currently set to appear in the list view, as can be seen in the next illustration. If you want to change this default, tap on the line that you would prefer to show as the default.

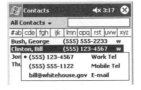

Tapping any contact name or phone number in the list will open the contact's detail information, as shown in Figure 5-16.

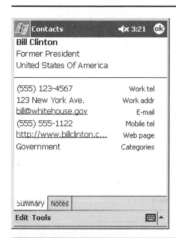

5

FIGURE 5-16   Tapping a contact name or number will open that individual's contact information window.

The Summary tab shows all the contact information you have for the contact. The Notes tab contains any notes that you have for the contact. Notes can include text, drawings, images, and sound recordings. Tapping the Edit menu will enable you to enter and change any of the information displayed here. Tap Tools in the menu bar to change your view (on the Notes tab only), delete the contact, send an e-mail to the contact, or beam the contact to another Pocket PC.

Tapping and holding any name in your list of contacts will open up a shortcut menu via which you can copy or delete the contact, send an e-mail to the contact, or beam the contact to another Pocket PC.

Entering a New Contact

To add a contact to your list, tap the New menu at the bottom of the Contacts dialog box to open the new contact form, shown here:

From this window you can enter an entire range of information. These fields mirror the fields found in the desktop version of Outlook, allowing seamless synchronization of information.

A number of the fields are contractions of information held in multiple fields. For example, the Name field is a combination of the Title, First, Middle, Last, and Suffix fields. As you enter a name, Contacts will try to place the appropriate names into the appropriate fields. If it is unsure, it will display a red icon with an exclamation mark at the end of the line. All combination fields include a drop-down arrow at the end of the field. If you tap the arrow, all the subfields involved will be displayed and you will be able to enter the data into each subfield, as shown in this illustration:

Date fields, such as Birthday and Anniversary, enable you to select a date from a drop-down calendar, as shown in Figure 5-17. If no date is selected, the field will show None. The drop-down calendar also has options below the specific dates to select Today or None.

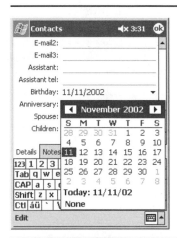

FIGURE 5-17   Date fields include drop-down calendars to make selecting a date easier.

The Categories field is another unique field. It displays the category, or categories, that you have assigned this contact to. When you tap the field, it will open up a separate form in which you can select all the categories you want to apply to this contact from a list of categories. You can select multiple categories by selecting multiple check boxes, as shown here:

If the category that you want isn't in the list, you can add a category (or delete one you no longer want) using the Add/Delete tab at the bottom of the categories dialog box shown here:

This tab features a list of all the categories. You can select a specific category and tap the Delete button to remove a category. To add a category, place the cursor into the text box at the top of the form, enter the category name, and then tap the Add button.

Categories in Pocket Outlook are synced over from your desktop Outlook installation. Setting up and managing your categories is easier on the desktop, so you should do the bulk of your planning there instead of on your iPAQ.

Customizing the Contact Manager

Even on the Pocket PC, you can customize a few options in your software. This list is limited in the Contacts application, but you can change a few items in the view as well as some default information for when you are entering details.

Selecting Tools | Options will open the Options dialog box, shown in the next illustration, where you can make changes to your Contacts application.

The three check boxes allow you to show or hide the ABC boxes, show contact names only (that is, don't show phone number or e-mail address), or switch to a larger font if you find the standard size hard to read.

You can also change the default area code, which is automatically included with every new contact you enter, and default country.

There are three options you can set in ActiveSync on the desktop PC for your Contacts:

Sync All Contacts   This default setting will ensure that any modifications made to contacts in either your iPAQ or your desktop are all up to date.

Sync Only The Following Contacts   This option enables you to choose only specific contacts to synchronize. This is very limiting because any new contacts added to your iPAQ will not be automatically sent over to your PC.

Sync Only Selected Categories   This setting enables you to select only specific categories of contacts to synchronize. This can be useful if you synchronize with multiple desktop systems or if multiple people are sharing the same iPAQ.

Keeping in Touch with E-mail

For the Internet, e-mail is the killer application. It was e-mail that drove people to get Internet connections to every corporate desktop and in every home. Many PDA experts expected that being able to get e-mail anywhere, anytime, would be the driving force that would cause millions to adopt PDAs. This ended up being a bit of a pipe dream as most PDAs, particularly up until now, were not wirelessly connected, and so e-mail could only be sent or received while your PDA was attached to your computer with a sync cable.

Out of the box, your iPAQ is not wirelessly enabled, but it can sync your Outlook Inbox with its own Inbox application, allowing you to take your e-mail with you. With some simple wireless add-in products, you can easily extend your iPAQ to allow you to send and receive your e-mail anywhere, at any time. For details about wireless iPAQ, see Chapter 9. This section will focus on the specifics of using the Inbox application, whether you are wirelessly connected or not.

Setting Up Your Inbox and Services

There are two ways to work with e-mail on your Pocket PC: through your ActiveSync connection or by connecting to an external mail server.

E-mail with ActiveSync

ActiveSync will keep a copy on your Pocket PC of the messages in your current desktop Outlook folders. All of the setup for this is done in your ActiveSync application on your PC. With each synchronization, the appropriate messages are transferred to your iPAQ so that you can read them when you are disconnected. You can also compose replies to the e-mail you read, and these will be sent by your desktop version of Outlook the next time you synchronize your iPAQ.

   Remember that your Inbox will only synchronize with one desktop Outlook partnership, so if you are syncing with multiple desktops, as discussed in Chapter 2, make sure you set up your partnerships correctly and sync with your Inbox partner first. For more information, see "Syncing to Multiple Desktops," in Chapter 2.

To set up ActiveSync synchronization of your desktop, open ActiveSync on your PC, and select the check box beside Inbox, as shown in Figure 5-18.

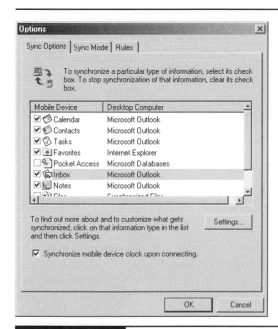

FIGURE 5-18   To synchronize your Pocket Inbox with your desktop Outlook, select the Inbox check box in the ActiveSync setup.

After selecting the check box, you will want to adjust the settings for your mail synchronization. Click the Settings button to open the Mail Synchronization Settings dialog box, shown in Figure 5-19.

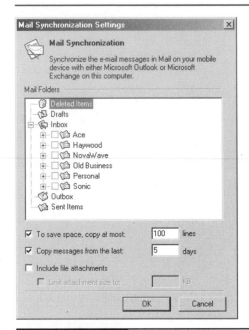

The Mail Synchronization Settings dialog box enables you to determine what is stored on your iPAQ.

From here you can specify which subfolders you want to be synchronized with your iPAQ. Select the check box before the name of any subfolder whose messages you want copied to the Inbox program on your iPAQ. Then you can specify whether you want only a limited number of lines of a message to be copied to your iPAQ. The purpose of this is to reduce the amount of data stored on the device so you don't run out of room. However, I recommend not selecting this option because if, just once, you receive an important long message, and it is truncated, you might get so annoyed you will toss your iPAQ into the nearest dumpster. Instead, I recommend keeping only a limited number of days of messages. By default, the system will only synchronize five days of messages, or one working week. I find that even three days of messages is sufficient, unless I am on the road for an extended period of time. The Include File Attachments option enables you to automatically copy file attachments to your Pocket PC, or leave them unless you request them. Attachments can quickly fill up the memory of your device, so by default this option is turned off, and I would usually recommend that you leave it off. You can request to have attachments downloaded from your iPAQ as needed.

NOTE   *Note that Sent Items and Drafts folders cannot be synced with your desktop Outlook program.*

Connecting to a Mail Server

Your iPAQ can also be configured to connect to other types of mail servers and bypass your desktop Outlook program altogether. In order for this configuration to work, your iPAQ must be able to connect to the Internet. You can connect your iPAQ to the Internet in one of three ways:

Wireless connection   Through a third-party wireless modem or network card, you can connect to the Internet from almost anywhere.

Wired connection   Through a third-party network card, you can get onto a corporate or home network with an Internet gateway.

ActiveSync connection   If the desktop PC that you ActiveSync with has an Internet connection, you can use the pass through option (discussed in Chapter 2) to connect to an outside mail server.

You must set up the properties of the outside mail server by configuring a new service on your iPAQ. From the Services menu, select New Service. This will open the E-mail Setup Wizard, which will help you configure your service. The first window asks you for your e-mail address, as shown here:

Enter your e-mail address in the box provided, and then tap the Next button to bring up the second window of the wizard, as shown here:

Here the wizard will attempt to automatically configure your e-mail service by reading from a configuration file kept on the Microsoft servers. A number of the major ISPs are referenced there. If you are not using a major ISP, or cannot be configured automatically, you can tap Skip to configure the service yourself. Tap Next to open the third window of the wizard, shown in this illustration:

In this window you will enter your user information, including your full name, user name, and password. You have the option to save the password and not be prompted each time it tries to synchronize your e-mail. When you have entered all your information, tap Next to open the fourth window of the wizard, as shown here:

In this window you will configure your server type and name for this service. There are two types of servers you can connect to: POP3 and IMAP4. The name you choose for the service can be anything you like, but should be descriptive enough to let you differentiate it from your other mail services (if you are connecting to more than one).

POP3 is supported by almost every mail server that you might connect to. It is an older protocol, but widely supported. With POP3, your e-mail is copied down to your device. There is little intelligence in the protocol for handling folders or synchronization with the server.

It is very likely that the mailbox being accessed by your handheld is also accessed from one or more desktops. In this case, it is probably better to use the newer, more efficient, IMAP4 protocol. In my situation, I have an office e-mail service that is run from a Microsoft Exchange server. At work, my desktop accesses the exchange server through Outlook. I have a computer at home with a cable modem that keeps synchronized with my mail server using IMAP4. This way, no matter which desktop system I am using, when I read, compose, delete, or file messages, it is in one common message store that all my systems share. When I chose to connect my iPAQ to this message store, IMAP4 was the obvious choice, as it would participate in this tidy little family of e-mail handlers by synchronizing with the central Microsoft Exchange message store.

When you have entered the relevant account information, tap Next to open the wizard's final window, as shown here:

The fifth and final window of the wizard (unless you choose to set options!) is where you will specify the Internet address of your mail server. You must specify the address of your POP3 or IMAP4 server in the Incoming Mail box. Mail is always sent using a specific protocol called SMTP (Simple Mail Transfer Protocol). In order to send mail, you must have an address for an SMTP server, which is the one that you will enter in the Outgoing Mail box. Usually this server will be the same as your incoming mail server, but not always. Check with your ISP or system administrator if you do not know what to enter in these boxes. If your mail server uses a network connection that requires a specific domain to connect to, you will enter that value in the Domain box.

From this window you can access an additional three options windows to configure such items as changing the time intervals for downloading new messages, downloading attachments, and limiting what portion of a message is downloaded. Tap the Options button to open the first window, as shown here:

The first Advanced Option window enables you to set the frequency to check for new messages. By default it will check every 15 minutes. You can clear the check box to have the Inbox only check for new messages when you specifically request it. If your outgoing e-mail server requires authentication, you can select that check box. Authentication requirement is becoming more and more common as junk e-mail continues to grow as a problem. You can also specify a specific connection by which to send outgoing messages in the Connection drop-down list. When you have set the options you want, tap Next to move on to the second Advanced Options window, as shown here:

The second Advanced Options window lets you set how much of the message you want to bring back. The drop-down list enables you to choose whether you want to download the message headers only or a full copy of the message. If you are downloading only the headers, you can choose to include a specific amount of the message. By default you will download the first 2KB, but you can download more (or less) by changing the number in the box. The second check box lets you choose to receive the attachments to a message (by default they are not brought into the Pocket Inbox) and alternatively to pick a maximum size for any attachments you are going to download. When you have finished setting these options, tap Next to open the last window.

The third and final window is very simple. It enables you to set a maximum number of days of messages to hold in your Inbox. I recommend only holding three days of messages, which just so happens to be the default.

Your new e-mail service is now fully configured and ready to be used.

Navigating Your Inbox

When you open the Inbox, it will open the inbox of the last e-mail service you used. You will see the list of e-mail messages, as shown in Figure 5-20.

If an e-mail message has been read it appears in normal text; an unread message appears in bold. You can see whom the message is from, the time/date received, the size, and the subject. The envelope icon to the left of any message provides a great deal of information about the message as well:

- If the bottom-right corner of the envelope is missing, this means that the message has not been downloaded from the server. If it is there, then the message has been downloaded.

- A closed envelope indicates an unread message. An open envelope indicates the message has been read.

- A paper clip attached to the envelope means that the message includes attachments.

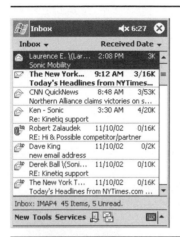

FIGURE 5-20   Opening the Inbox application will show you the messages from the last e-mail service you used.

At the top left you can tap the drop-down arrow to choose which e-mail service and inbox you want to look at, as shown here:

Tap the drop-down arrow on the top right to change how the messages in the current folder are sorted. By default they are sorted by received date, but you can also choose to sort by the sender or subject, as shown in this illustration:

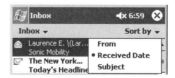

The very bottom of the window contains a status bar that will indicate what operation is currently being performed. If no operation is being performed, it will indicate which mail service you are viewing, the total number of messages, and the number of unread messages.

Below the status bar is the menu bar. The icons to the right of the menu options will, left to right, connect this mail service to its server (assuming you are connected to the Internet) and check for new mail.

Reading a Message

To read a message, tap on it with the stylus. This will open the message details, as shown in Figure 5-21.

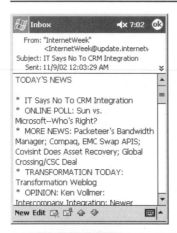

FIGURE 5-21   An open e-mail message.

The top section of the window contains the header of the message. In its default, short view, you can see who sent the message, the subject, and when it was sent. To see the longer header information, tap the two down arrows in the bottom-right corner of the top section. This will display the To, Cc, and size information.

You can read the message by using the scroll bar on the right side of the window to move up and down within the message. Alternatively, you can use the hardware control disc to scroll the message up or down.

From the menu bar you can use the blue up and down arrows to scroll to the next or previous message. Tapping the envelope with a red × on it will delete the current message. Tapping the envelope with an arrow on it will enable you to reply to the message.

The Edit menu contains several commands:

Mark As Unread   This command returns the message to bold in the message list, as though it had never been read.

Mark For Download   This command will cause the entire contents of the message to be downloaded from the mail server the next time you are connected.

Move To   Use this command to move the message to a folder.

Language   This command enables you to select the language font for the message. This is useful if you receive messages in other languages.

Select All   With this command you can select all the text in a message if you are in edit mode.

Copy   This command copies any selected text to the clipboard for pasting somewhere else.

Edit My Text Messages   Use this command to change the predefined My Text Messages list (for details, see "Using My Text Messages," later in this chapter).

Handling Attachments

E-mail attachments are used all the time to send Word documents, spreadsheets, and more. Being able to receive, read, and work with these attachments on your Pocket PC makes it a very powerful tool. Attachments to e-mail messages appear in a separate area below the main body of the message, as shown in Figure 5-22.

FIGURE 5-22   E-mail attachments appear in a separate area below the main body of the message.

To the left of the icon for the attachment is an arrow. The arrow is gray if the attachment is not downloaded. It is green if the attachment has been flagged for download. Tapping the attachment icon will cause it to be flagged to be downloaded, and if it has been downloaded, it will open the attachment. You can tap and hold the stylus on the attachment to perform a Save As operation if the attachment has been downloaded.

 *Once an item is flagged for download, it is not actually downloaded until your next send/receive cycle. You can manually initiate this cycle by tapping the connect to server or check for new mail icons in the menu bar at the bottom of the window.*

Composing a Message

To create a new message, simply tap New at any time. This will open the New Message window, as shown in Figure 5-23. The top box contains a very minimalist header row with only To and Subject fields. You can enter the e-mail address of the person to whom you want to send the message to, or you can select a contact from your Contacts application by tapping the To field, as shown here:

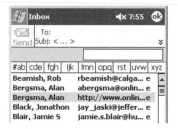

Alternatively, you can access the contacts list by tapping the contact icon (the one that looks like an ID card) in the menu bar. To select more than one recipient, just keep tapping until you are done. When you are finished, tap in the Subject field to make the list of contacts go away.

FIGURE 5-23   Tapping New will open a window for creating new messages.

Entering Extended Header Information

To enter extended header information you can tap the double down arrow on the bottom right of the header area. This will cause the header area to expand to show Cc and Bcc rows as well as enable you to select which e-mail service you want to send your message from (if you have more than one registered). The expanded header area will look something like this:

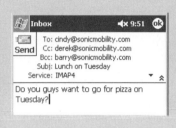

At any time you can tap in the message body and enter the text of your message. A slick trick that I like is to record a quick voice memo and e-mail it to someone as a .WAV file. You can do this by tapping the record icon (the cassette tape) on the menu bar. This will open up the full record toolbar, as shown in Figure 5-24. From here you can use the built-in iPAQ microphone to dictate a quick message, which will be attached as a .WAV file to your e-mail message. What a great way to whip out a quick note to someone when you don't have time to try to write it down. We can all talk much faster than we can type, especially on a miniaturized virtual keyboard!

FIGURE 5-24 Voice attachments are a great way to send a quick note to someone when you are on the move and don't have time to type.

When you have finished composing your message, tap the Send button in the top-left corner to send your message to your Outbox for transmission next time you are connected to your service.

Using My Text Messages

Many e-mail messages can be replied to with a very short message. Pocket Outlook has a handy function called My Text Messages, which helps you respond very quickly to your e-mail. My Text Messages provides a list of common replies, which you can select with one tap and drop into your message. To access My Text Messages, tap My Text to open a pop-up list of standard messages, as shown in Figure 5-25. The list includes convenient one-word responses such as Yes and No, as well as status updates such as "I can't talk right now," "I'll be right there," and "I'm running late."

FIGURE 5-25   A set of standard responses can be inserted into your message with the My Text command.

You cannot change the total number of items in this list, but you can change ones that you don't use often into something that may be more useful to you. To do so, select Edit | Edit My Text Messages. This will open the My Text Messages dialog box, shown next, where you can select any item and change it.

Note that your My Text messages are shared between the MSN Messenger client and the Inbox application.

Customizing Your Inbox

You can edit or modify a number of areas in the Inbox application. One thing to keep in mind is that if you need to change the basic properties of your e-mail service, you cannot do this while you are connected to it. If you need to change the name of a mail server or something fundamental, you must be disconnected from your service, then you can go to the Tools menu and select Options. This will open the dialog box shown in Figure 5-26. From here you can select any service in the list to modify. You will notice that ActiveSync is not in the list. This is because that is the one mail service that is set up from the PC, not from your iPAQ.

FIGURE 5-26   To edit the base properties of a service, select it from the list in the Inbox Options dialog box.

Notice that there are four tabs at the bottom of the Inbox Options dialog box. These tabs let you open other dialog boxes with other settings. On the Message tab, shown in Figure 5-27, you configure options for what part of the message body to include when replying and how to format it. You can choose to keep a copy of sent messages in the Sent folder, what action to take after deleting a message, and how to dispose of deleted items.

The Address tab, shown in Figure 5-28, enables you to customize how Pocket Inbox does address lookups. It can select addresses from all e-mail fields in your Contacts folder, or only a specific field. You can also set it to look up e-mail addresses against a Contacts folder on a mail server (if the mail server supports this action).

FIGURE 5-27   The Message tab under Options lets you set behavior when working with messages like what to do after a delete, how to reply, and when to empty deleted items.

FIGURE 5-28   Customize how addresses are looked up with the Address tab under Options.

The final tab of the Inbox Options dialog box, Storage, simply allows you to select a check box to store attachments to e-mail messages on an external storage card if you have a CompactFlash or other external storage card.

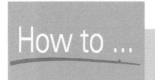

Do Name Lookups Against an External Mail Server

If you want to perform name lookups on a mail server that isn't one of your base e-mail services, you can do this by tapping the Add button on the Address tab of the Inbox Options dialog box. This will open the dialog box shown in the following illustration. You must specify the directory and server to search for the names. There is a very good chance that the server may require you to log on and authenticate. If so, select the authenticate check box and fill in your user name and password.

Keeping on Top of Your Tasks

If you are like me, you have many tasks that always seem to run in parallel; keeping track of those tasks can require a Herculean effort. In fact, I found that every time I had something to add to my task list, I couldn't find the list, so I would start another one. Next thing I knew, I had several to-do lists going at the same time!

Now I keep all of my to-do tasks organized in my Pocket PC, which seamlessly integrates them with my desktop version of Outlook. Life is good!

Navigating Your Tasks

You open the Tasks application by tapping Tasks in the Start menu, or by navigating to it from the Today page by tapping the Tasks item in the list. Either action will open the main Tasks window, shown in Figure 5-29.

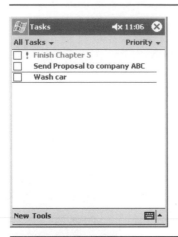

 FIGURE 5-29 Keep track of all of your to-do items in the Tasks application.

Tap the drop-down arrow on the top left of the window to view a subset of task. Your choices include the following:

All Tasks   A list of all tasks.

Recent   A list of tasks you have looked at most recently.

<Category>   A list of all the categories that you have assigned to tasks. You can view any single category you select.

No Category   A list of any tasks that do not have specific categories assigned.

Active   A combination with one of the above lists to show only the subset of tasks that are active.

Completed Only   Like the Active option, works with the other list items to further subcategorize by completed items only.

> NOTE *By default, only active items are kept on your iPAQ so that when you next sync your device, any completed items will be removed from the iPAQ, although a full record is still kept in your desktop Outlook. Details on customizing this ActiveSync configuration option can be found in sidebar "How to Customize Tasks," later in this chapter.*

Tap the drop-down arrow on the top right to sort the list of tasks. By default they are sorted by priority. You can also choose to sort by Status, Subject, Start Date, or Due Date.

The check box to the left of each individual task allows you to mark a task as completed, thus changing its status.

Tapping on a specific task will allow you to view the details for that task, as shown here:

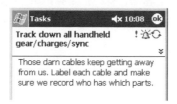

There is a line about one-third of the way down the page. Above this line are the details of the task properties. Below the line are any notes that you have entered for the task. You can tap Edit to change any of the task properties, or to enter notes for the task. The Tools menu contains commands to delete the task or beam it to another device.

Creating a New Task

You can add a new task to the list by tapping New in the menu bar or by using the entry bar. The New command will open the new task dialog box, shown in Figure 5-30.

FIGURE 5-30   Use the new task dialog box to add a task to your to-do list.

You can enter information in the following fields in the new task dialog box:

Subject   The name of the task that you need to perform.

Priority   Normal (default), High, or Low. Selecting High will cause a red exclamation mark to be displayed next to the task in the list. Selecting Low will cause a blue down arrow to be displayed next to the task.

Status   Either completed (active) or not completed.

Starts   Defaults to none, but can be set to any date when the task should become active. This allows you to put future tasks on your list that you don't want to appear until a specific date. Note that if you assign a start date to your task, it will also automatically receive a due date.

Due   Defaults to none, but can be set to any date that the task needs to be finished by. If the current date is past the due date, the task will appear in red in your task list.

Occurs   Allows you to set recurrence for a task, just as you do for an appointment. For example, I give my dog medication on the first of every month, so I could set a recurring task that starts on the first of November and recurs on Day 1 of every month, which will make that task appear on my task list on the first of every month.

Reminder   Enables you to set a reminder alarm so that your iPAQ will announce a task and remind you to finish it. This can only be set if your task has a due date. After choosing the reminder option, you can tap the date to select a date from the calendar.

Categories   Enables you to place this task in a category. The categories will be the same as those that you have set up for appointments and contacts. All Pocket Outlook programs share the same categories list. You can assign multiple categories to a task. This is particularly useful if you have a very large number of tasks in your list and need to be able to see the various subsets. You could enter all the groceries you need to pick up as separate tasks and then categorize them under a group called Shopping List.

Sensitivity   Normal (default) or private. Setting this as private means that if you are sharing your calendar with people on a Microsoft Exchange server, they will not be able to see the details of this task. They will merely see that a task exists and that it is private.

Notes tab   This is a separate tab where you can add any notes you like to a task. Like the notes in other Pocket Outlook applications, your Inbox notes can include text, drawings, and audio recordings.

When you are finished setting up your new task, tap OK in the upper-right corner to have the task added to your list.

An alternative way to add tasks is to change the standard interface to show the *entry bar*. To view the entry bar, select Tools | Entry Bar. Making this selection again will hide the entry bar. When the entry bar is visible, a new line will appear below the bar that contains the category and sort drop-down lists, as shown in this illustration:

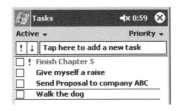

When you use the entry bar, you simply enter a new task by entering the task name into the edit box. You can select the priority by tapping the exclamation mark or down arrow icons to the left of the entry box. Tapping in the list area will cause your new task to be created. I like this feature because I often add new tasks to my list on the fly as they come to mind. When you create tasks this way, all the other properties of the task are defaulted (normal priority, no recurrence, no due date, normal sensitivity, and so on).

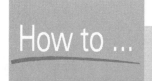

Customize Tasks

There are only a few options to choose from when customizing the iPAQ interface for the Tasks application. To modify the interface, choose Options from the Tools menu to open the Tasks Options dialog box, shown here:

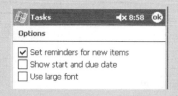

The first check box enables you to configure the system to automatically set reminders for any new tasks you create. Selecting the second check box will make start and due dates visible, as shown in the following illustration. This feature is useful, but means that you can only view half as many tasks in your list at any given time.

The final check box enables you to use a slightly larger font if you find the default font a little too small to read.

Other options to be aware of are those that you can set on the ActiveSync module on your PC. The options in ActiveSync can be reached by opening the ActiveSync application and then clicking the Tasks line in the detail area. This will open the Task Synchronization Settings dialog box, as shown in Figure 5-31.

How to ... Customize Tasks (continued)

There are three options you can set in ActiveSync:

Synchronize All Tasks This setting will synchronize all tasks on both the iPAQ and the desktop.

Synchronize Only Incomplete Tasks This default setting will synchronize only tasks that are not yet completed. Once completed, it will only leave information on the PC, not on your iPAQ.

Synchronize Only The This setting enables you to set the number of past weeks to synchronize (defaults to two weeks) and the number of future weeks (defaults to all).

Synchronize Only Those Tasks In The Following Selected Categories This setting enables you to select only specific categories of tasks to synchronize. This can be useful if you synchronize with multiple desktop systems or if multiple people are sharing the same iPAQ.

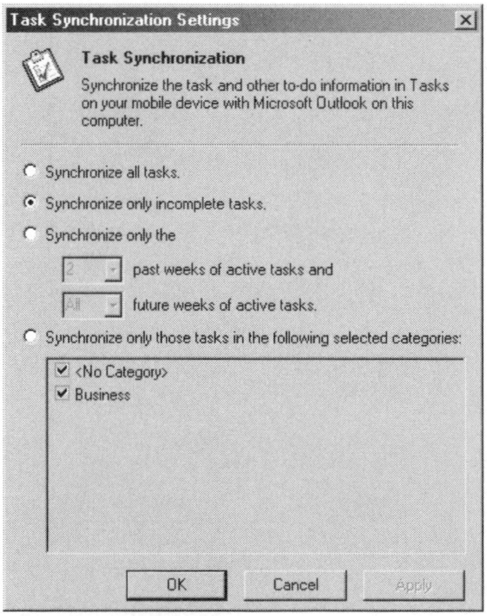

FIGURE 5-31 Options for Task synchronization can be set in the ActiveSync Task Synchronization Settings dialog box.

Keeping Track of Your Notes

The Notes program is another very useful tool for helping to eliminate the scraps of paper in your life. If you need to jot something down, or find yourself in a meeting for which you must take notes, or need to make a quick dictation, you can do all of this with Notes.

Navigating Your Notes

The Notes application can be accessed from the Start menu. Launching Notes will open a list showing all the Notes files in your My Documents folder, as shown in Figure 5-32.

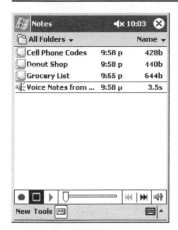

FIGURE 5-32   Each note is stored as its own file in the My Documents folder on your iPAQ.

Notes are shown with their first line as their title (which can be modified after saving the note the first time), the date or time they were created, and their size. The icon on the left will show you if it is a regular note or an audio file. If the note is an audio file, its size will show as the number of seconds of the recording. To open and view a particular note, simply tap it with your stylus. If you tap and hold a note, the shortcut menu gives you the option to create a copy of the note, delete the note, select all the notes, e-mail the note, beam the note, or rename/move the note.

An open note can be edited at will. The commands on the Edit menu enable you to perform operations such as cut, copy, paste, undo, redo, clear, and select all. You can tap the cassette tape icon to embed an audio recording within a text note. The pencil icon that appears at the bottom of the window when editing will drop you into Writing or Drawing mode where you can handwrite text or draw an image. If you handwrite text, you can select the text and choose Recognize from the Tools menu to have the handwriting interpreted into text. If the Recognizer gets a word wrong, you can tap and select the word and then choose Alternates from the Tools menu to see a list of alternate words to select from.

The Tools menu also includes commands to e-mail or beam the note, to change the current zoom factor from 75% to 300%, and to rename, move, or delete the note.

Creating a New Note

To create a new note, you can tap New on the menu bar at any time. Or, from any application, at any time, you can press the Record hardware button on the iPAQ to begin creating a new voice note immediately.

Your new note will open in the default entry mode that you have chosen. Out of the box, your iPAQ is configured to be in Writing mode, where you can draw and write characters on the screen. The default mode can be changed in the Notes Options dialog box (for details, see the sidebar "How to Customize Notes"). The Notes entry mode looks and works identically to the entry mode discussed in the Chapter 3. Once you have created the note you desire, you can tap the OK button to save the note. By default it will be saved in the My Documents folder using the first line of text that you entered as the filename.

 **Customize Notes**

You can customize the Notes application by selecting the Options command from the Tools menu. The Notes Options dialog box will open, as shown in Figure 5-33.

You can set the following four options:

Default Mode   This is the mode that the system will drop into whenever a new note is opened. You can select Writing mode, which enables you to write characters (and draw), or you can select Typing mode, which only selects typed characters or recognized characters from the soft input area.

Default Template   You can select a standard template to use for each new note that is created. By default, a blank template is used, but you can select a template for meeting notes, memo, phone memo, or to-do. This type of note will be the one that is created every time, so unless you generate a lot of one type of note, you probably should not change this option.

Save To   This option enables you to choose to save your notes to the main memory of your iPAQ or to an external storage card if you have one plugged in.

Record Button Action   By default, when you press the hardware record button, the application switches to the Notes application and a new voice recording is created. The other option available here is to remain in the current program.

FIGURE 5-33   The Options dialog box for Notes lets you configure the default
behavior of the Notes application.

5

How to...

■ Download and install Pocket Money

■ Manage your accounts

■ Work with the account register

■ Manage your investments

■ Categorize your financial information

■ Manage your payees

■ Protect your information with passwords

■ Set ActiveSync options to sync with desktop Money

This chapter will focus specifically on what you can do on your iPAQ with Pocket Money. It is not our intention to teach you how to use Money, but rather to show you how your Pocket PC can factor into your personal financial management.

What Can You Do with Pocket Money?

Pocket Money was released after the general release of Pocket PC 2002. As such, it is not part of your standard install. You must download it from Microsoft in order to install it on your iPAQ (discussed in the next section).

Once you have installed Pocket Money, you can see a summary list of all of your accounts and balances, see the details of a specific account, monitor all of your investments, set and manage categories for tracking your expenses, and manage your list of payees that you make payments to.

Downloading and Installing Pocket Money

To get Pocket Money, you can download it for free from the Microsoft website at **http://www.microsoft.com/mobile/pocketpc/downloads/money.asp**. Before you download the file, you must have already installed Microsoft Money on your desktop PC, otherwise the two programs will not synchronize properly.

Account Manager

The primary window of Pocket Money is the Account Manager, as shown in Figure 6-1.

FIGURE 6-1   The Account Manager window shows you the list of all of your accounts and the current balance.

In the Account Manager window is a list all of your accounts with their current balances. The net balance of these accounts is displayed at the bottom of the window, which, if you have every account entered, will be your approximate net worth. Tapping on a checking, savings, or credit card account will take you to the Account Register for that account. Alternatively, you can navigate through the Pocket Money options by using the drop-down menu in the top left of the window as shown here:

At the very bottom of the window is the menu and icon bar that you can also use to navigate through the different Pocket Money windows. Tapping the New command in the Account Manager will enable you to set up a new account in Money. The dialog box that opens will give you the opportunity to fill in all the required information for the account:

Name   The name that will let you tell this account apart from the others in your list.

Account Type   Bank, cash, credit card, or line of credit.

Opening Balance   The balance in the account at the time you create it.

Credit Limit   The limit on the account if it is a credit card or line of credit.

Interest Rate   The rate that you are charged or credited on any account balances.

Display Account On Today Screen This check box allows you to have the account show up in the Today screen with the current balance. This is very useful for tracking your most commonly used accounts.

In addition to the required information, you can include the following optional information: account number, institution name, contact name, and phone number.

Account Register

The Account Register window, shown in Figure 6-2, can be accessed by tapping any account in the Account Manager window. Each entry in the register consists of two lines. The top line shows the date and the amount of the transaction. The second line shows the party involved in the transaction (who the money was paid to or received from) along with the current balance in the account after the transaction.

FIGURE 6-2   Manage individual transactions in the Account Register window.

The bottom of the window will show you the current balance in the account. You can switch between accounts using the drop-down list in the top-right corner of the window. You can see the details of any transaction by tapping it with the stylus. This will open the transaction detail dialog box shown here:

The Type field will define the transaction as being either a withdrawal, deposit, or transfer. The Account field lets you put the transaction into any of your existing accounts. The Payee field remembers all of your current payees (managed as a separate list, as described below). It will automatically try to match what you type in this field with the available list of payees. The Date field lets you enter a date for the transaction. The Amount field stores the amount.

On the Optional tab you can enter or modify additional information about the transaction including the following:

Check Num   The number of the check (if paying by check).

Category   The expense or income category for tracking and reporting purposes.

Subcategory   A subcategory for the category selected above.

Status   A status of blank, R (for reconciled), C (for cleared), or V (for void).

Memo   Your personal notes on the transaction.

The Split command at the bottom of the Optional tab in the transaction detail dialog box allows you to define different categories and subcategories for different elements in the transaction, as shown in Figure 6-3.

6

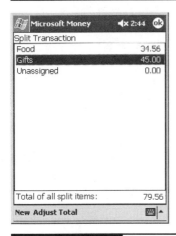

FIGURE 6-3   The Split window allows you to define different categories and subcategories within a transaction.

In this example, we have taken our total bill of $79.56 at Safeway and categorized $34.56 of it as Food, and $45.00 as Gifts. The Unassigned line will show you the total amount of the transaction that you haven't assigned to a category yet. You can add new sub-elements by tapping New. If you enter the split amounts and realize that you have entered the total amount of the transaction incorrectly, you can tap Adjust Total and have Pocket Money adjust the total of the transaction to match the sum of your split items. Tapping OK will return you to the transaction dialog box.

Tapping New on the menu bar in the Account Register window will open up a blank transaction where you can enter all the new information on the fly. This is convenient for recording transactions while you are at the checkout instead of trying to remember them all later.

Categories

The Categories window allows you to maintain the set of categories and subcategories used by Money. The full list of categories and subcategories is displayed when you enter the window, as shown in Figure 6-4.

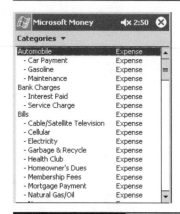

| FIGURE 6-4 | Display all the categories and subcategories available to you in the Categories window. |

 *Categories cannot be edited in Pocket Money. This activity is reserved for the full desktop version of Money. You are restricted to creating new categories and deleting existing categories.*

Tapping and holding the stylus on any category or subcategory will open a shortcut menu enabling you to delete that item from the list. If any transactions exist on your device that use this category, then you will not be able to delete it. Tapping a particular item in the list will open up a dialog box for you to view the properties of the category, as shown here:

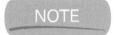 *To create a new category, tap New in the menu bar at the bottom of the categories list. This will open up a blank version of the window shown in the preceding illustration allowing you to specify a category name, type (expense or income), and whether it is a subcategory of another category. You can also add a memo to give a longer description of the category.*

Investments

One of the most useful features of Pocket Money if you invest or trade regularly in the stock market is the ability to manage your portfolio from your iPAQ. The Investments window will show your current portfolio of investments that you have chosen to sync over to your iPAQ. You can keep up to date on the current prices of your stocks while on the move if you have a wireless connection (for details, see Chapter 9).

6

 *You will not see each individual investment account in Pocket Money. Instead, it will sync specific securities that you want to monitor from your iPAQ. You set this up in the ActiveSync options, as described in "Money ActiveSync Options," at the end of this chapter.*

Selecting Investments from the drop-down list in the top left of your window, or tapping the Investments icon in the icon bar at the bottom of the window will open the Investments window, as shown in Figure 6-5.

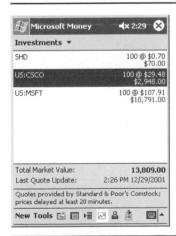

FIGURE 6-5 The Investments window allows you to track your individual stocks and see how they are performing.

Each investment that you are tracking is shown on its own line. The stock symbol is shown along with the number of shares that you are holding and the last known price. Below that you will see the current market value of your holdings. At the bottom of the window you will see the total market value of your tracked portfolio as well as when the last price quote update was completed. If you are connected to a computer with a sync cable or have another connection to the Internet (Ethernet card or wireless access), you can get a price update at any time by tapping on the Update icon in the icon bar (the last icon on the right, with a green downward-pointing arrow).

Tapping any specific investment will open a detail dialog box for that investment, as shown here:

Microsoft Money	◀× 2:35 ok
Investment Name:	Microsoft
Investment Symbol:	US:MSFT
Last Price:	107.91
Shares Held:	1.00
☐ Display investment on Today screen	

You can see the full name of the investment, the last known price, and the number of shares held. You can also flag this particular stock so that it shows up on your Today screen (for those particularly volatile stocks!). Tapping New in the menu bar at the bottom of the Investments window will also bring you to this dialog box so that you can enter a new investment to track. Tapping and holding on a specific investment will give you a pop-up menu allowing you to delete it from your list of investments.

If you delete an investment from your list, it will only be gone temporarily. Next time you synchronize, it will be back. To stop an investment from syncing over to your iPAQ, you must set it to not sync in the ActiveSync options (discussed in "Money ActiveSync Options," later in this chapter). To remove an investment from your portfolio permanently, you must do it from the desktop version of Money.

Payees

Pocket Money will keep your full list of payees synchronized on your iPAQ. You can see this list by selecting the Payees command from the drop-down list on the top left of the window or by tapping the Payees icon in the icon bar (the image of a person). This will open the Payees window, as shown in Figure 6-6.

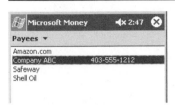

FIGURE 6-6   Open the Payees window to view the complete list of payees
                        synchronized on your iPAQ.

In this list you can see the names of your payees and also their phone number (if you have
one on file). Tapping on any given payee will allow you to see and edit the details of that payee
as shown for Company ABC here:

Tapping New in the menu bar will open a blank version of this window, in which you can
enter the information for the new payee.

   *Whenever you enter new payees in the Account Register window, they will
automatically be added as payees in the Payee list. You do not need to
manually add every payee prior to using them in the Account Register.*

As with categories, tapping and holding a specific payee will delete that payee; however, if
you have used that payee in any transaction (even if the transaction is not synced over to the
Pocket PC) the payee will not be permanently deleted and will reappear the next time you sync
your information.

Money Options

Selecting Options from the Tools menu will take you to the Pocket Money options dialog box,
shown in Figure 6-7.

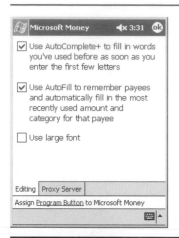

The Pocket Money options dialog box lets you customize how Pocket Money works.

Here you have two tabs to work with: Editing and Proxy Server. The Editing tab lets you set three options:

Use AutoComplete   Selecting this option will cause Pocket Money to try to match any entries that you are entering as they are being typed. This saves you from having to type in the whole payee name or category name if it has been used before.

Use AutoFill   Selecting this option will cause Pocket Money to remember the most recently used amount and category for each payee; the next time you enter that payee in a new transaction, Pocket Money will automatically fill in the amount and category. This is very useful for regularly occurring transactions such as rent, phone bills, and so forth.

Use Large Font   Selecting this option will cause a larger font to be used in all windows. This makes each window easier to read, but reduces the amount of data that can be shown at one time.

On the Proxy Server tab you can specify whether you want Pocket Money to access the Internet via a proxy server when updating information (such as investment prices). Your system administrator will tell you if this is necessary. In general, it is only an issue if you are working in a protected corporate network. You will need to select the check box to tell Pocket Money to use a proxy server and then fill in the HTTP (HyperText Transfer Protocol) address (such as **http://sonicproxy.sonicmobility.com**) and the port number to use.

At the very bottom of the options dialog box is a link that when tapped will allow you to link one of the hardware buttons on your iPAQ to Pocket Money. For example, if you do not use the voice recorder button on the side of the iPAQ, you could set it to launch Money (or any other application that you use frequently) instead. The link takes you to the appropriate Settings option to change your hardware button settings.

Setting a Money Password

Your financial information is private and sensitive information. If you have not already secured your iPAQ from unauthorized use by using a device password or one of the other techniques described in Chapter 8, you can add a password specifically to the Money application to prevent unauthorized access (or if you are particularly paranoid, you can use all of the above for extra levels of security).

To set a password for Pocket Money, once you are in Pocket Money, select Password from the Tools menu. A dialog box will appear in which you can set and confirm the password you want to use. From this point on, you will be asked to enter the password whenever you start Pocket Money.

TIP

Remember that applications on a Pocket PC tend to keep running even when you have tapped OK to close the application. They just become idle. So closing Pocket Money and powering off your iPAQ does not necessarily mean that your password will stop someone from coming to your iPAQ, turning it on, and looking at your accounts. You must specifically close the task in order to log out. This can be done from the iTask application that comes with your iPAQ. On all versions of the iPAQ except the 38xx series, you do this by pressing the rightmost hardware button, which will open a list of all open applications. From this list, if you tap and hold on a specific application you will see a pop-up menu allowing you to close that particular application/task, close all applications/tasks, or close all background applications/ tasks. On the 38xx series, you can run the iTask software from the Programs folder and accomplish the same result. (See Chapter 7 for more details on using iTask to shut down applications.)

Also remember that setting a password will not stop the account balances and information that you have requested from being displayed on the Today page when the iPAQ starts up.

6

Money ActiveSync Options

To optimize the use of Pocket Money, you must set up the correct information in the ActiveSync program. Double-click the Microsoft Money line in the Details area of ActiveSync to open the options dialog box, shown in Figure 6-8.

The most important piece of information in this dialog box is the pointer to the Microsoft Money file that you wish to synchronize with. This path can be changed by clicking the Browse button and navigating to the appropriate file.

In the bottom half of the dialog box are three tabs: Transactions, Investments, and Tools. On the Transactions tab you can select the accounts you want to synchronize over to your iPAQ as well as set an option to synchronize all transactions (synchronizing all transactions is time consuming and memory intensive on your iPAQ, so it isn't recommended unless you have very small financial files) or synchronize only a set number of previous weeks of transactions (from none to 52 weeks of previous transactions; the default is 4 weeks).

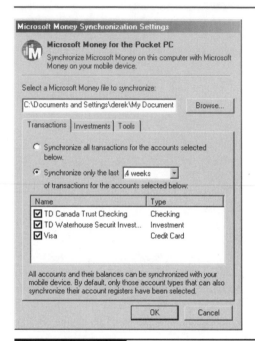

FIGURE 6-8   Use the Microsoft Money Synchronization Settings dialog box to set the ActiveSync options.

On the Investments tab you can choose to synchronize over to your iPAQ all of your investments or only specific investments selected from the list.

The Tools tab gives you two tools to help you with managing your Pocket Money install. The first tool will perform a full synchronization between your iPAQ and your desktop version of Money. If things get out of sync, or if you have changed the file you are using on your desktop, click this to resync all of your data. The second tool allows you to remove all Pocket Money data from your iPAQ. It is important to remove this data before you give your iPAQ to someone else or send it in for servicing. This tab also has a check box to tell ActiveSync to remember your Money password and use it next time you sync data.

Part II

Optimize Your iPAQ Pocket PC for Maximum Productivity

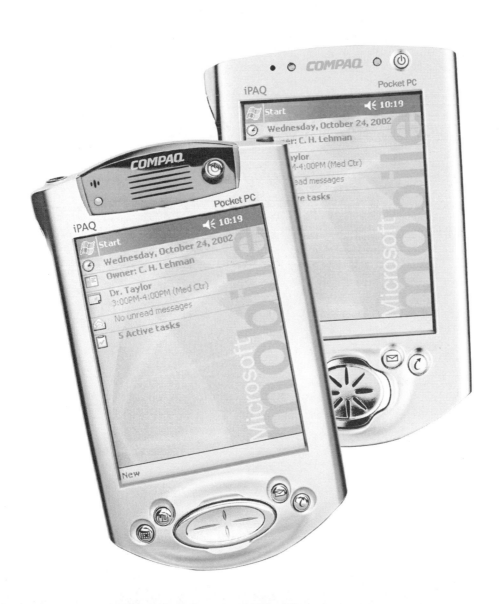

Chapter 7

Optimize Your iPAQ Pocket PC— Better, Faster, and Longer

How to...

■ Control running applications

■ Manage the iPAQ's built-in memory

■ Increase your iPAQ's storage

■ Maximize your iPAQ's battery life

There is an old saying in the computer industry: "What Intel giveth, Microsoft taketh away." That is not to say that if your iPAQ slows down, it's Microsoft's fault. Far from it. This is just another way of saying that no matter how fast the processors become and how much memory our devices have, there will always be a better and faster model on the horizon. So until the future iPAQs with 512MB of RAM and 1 GHz Intel Xscale processors arrive, we have to live with our "slow" 206 MHz iPAQ.

One of the strengths of the iPAQ is its ability to multitask. That is to say, its ability to run multiple programs at the same time. This can be both a blessing and a curse. Being able to run Word, then switch to Excel without saving and exiting Word, and then switch back is something that we have gotten used to in the desktop world. Our iPAQs work the same. But as we run more and more programs, the processor has to perform more and more tasks, and the iPAQ appears to slow down.

In a desktop environment, we have hard drives. This allows the operating system to "free" up memory by saving portions of it to the disk (called paging). In the Pocket PC world, we do not have that luxury because all of the iPAQ's software is stored in either ROM or RAM. Therefore, all of our programs need to be stored in that memory (although the storage cards available for the iPAQ today make this easier to live with).

One of the problems with the iPAQ (and all other Pocket PC devices) is that as applications are executed, they take up more storage and therefore slow down the device. This chapter will deal with some of the tasks that you can perform to ensure that your iPAQ will run better, faster, and longer.

Although we could try to divide this chapter into Better, Faster, and Longer sections, it makes more sense to group the Better and Faster sections together and leave the Longer section apart. As you will see, better and faster go hand-in-hand.

Optimizing your iPAQ is one area in which the older iPAQs (running Pocket PC 2000) and the newer ones (running Pocket PC 2002) differ significantly. We will therefore cover both iPAQ/operating system combinations, and we will illustrate the differences between them.

Controlling Running Applications

Both versions of the Pocket PC operating system are lacking a way for you to easily and quickly control which applications are running. Though they both have the Memory control panel, it is lacking in what it can do and how easily accessible it is. For this reason, Compaq decided to include special applications for controlling the running applications quickly and easily.

QMenu

The original iPAQ shipped with a piece of software installed in ROM called QMenu or Compaq Menu. QMenu performed two tasks. First, it allowed you to control the applications currently running on your iPAQ. You could choose to stop a single application or all the applications running on your device, as well as choose the application that you would like to switch to. QMenu's second role was simply as a shortcut to some of the control panels you might need on a regular basis. What's interesting is that most of these control panels fall into the Better, Faster, or Longer category.

There are a couple of ways to launch QMenu. You can either navigate to it in the Program menu (Start | Programs | QMenu), as illustrated here, or press the "Q" button on the front of the iPAQ (just to the right of the Navigation pad).

When you run the QMenu application, you will see a menu similar to the one shown in Figure 7-1. At this point, you can perform one of the following actions:

- Close the active task
- Close all tasks
- Switch to a running application
- Run File Explorer
- Run the Power control panel
- Run the Volume control panel
- Run the QUtilities program
- Run the Backlight control panel

In this section, we will look at the first three actions in the preceding list. The other options will be covered later in this chapter.

FIGURE 7-1   The QMenu menu allows you to control many features of your iPAQ.

If you choose the Close Active Task command, then the application (or task) that is running below QMenu, Pocket Excel in this example, will close. QMenu will then close. Note that you will not be asked to confirm this process. It will simply close the application, and you will lose any modifications or data that the application has stored but that you haven't saved.

The Close All Tasks command simply closes all the currently running applications. Again, QMenu will close and all applications will be terminated without any confirmation on your part. This command provides a very quick way to clear the deck—get the iPAQ into a state where no applications are running.

While there is no option to switch applications, this can be easily done. If you want to switch to another application, simply tap the desired application from the QMenu menu.

iTask

New to the native Pocket PC 2002 iPAQs (37*xx* and 38*xx* series) is a new application that replaces QMenu called iTask. iTask is similar to QMenu in its ability to control running applications on the iPAQ. Where it differs is in the ability for you to customize its menus. Before we look at this customization, let's look at some of the built-in features of iTask.

iTask can be launched from the Program menu, as shown in the following illustration, by navigating to Start | Programs and tapping the iTask icon. It can also be launched by pressing the iTask button on the iPAQ (located on the far right of the Navigation pad). This button will be labeled with the same icon as the iTask application.

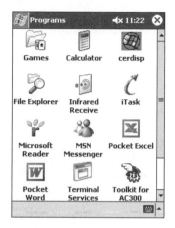

You will notice that iTask is divided into two sections, as shown in Figure 7-2. In the upper part of the menu the running applications are listed, whereas the lower section displays three buttons.

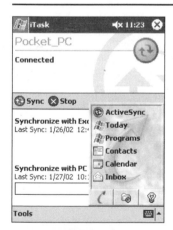

FIGURE 7-2   iTask enables you to control running applications.

Much like with the QMenu application, iTask enables you to close a selected task or application as well as close all tasks. A new feature also allows you to close the background tasks. To close a selected task, simply tap and hold the name of the application that you want to close. A new menu will appear, as shown in Figure 7-3. Choose Close This Task from the menu, and the application will close. As with QMenu, no confirmation is required to terminate the application.

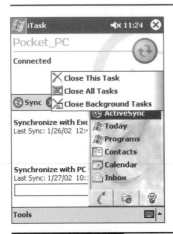

FIGURE 7-3   The iTask menu opens when you tap and hold a task or application name.

To close all tasks, simply tap and hold any application listed in the iTask menu, and choose Close All Tasks from the menu. All running applications and tasks will terminate. Again, no confirmation is required. Be aware that some items on the iTask menu can never be closed. These include Today, Programs, and ActiveSync. Some of these tasks can be closed manually by tapping on the close or OK button in the top-right corner of the screen.

You may find that an application you launch is running extremely slowly because of the number of other applications running at the same time. With the previous Pocket PC operating system (Pocket PC 2000), your only real option was to either close all the applications using the QMenu program (and then re-launch your desired application) or close each of the other applications manually through the Memory control panel (covered later in this chapter). With iTask, you can simply tap and hold the application that you would like to keep running and choose Close Background Tasks from the menu. This will terminate all running applications except for the one you selected.

Configuring iTask

One of the coolest features of the new iTask application is your ability to configure it. As we mentioned previously, there are three buttons on the bottom of the iTask window. By default, these are known as (from left to right) the iTask, Settings, and Brightness buttons. You can modify these buttons, the commands that appear on the buttons, and their icons.

But first, let's list the options that are set by default on the 37*xx* and 38*xx* series devices. The menus accessed by tapping the Settings and the Brightness buttons are the same for both these series.

The Brightness menu simply covers the Backlight control panel, whereas the Settings menu, shown in the following illustration, includes the following commands:

- Backlight
- Buttons
- Memory
- Menus
- Power
- Regional Settings
- Remove Programs
- Sounds & Notifications
- Today Settings

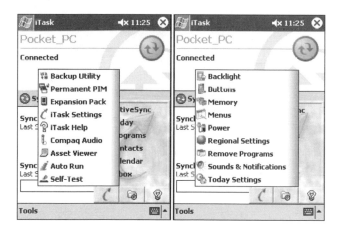

The iTask option enables you to control many tasks on your iPAQ. The 37*xx* series iTask menu contains the following options:

- CF Backup
- Save Contacts
- Expansion Pack
- iTask Settings
- iTask Help

■ Microphone AGC

■ Asset Viewer

■ Auto Run

The 38*xx* series iTask menu, shown in the following illustration, contains the following options:

■ Backup Utility

■ Permanent PIM

■ Expansion Pack

■ iTask Settings

■ iTask Help

■ Compaq Audio

■ Asset Viewer

■ Auto Run

■ Self-Test

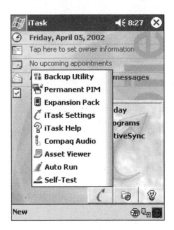

As we mentioned, the options that exist on the iTask menus can be configured by you. To do this, open the iTask Settings control panel, shown in Figure 7-4, in the System section.

To add an application to iTask, choose the menu where it is to be displayed from the Label drop-down list, choose its location on the menu (from the Menu Item drop-down list), and choose the application from the Replace With drop-down list. You can also choose the icon to be displayed on one of the three buttons in iTask from the Icon drop-down list. Be aware that each of the three menus is limited to ten items.

FIGURE 7-4   Use the iTask Settings control panel to modify your iTask menus.

Optimizing Memory

It is important for you to understand how the iPAQ uses its memory for operation. When the 32MB version of the iPAQ came out, it was heralded as having more than sufficient capacity to do everything imaginable with the Pocket PC. It then became clear that since the applications are stored in the iPAQ's RAM, as you added more applications, you quickly ran out of memory. The 64MB models solved that by doubling the iPAQ's storage. Remember that the iPAQ's RAM is used to store both programs and data (programs are applications that are running on the device, whereas data is the files that are stored in RAM).

NOTE   *Although we cover some information on storage in this chapter, Chapter 14 covers storage in much greater detail.*

The Memory control panel (launched from the System section of your iPAQ's Settings) has three tabs: Main, Storage Card, and Running Programs. We will now look at each of these tabs in detail.

The Main Tab

The Main tab in the Memory control panel enables you to control the percentage of the total memory that is used for storage and for programs. As you will notice in Figure 7-5, by simply moving the slider to the left, you will increase the amount of memory used for storage, whereas moving it to the right will increase the amount used for programs. The blue bar underneath the slider shows the total amount of free memory.

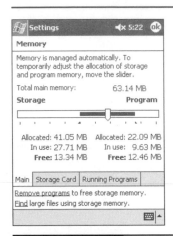

FIGURE 7-5   The Main tab of the Memory control panel allows you to control the way your iPAQ stores data and applications.

It is important for you to note that although the iPAQ has RAM (32MB, 64MB, or more), it assigns this RAM differently. If the memory is used for storage, then only data files can be stored on it and applications cannot be executed from that memory section. Applications are executed from the programs section of memory. If an application is stored in the storage section and you execute it, it will be copied to the program section first. You will notice this when you launch a large application from a storage card on your iPAQ. You will notice that there will be a delay on the iPAQ before the application starts.

The Storage Card Tab

It will become clear to you as you use your iPAQ that 64MB of memory is just not enough. You will most likely find yourself requiring more storage memory. Chapter 14 covers some of the external storage solutions that exist for the iPAQ today, but for now we will look at the Storage Card tab of the Memory control panel, shown in Figure 7-6. On this tab you can view any storage cards and devices that are installed on your iPAQ and find out the amount of free or used space that exists on them. You will also notice a category for RAM called *Extra*. This is an upgrade that was performed on this iPAQ to increase its physical memory. More on this upgrade in Chapter 14.

You will notice that the iPAQ "sees" all storage external to the built-in memory as a Storage Card. This is true if it is a MultiMedia Card (MMC), Secure Digital (SD) card, CompactFlash (CF) card, a hard drive, or upgraded memory.

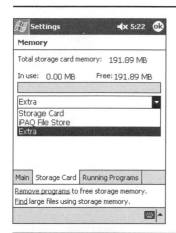

FIGURE 7-6   The Storage Card tab of the Memory control panel allows you to view the configuration of your storage cards.

If you have one of the newer iPAQs (37*xx* or 38*xx* series), you will notice that there is a mystery "storage card" that appears on the device. This storage card is called the iPAQ File Store and is approximately 6.59MB in size.

The solution as to where this storage comes from is an easy one. Most of the original iPAQs shipped with 16MB of ROM. It is in ROM that the operating system was stored. A few lucky iPAQ owners got one of the original iPAQs with 32MB of ROM. The reason for the different ROM sizes is that when they iPAQs were built, 16MB ROM chips were not available and 32MB ones replaced them. Because the operating system required less than 16MB of storage, this was never an issue.

With the release of Pocket PC 2002, however, the operating system grew to be greater than 24MB (because it included MSN Messenger, Terminal Services, and Microsoft Reader). Because the iPAQ has the ability to store information in ROM (for upgrades of the operating system you can flash—overwrite the iPAQ's memory—the ROM), Compaq decide to make the extra ROM available to the user. This extra ROM appears as the "iPAQ File Store." There is one aspect, however, that differentiates it from RAM. Because it is ROM and can be flashed, it is semi-permanent. What this means to you is that any program that you store in the iPAQ File Store will be retained even if you lose battery power completely and all the data/applications in the iPAQ. It is therefore recommended that you store data or applications that you always require on your iPAQ, such as network card drivers. You can also make your contacts and appointments permanent by storing them in this flash ROM, but more on that later in this chapter. Although you can use it to store applications, you may only want to use it for data. If you install applications to it, then lose power on your device and it hard resets, you won't be able to use the applications in the File Store because the registry entries will be gone, DLLs in the /windows directory will be gone, the icon will be gone, and so forth.

Going back to the storage cards, you can simply view the size of the storage cards in this control panel without making changes to it. The process involved in storing information to a storage card or the iPAQ File Store is covered later in this chapter.

The Running Programs Tab

While the iTask application is available for you to control running applications (as well as to launch them), the Pocket PC operating system has a feature for controlling running applications built-in. This is the Running Programs tab of the Memory control panel, shown in Figure 7-7.

FIGURE 7-7 The Running Programs tab of the Memory control panel allows you to control the running programs.

Like the Task Manager in Windows NT or Windows 2000, this tab enables you to view all the programs that are currently running in memory, as well as to control them.

As you can see in Figure 7-7, a list of all running programs is presented to you. You then have one of three options: Activate, Stop, or Stop All. If you select an application from the list and tap the Activate button, the Memory control panel will close and the selected application will be brought to the foreground. By selecting an application and tapping on the Stop button you will terminate it. And by tapping the Stop All button, you will force the iPAQ to terminate all non-operating system programs.

The Memory control panel contains two other options: Remove Programs To Free Storage Memory and Find Large Files Using Storage Memory.

You can use the Remove Programs option (simply by tapping the link at the bottom of the Memory control panel) to remove (or uninstall) applications from your iPAQ. You will then be presented with a list of the installed applications, as shown in the illustration on the following page. When you tap an application, a confirmation dialog box will appear, at which point you can choose to remove the application from your iPAQ. Be aware, however, that this only removes the application from the iPAQ. Because most applications are installed from a desktop system, you will need to uninstall the application on the desktop too.

Most Pocket PC applications install themselves on the desktop first, at which point, ActiveSync transfers the application to the iPAQ and installs it. These applications are usually installed in directories directly below the ActiveSync directory (C:\Program Files\Microsoft ActiveSync, for example). If you want to uninstall an application, simply follow these steps:

1. Connect your iPAQ to your desktop.

2. Make sure that ActiveSync recognizes the iPAQ and connects to it.

3. Choose Add/Remove Programs from the Tools menu in ActiveSync.

4. Select the application to be removed in the Add/Remove Programs dialog box, shown in Figure 7-8.

5. Click on the Remove button.

6. Click the OK button to confirm the application's removal. The application will now be removed from both the desktop and the iPAQ.

Because the iPAQ has a finite amount of memory, Microsoft included a little utility to allow you to quickly find files on your iPAQ based on some criteria. This utility is launched by tapping the Find link at the bottom of the Memory control panel, which opens a window like the one illustrated here:

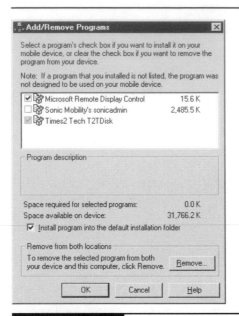

FIGURE 7-8   Removing applications on both the desktop and the iPAQ

You can type in a search field under the Find field or simply search for all files that fall into the criteria set in the Type field. You can choose from the following file types:

- All data
- Calendar
- Contacts
- Help (only in Pocket PC 2002)
- Inbox
- Larger than 64KB
- Notes
- Pocket Excel
- Pocket Outlook
- Pocket Word
- Tasks

You will notice that Microsoft has included most of the files that will require a large amount of storage space on your iPAQ, such as Pocket Excel and Pocket Word files.

Permanent PIM

Since the newer iPAQ models have extra storage available in the non-volatile ROM, an application exists to enable you to store some of your most important information in it. Compaq decided that the information most people will want to ensure they do not lose will be their appointments and their contacts. For this reason, they included the Permanent PIM control panel.

The Permanent PIM control panel, shown in Figure 7-9, enables you to control whether your contacts and/or appointments are to be stored in non-volatile ROM. By selecting the desired check boxes, you can ensure that this information is retained even if the iPAQ's battery runs out completely.

7

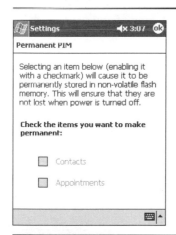

FIGURE 7-9   Storing your contacts and appointments in non-volatile ROM

Installing Applications on the iPAQ

Most Pocket PC applications will automatically launch the Add/Remove Programs utility covered earlier in the chapter. Some, however, do not, or you might not have your iPAQ synced with the desktop when the application attempts to install. For this reason, in this section we will cover the process of installing an application to both the iPAQ's main memory and a storage card.

Installing to Main Memory

The process of installing to main memory is a simple one. All you need to do is launch the Add/Remove Programs utility of ActiveSync and answer Yes when asked whether you would like the application installed to the default directory, as shown here:

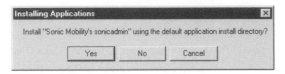

The application will now be installed into main memory and into the directory specified by the application vendor.

Installing to a Storage Card

The process of installing an application to a Storage card (including the iPAQ File Store) is almost as easy as that of installation to main memory. The only difference is that when presented with the prompt shown earlier, simply answer No. The dialog box shown in Figure 7-10 will open, where you can choose which storage card (assuming that multiple ones are available) the application is to be installed to.

FIGURE 7-10   Select or enter the name of the storage card you want to install the application to in this dialog box.

Maximizing Your iPAQ's Battery Power

One of the biggest misconceptions about the iPAQ and other Pocket PC devices is that they have zero battery life. Although it is true that the iPAQ uses more battery power than, say, a Palm device, it is important to remember that several things set the iPAQ apart from such devices. First and foremost is the iPAQ screen, which is arguably one of the best handheld screens on the market.

The iPAQ screen is lit from the side and requires quite a bit of power to maintain. For this reason, several features have been built into the iPAQ to enable you to control the brightness of the screen, as well as how the iPAQ will react to different power situations, such as when on battery power and connected to AC power.

Conserving Battery Power

Two different control panels are used for controlling power usage in the iPAQ: the Power and the Backlight control panels. Each of these is covered in detail in the next sections.

The Power Control Panel

The Power control panel simply allows you to view the current battery status and control what the device should do when on battery power or when connected to external power. As can be seen in the following illustration, the top half of the control panel displays the battery status (with the Main battery and an External battery if one exists). The bottom half allows you to set whether the iPAQ is to be turned off after inactivity if on battery or external power, and the amount of time before the iPAQ is to be turned off.

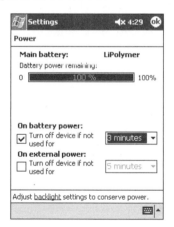

The Backlight Control Panel

The Backlight control panel contains three tabs: Battery Power, External Power, and Brightness. The first two tabs, Battery Power and External Power, are identical in all iPAQ models, whereas the Brightness tab is different on the 38xx series.

The Battery Power tab, shown in Figure 7-11, enables you to configure the threshold at which the backlight is to be turned off when the device is not in use and whether to turn the backlight on if the screen is tapped or a button is pressed.

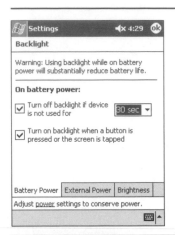

FIGURE 7-11   The Battery Power tab for monitoring your iPAQ's configuration when running on battery

The External Power tab, shown in Figure 7-12, is used to configure the same settings as the Battery Power tab, except when the iPAQ is running on external power.

FIGURE 7-12   The External Power tab for monitoring your iPAQ's configuration when running on external power

The last tab, the Brightness tab, differs depending on which model of iPAQ you have. If you have a 36xx or 37xx series iPAQ, the tab will appear as shown in Figure 7-13. There are six options for brightness levels, and a Power Usage graphic is displayed on the right. The following options are available:

- Automatic
- Super Bright
- High Bright
- Med Bright
- Low Bright
- Power Save

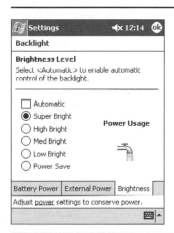

FIGURE 7-13   The Brightness tab on the 36*xx* and 37*xx* series iPAQ for controlling the brightness of your iPAQ's screen

The Power Save option will simply turn the backlight completely off. This setting will conserve the most battery life out of your iPAQ. The four different Bright settings are simply different levels of brightness. The top option, Automatic, allows the iPAQ to choose the brightness level automatically. This is done by using an ambient light sensor, which is located to the left of the Compaq logo. The iPAQ will brighten the display in dark environments and turn it off in bright environments.

As we mentioned, the Brightness tab differs significantly on the 38*xx* series iPAQ, as Figure 7-14 illustrates. On the 38*xx* series iPAQ, you can choose the brightness levels differently on battery or external power. It also offers many more levels of brightness. As with the 36*xx* and 37*xx* series iPAQs, an automatic option is available, and it too uses an ambient sensor.

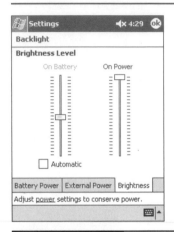

FIGURE 7-14   The Brightness tab on the 38*xx* series iPAQ is very different than the previous versions.

You can quickly turn the backlight on or off by pressing and holding the power button.

Emergency Power

Several solutions exist for extending the battery life of your iPAQ. We examine three different solutions in this section, although many others exist.

The first product that you should be aware of is called Instant Power (**www.instant-power.com**). This solution is unique in that it uses a zinc-air cell to charge the iPAQ. The zinc-air cell is stored in a sealed bag. When you need to charge your iPAQ, simply remove the cell from the bag and plug it into the iPAQ. The cell will then start to react with the air and produce enough power to charge the iPAQ three times. When you are done with the cell, simply store it in a special bag until the next time you need to use it. It remains usable in the bag for two to three months.

The second product is not specifically a battery product, but a dual CompactFlash expansion sleeve. We mention it here because it has removable batteries. This capability has always been lacking with the iPAQ and is finally available with the Nexian Dual CF and Power Pak for the iPAQ (**www.nexian.com**).

The final product covered here is a new battery for the iPAQ that replaces the existing one. To install this battery you have to open your iPAQ (possibly voiding your warranty, but then again, if it was under warranty and your battery failed, you would probably send it back to Compaq). This battery also has a vibrate option, which means you can be silently notified by your iPAQ when events, such as appointments, take place. This do-it-yourself battery is available from **www.kingrex.net**. More on these extra add-ons in Chapter 15.

Chapter 8

Secure Your iPAQ Pocket PC

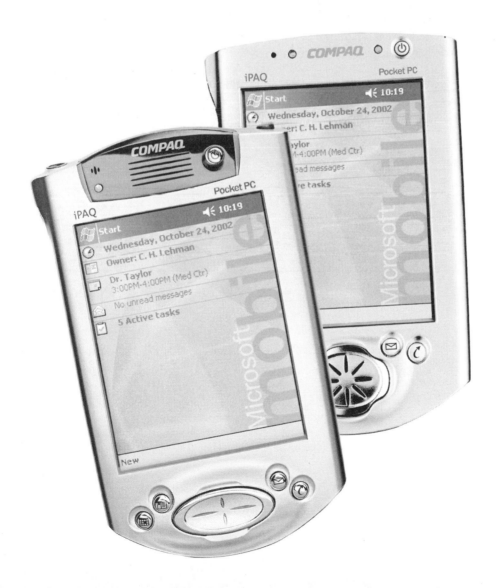

How to...

- Secure your iPAQ with a password
- Upgrade the built-in iPAQ security
- Use hardware security products with your iPAQ
- Sign into your iPAQ with your signature

By now, you'll have gotten a sense of the power of the iPAQ. It is more than a handheld PDA; it is a handheld computer. It offers laptop/desktop–like capabilities in many arenas for a fraction of the cost. There is, however, one problem with it. It is portable.

"Why is that a bad thing?" you might ask. Well, because the iPAQ is so portable and powerful, you will probably use it all the time, which increases the chance that you will lose it or it will be stolen. Particularly if you are storing sensitive data, such as bank account numbers, personal documents, lists of passwords or PINs (personal identification numbers), and correspondence on your iPAQ, you will want to ensure that no one can access that information. How can you make your iPAQ more secure? It's easy, if you take some simple precautions.

This chapter will discuss some of the tools (both built-in and third-party) that can be used to secure your iPAQ. Losing your iPAQ will always be an inconvenience, but you can make sure it isn't a disaster.

Using the Built-In Security Tools

All iPAQs have a built-in password utility, which you can access on the Personal tab of the Settings window, shown in Figure 8-1. To open the Settings window select Start | Settings.

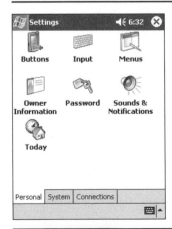

FIGURE 8-1   Control your iPAQ's settings with the Personal tab of the Settings window.

The Password application will look different and have different capabilities depending on which version of the Pocket PC operating system you have (which is not necessarily determined by which iPAQ you have). The version that shipped with the original Pocket PC operating system (now called Pocket PC 2000) was very basic in its function. You were simply able to enter in a four-digit PIN-type password to secure your iPAQ (as shown in Figure 8-2). As you can imagine, if someone was going to go to all the trouble of stealing your iPAQ, then a few hours in front of the television guessing which of the 10,000 combinations you chose is not a huge deal. To avoid this scenario, Microsoft implemented a system where after five tries, the timing between entries would double. Every failed entry would cause it to double again. This means that after 15 failed tries, you would have to wait 2 minutes before you could try again, and that to try 50 combinations would take a full day.

FIGURE 8-2   Set your password for a Pocket PC 2000 iPAQ through the Password dialog box.

To set a password, simply launch the Password utility, enter a four-digit number, and reset the device. The next time you power the iPAQ on, you will notice a similar keypad displayed on the screen, at which point, you will need to enter the password to gain access to the iPAQ. If you own a Pocket PC 2000 iPAQ and would like a more secure password utility, consider the strong password protection offered by Microsoft's Password PowerToy, available at **http://www.microsoft.com/mobile/pocketpc/downloads/powertoys.asp**.

Should you ever forget your password, you have one of two choices. You can sit in front of the television and try to guess your password, or you can perform a hard reset of the device (see Appendix A for direction on how to perform a hard reset).

With Pocket PC 2002, Microsoft provides a much more powerful Password utility. As Figure 8-3 illustrates, you are given one of three different options in this new dialog box. You can choose to not have a password, use a four-digit password, or use a strong alphanumeric password.

FIGURE 8-3   On a Pocket PC 2002 iPAQ, the Password dialog box is slightly different.

The first option of the dialog box is straightforward. No password is set, and therefore anyone can access the device. The second option is the same as the one offered by the Pocket PC 2000 operating system. You must enter a four-digit password to access the iPAQ, as shown in Figure 8-4.

FIGURE 8-4   Use the numeric keypad in the Password dialog box to choose a four-digit password.

The final option enables you to choose a password that uses an alphanumeric sequence (similar to what you would use on the Internet or at work). As you can see in Figure 8-5, you use the keyboard (or another mode of data entry) to choose and confirm your password.

FIGURE 8-5   If you select the Strong Alphanumeric Password option, a keyboard will appear that you can use to enter your password.

No matter what type of password you choose with Pocket PC 2002, if you forget it or lose it, you will need to perform a hard reset of the iPAQ to access your data, just as you would with earlier versions of the operating system.

Once you enable any of the password options, you will be presented with a password prompt (shown in Figure 8-6) when you attempt to synchronize with your desktop via ActiveSync. As you can imagine, all this security would be for naught if all you had to do was sync the data over to a desktop.

FIGURE 8-6   If your iPAQ has a password assigned to it, you will have to enter it before ActiveSync can connect to it.

8

Extending the Built-In Security

For many people, iPAQ's built-in password security is just not good enough. If you are one of those people, several software and hardware products are available to serve your needs. Two extremely similar software products, Sign-On by CIC and PDALok by Penflow, enable you to not only use the PIN-type password, but also your signature to secure your iPAQ. The hardware products offered by BioSentric Solutions enable you to use your fingerprint for iPAQ security.

Sign-On

Sign-On by CIC (**www.cic.com**) is a security utility that enables you to use your signature as well as a password to lock your iPAQ. After you install Sign-On, the Sign-On icon replaces the Password icon on the Personal tab of the Settings window, as shown in Figure 8-7. (Don't worry, the Password icon reappears if or when you uninstall the program.)

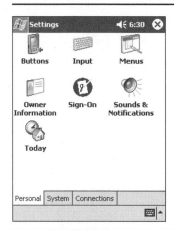

FIGURE 8-7   Once Sign-On is installed on your iPAQ, an icon will appear on the Settings window.

Before you can use Sign-On's signature feature, you need to "enroll" your signature, that is, train the application to recognize it, by writing your signature on the screen three times, as you can see in Figure 8-8. You can then test the signature, as well as set a four-digit PIN-type password for ActiveSync (and, if desired, startup).

PDALok

PDALok from Penflow (**www.pdalok.com**) is very similar to the Sign-On product. The only real difference is that PDALok requires that you write the signature six times before the application will enroll it (see Figure 8-9). As with Sign-On, the PDALok icon replaces the Password icon in the Settings window.

FIGURE 8-8   Enrolling your signature with Sign-On

8

FIGURE 8-9   Enrolling your signature with PDALok

TIP

Before you even think about using one of these tools, make sure that you have completely backed up your iPAQ. After configuring PDALok to recognize my signature, I tried unsuccessfully to unlock my iPAQ—although the signature was validated, the program would not let me in to the device. I am unclear as to whether this was a conflict with the operating system or a problem with the application.

BioSentry and BioHub

BioSentric Solutions (**www.biocentricsolutions.com**) offers two different hardware options for the iPAQ: BioSentry and BioHub. Both of these products will scan your fingerprint and grant you access based on the fingerprint. The only difference between the BioSentry and BioHub solutions is the former is an iPAQ expansion sleeve and the latter is a CF card–based solution. The BioSentry sleeve has a built-in Compact Flash slot to enable you to add memory storage to your iPAQ. Both offer 56-bit, triple DES encryption and half-a-second matching time.

Browsing the Internet Securely

Many of us now rely on the Internet for help with our day-to-day tasks. Just as e-mail has become a must for many professionals today, Internet banking has become a "can't live without it." The problem with doing so from the iPAQ is that out of the box, Pocket Internet Explorer (PIE) is not running at 128-bit encryption. Without this level of encryption, most banks (at least the reputable ones) will not allow you to access sensitive information, such as your account information. The same is true for just about any purchases that you may complete online.

If your iPAQ has the Pocket PC 2002 operating system (or has been upgraded to it), you will not need to install the High Encryption Pack because PIE will already support it.

*Microsoft was aware of this shortcoming of PIE and released the Microsoft High Encryption Pack for Pocket PC v1.0. The High Encryption Pack (which is available as a free download from **www.microsoft.com/mobile/pocketpc/downloads/ ssl128.asp**) extends the functionality of PIE to allow it to encrypt/decrypt data using 128-bit encryption. You will only need this download if your iPAQ runs the Pocket PC 2000 operating system.*

Now when you navigate to a secure site, you will be allowed to perform the desired transactions. If you need to find out whether the connection used is a secure one, simply check the properties of the page (choose View | Properties) from PIE. You will notice that in the Security field, the page will be listed as Secure, as shown in Figure 8-10.

Another giveaway that you are on a secure web page is the Security prompt message that appears when you try to leave a secure page to go to an insecure page. This message box, shown in Figure 8-11, warns you that you are leaving a secure connection and gives you the opportunity to change your mind.

Securing Your Personal Data

When it comes to storing personal information on your iPAQ securely, there are two products that perform the task perfectly: eWallet from Ilium Software (**www.iliumsoft.com**) and CodeWallet Professional from Developer One (**www.developerone.com**).

FIGURE 8-10   You can check the web page's Properties sheet to determine whether it is secure.

FIGURE 8-11   The Security prompt includes options to continue leaving a secure page or return to it.

These products, known as electronic wallets, offer similar functions; they both enable you to store information about your bank, credit card, and frequent flyer accounts, information about insurance, health, and prescriptions, emergency numbers, and other personal data. Each account is treated as a card kept in your electronic wallet. You can easily secure all the cards, some cards, or the different categories of you wallet. Figure 8-12 shows eWallet and CodeWallet Professional in a side-by-side comparison.

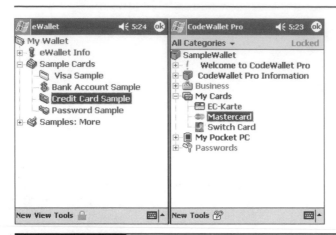

FIGURE 8-12   eWallet and CodeWallet Professional are two programs that let you store you important card information securely on you iPAQ.

You will immediately notice the similarities between the two products. One difference that stands out is that with CodeWallet Professional any locked category or card appears in red. This enables you to see at a glance which are password protected and which are not.

eWallet includes the following card types:

Bank account	Lens prescription
Calling card	Library card
Car info	Membership info
Clothes sizes	Note card
Combination lock	Passport info
Contact	Password
Credit card	Picture card
Driver's license	Prescription
Emergency numbers	Serial number
Free form	Social Security number
General purpose	Software serial number
Health numbers	Voice mail info
ID card	Voter card
Insurance policy	Website

CodeWallet Professional includes these card types:

Bank account	Personal insurance
Calling card contact	Prescription
Contact favorites	Security System
Credit card	Social Security card
Dining: restaurant	Software license/key
Dining: take-out	Stock/Investment
Emergency numbers	Travel: car rental
Event	Travel: flight detail
Exercise	Travel: flight summary
Gift ideas	Travel: ground transportation
Home services	Travel: hotel
ID/Account number	Travel: long-term parking
Insurance policy	Travel: places
Internet service provider	Vehicle: dealer
Library card	Vehicle: driver's license
Local government	Vehicle: maintenance
Lock combination	Vehicle: profile
Notes	Voice mail codes
Online shopping account	Warranty
Passport	Web favorites
Password	Website

Both products have a desktop component to them. eWallet's desktop companion (shown in Figure 8-13) is included with the eWallet suite. The desktop version offers all the functionality of the iPAQ version, plus the ability to export records, back up the database, compact the database, and synchronize it with the iPAQ version.

The desktop version of CodeWallet Professional (shown in Figure 8-14) has all the features of its iPAQ counterpart, except that it can back up the database, export it to a text file, and create custom cards. When creating a custom card, you have the ability to choose all the fields and properties for the new card.

You can purchase the Pocket PC and the desktop versions of these applications separately or together in a Mobile Sync Pack.

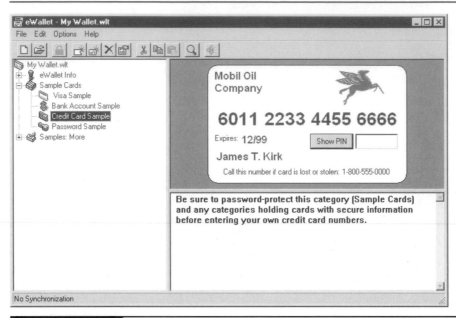

FIGURE 8-13 Instead of adding cards on your iPAQ, you can use eWallet on the desktop.

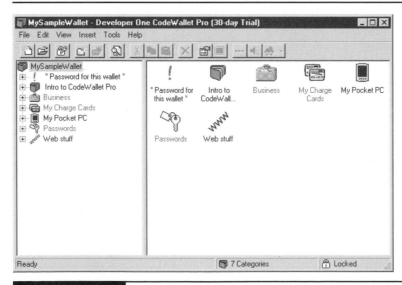

FIGURE 8-14 Simplify your Card entry process by using CodeWallet Professional desktop edition.

Chapter 9

Connect Wirelessly with Your iPAQ Pocket PC

How to...

- ■ Set up your iPAQ to connect to a wireless network
- ■ Select from the various wireless networks available
- ■ Choose the sleeves and cards that are right for you
- ■ Install and configure the drivers for Sierra Wireless and Novatel wireless modems
- ■ Send and receive e-mail, chat, and surf the Internet through a wireless connection
- ■ Use a local wired or wireless connection

The future of all handheld computing lies in the arena of wireless connectivity. Eventually, every iPAQ will have built-in wireless capability. The most recent addition to the iPAQ line, the 3870, contains built-in Bluetooth wireless connectivity. This chapter will explain and evaluate different methods for getting your iPAQ connected to a wireless network. This will include real-time sending and receiving of e-mail from your handheld and surfing the Internet with Pocket Internet Explorer. In addition, we will discuss third-party software that can provide even more value on a wirelessly enabled iPAQ, such as wireless network systems administration. This chapter will also include an assessment of the different combinations of hardware that can be used to achieve a wireless connection from PCMCIA cards (CDPD, CDMA, CDMA 1xRTT, GSM, GPRS, Ricochet, and so on), and CompactFlash modems.

Connecting to Wireless Networks

With the exception of the 3870, none of the iPAQs have built-in capability to access a wireless network, and the 3870 only has the ability to access a Bluetooth wireless network. Bluetooth is short range and has yet to really take hold in the market. What this means is that in order to connect your iPAQ to a wireless network, you will need to add some external ingredients. If you want to use a private wireless network, you will be looking to acquire an 802.11b wireless LAN card and the necessary expansion sleeve to connect it to your iPAQ. Your options for this are covered in the next section, "Selecting the Hardware for Your Wireless Connection." The 802.11b cards will provide a bandwidth of 11 Mbps, but you must be within range of your wireless access points.

If you want to use one of the larger wireless networks that circle the globe, you will need to identify which wireless provider you will be using. Selecting your wireless provider will depend on where you reside, where you plan on using your wireless card, and how much bandwidth you need. Each wireless network carrier uses different protocols that have different transmission speeds. Without going into too much detail, Table 9-1 contains a comparison of the protocols that you can consider. For a full list of which carriers provide which protocols, their coverage, hardware requirements, and more, check **www.pocketpctools.com**.

Protocol	Bandwidth	Details
CDPD	19.2 Kbps	This protocol enjoys the widest coverage in North America at present. It is slow, but fairly reliable. Good for getting your mail and running applications, but not particularly practical for Internet surfing or e-mail with large attachments.
CDMA	14.4 Kbps	The CDMA protocol works like a standard dial-up modem on a PC, where you enter the number to dial, and you must have an existing account with that ISP in order to get Internet access. This protocol is also largely limited to North America.
GSM	9.6 Kbps–14.4 Kbps	GSM is the dominant protocol used almost everywhere else in the world. It has extensive coverage throughout Europe and Asia. Functionally it will work very much the same as CDMA with the need to dial up an existing ISP account to get Internet access.
GPRS	56 Kbps–118 Kbps	GPRS is the digital and data upgrade from GSM. Most GSM providers are moving to GPRS as this book is being written. The coverage is very good in Europe and Asia, but is still very sparse in North America. GPRS is configured in *channels*. Each channel supports 14.4 Kbps of data traffic. The carrier can configure the number of channels with each connection, up to eight. Most carriers are currently configuring four channels. Each channel supports data in one direction, so current GPRS offerings usually download data at 33.6 Kbps (three channels) and upload data at 14.4 Kbps (one channel). Alternatively, some carriers configure the service with 28.8 Kbps (two channels) in each direction. Both of these are called 56 Kbps service by the carriers. When the carriers choose to upgrade to eight-channel service, it will become a 118 Kbps service.
CDMA 1xRTT	56 Kbps–384 Kbps	CDMA 1x, or CDMA ONE service is an upgrade from current CDMA and CDPD networks. It is similar to GPRS and can be configured up to 384 Kbps, but initial offerings will likely be 56 Kbps.

9

TABLE 9-1   Wireless Network Protocols

Selecting the Hardware for Your Wireless Connection

After choosing the provider that you will use for your wireless connection, you will need to choose the hardware that you will connect with. There is a good chance that you might use two different protocols. For example, you might use an 802.11b card while you are in the office because it has much faster bandwidth and no air time charges. But when you leave the office, you may plug in a CDPD card connected to AT&T, which has much lower bandwidth, but much greater coverage range.

In this section we will look at the different hardware that you might select. In the next section will we show you how to set up two of these cards, the Sierra Wireless AirCard 300, and the Novatel Wireless G100.

Most of the wireless modems and LAN cards that you can choose from come in the form of a PCMCIA, or PC Card. These cards are interchangeable with your laptop standard, which is convenient when you want to share one wireless access account between your laptop and your iPAQ. There are also a number of CompactFlash cards emerging that support the 802.11b standard for wireless LAN. Table 9-2 presents the options by protocol.

Vendor and Model	Description
CDPD	
Sierra Wireless AirCard 300 for Handhelds	There is a version of this card for handhelds only, and one for handhelds and laptops. The primary difference is the power consumption of the cards. More information can be found at **www.sierrawireless.com/ProductsOrdering/300.html**.
Novatel Wireless Merlin Platinum Special Edition	This card is specifically designed for use in both handhelds and laptops and will drain less battery power from your iPAQ than the standard Merlin card. Maximum connection speed is 19.2 Kbps. More information can be found at **www.novatelwireless.com/pcproducts/merlinplatinumSE.htm**.
Enfora Pocket Spider	This is a CompactFlash CDPD modem that will work with your iPAQ CompactFlash expansion sleeve. More information can be found at **www.enfora.com**.
CDMA	
Sierra Wireless AirCard 510	This card is meant for both handhelds and laptops. It uses the CDMA protocol, which allows you to dial up an ISP with whom you already have a dial-up account. Check with your provider, but some of the CDMA providers, such as Bell Mobility in Canada, provide their own ISP dial-up service to their AirCard 510 customers. More information can be found at **www.sierrawireless.com/ProductsOrdering/510nb.html**.

TABLE 9-2   Wireless Modems and LAN Cards, by Protocol

Vendor and Model	Description
CDMA	
Others	Note that the dual band CDMA 1xRTT wireless modems described below can support the standard CDMA protocol and will likely be a better buy given that all CDMA networks are expected to upgrade to CDMA 2000 in the near future.
CDMA 1xRTT	
Sierra Wireless AirCard 550	This card operates on the CDMA 2000 networks, which have yet to be launched in North America but are expected to be operational by the summer of 2002. This version of the card offers single-band access to the North American PCS network. The theoretical top end data speeds of this card are 153 Kbps. More information can be found at **www.sierrawireless.com/ProductsOrdering/AC550-5551xRTT.html**.
Sierra Wireless AirCard 555	This is the dual-band version of the AirCard 550, which will operate on international CDMA 1xRTT networks as well as the North American networks. This modem can also connect to the circuit-switched CDMA networks at 14.4 Kbps. More information can be found at **www.sierrawireless.com/ProductsOrdering/AC550-5551xRTT.html**.
Novatel Wireless Merlin C201	This is a dual-band CDMA 1xRTT card with essentially the same functionality as the Sierra Wireless AirCard 555. One of the nice features of this card is that it appears it will ship with an integrated antenna, which means no long antenna to break, lose, or get in your way. More information can be found at **www.novatelwireless.com/pcproducts/merlinC201.html**.
GSM/GPRS	
Sierra Wireless AirCard 710	This is a single-band GSM/GPRS card that is suitable for North American usage only. One of the nicest features of this card is that the antenna is retractable and is stored internal to the card, making it less likely to get lost or damaged. More information can be found at **www.sierrawireless.com/ProductsOrdering/AC710-750GSM.html**.
Sierra Wireless AirCard 750	This is the tri-band version of the AirCard 710 and can function on any of the GSM/GPRS networks in the world. It loses the retractable antenna and instead features an external hinged antenna. More information can be found at **www.sierrawireless.com/ProductsOrdering/AC710-750GSM.html**.

9

TABLE 9-2   Wireless Modems and LAN Cards, by Protocol (continued)

Vendor and Model	Description
GSM/GPRS	
Novatel Wireless Merlin G100	This is a single-band GSM/GPRS card that is suitable for North American usage only. It features up to 53.6 Kbps throughput in areas featuring GPRS coverage, and 14.4 Kbps in areas offering only GSM coverage. More information can be found at **www.novatelwireless.com/pcproducts/g100.html**.
Option Wireless Globetrotter	This is a universal tri-band GSM/GPRS card that is suitable for worldwide use. It also has a headset plug-in, which enables you to use your iPAQ as your cell phone and make voice calls. The antenna is fully internally retractable, which is very practical. More information can be found at **www.option.com**.

TABLE 9-2   Wireless Modems and LAN Cards, by Protocol (continued)

Note that there are several companies now promising GPRS cards in the very near future; however, many of these do not yet have compatible drivers for the Pocket PC. Other companies getting close with their cards include Xircom (**www.xircom.com**) and CET Technologies in Singapore (**www.cet.st.com**).

Other Hardware

Of course, to make any of the previously mentioned modems work, you will require an expansion sleeve. All the expansion sleeves are discussed in detail in Chapter 13. You can get an expansion sleeve from Compaq that includes a built-in GSM/GPRS modem.

Setting Up Your Wireless Modem

In this section we will show you how to install and configure your wireless cards. We will explain one CDPD card and one GPRS card from each of the two major manufacturers, Sierra Wireless and Novatel Wireless. The other cards and vendors will be similar.

Setting Up a Sierra Wireless AirCard 300: CDPD

The Sierra Wireless AirCard 300 is a Type II PCMCIA card. This means that you will need an expansion sleeve for your iPAQ that supports PCMCIA cards. Either the single or the dual sleeve will work. If you have all the equipment, then follow these steps:

1. Slide your iPAQ into the sleeve until it is firmly seated. You should see a window with the message "Initializing Expansion Pack" on the screen for a brief moment while

your iPAQ and your sleeve set up their communication. DO NOT insert the AirCard until after you have installed the drivers.

2. Connect your iPAQ to your PC with your ActiveSync cable, and make sure there is an active connection. Once this is established you are ready to install the drivers onto your iPAQ.

3. Install the necessary drivers for your AirCard. These likely came on a CD-ROM with your AirCard, but if not, you can download the latest drivers from the Sierra Wireless website (**www.sierrawireless.com**). Once you have the install program, run it, and the install should initiate through your ActiveSync connection to your iPAQ.

4. Once the drivers are installed, you MUST perform a soft reset of your iPAQ by pushing the recessed soft reset button on the bottom of the iPAQ. Simply turning the iPAQ on and off is not sufficient.

5. After you have completed the reset, disconnect your iPAQ from your PC.

6. Now you may insert your Sierra Wireless AirCard into the slot in the expansion sleeve.

The drivers are installed, but the system is still not quite ready to go. Now you must configure the system so it knows how to talk. Your wireless carrier should have provided you with some basic information:

Your IP address This is a static address in the CDPD world that is bound to your card.

Your DNS This can vary, but your carrier will have a DNS (name server) that they will recommend that you use.

Your "side" This is either A or B and is a setting that depends on how the carrier has their hardware/software set up.

If you don't have this information, you should contact your carrier and get it because you will need it to proceed any further.

With this information in hand, you are ready to run the Wireless Expert software:

1. Launch Wireless Expert from the Programs folder. The first page of the wizard gives you instructions and asks you to specify which carrier you are using, as shown in Figure 9-1. The carriers are all listed in the drop-down list.

2. The next page, shown in Figure 9-2, is where you will enter the information from your carrier. The EID number is read automatically from the AirCard. You must enter the NEI, which is the IP address your carrier gave you. Then you will enter the DNS for name resolution, and then choose your side designator. When this is all in, tap Next.

FIGURE 9-1   Choose the carrier that you have a wireless account with.

FIGURE 9-2   You must provide the IP address (NEI number) and DNS for name resolution that your carrier has provided to you.

3. The third page will run through and test each stage of your wireless connection. Once you see four green checkmarks come up, as shown in Figure 9-3, you are ready to go. If you see any red X marks, then something has failed in your setup. It may be because you entered the information wrong in step 2, or you aren't getting a strong enough signal from your current location, or your carrier hasn't set you up on its network yet. The software will guide you through troubleshooting any problems that occur.

Once you have successfully run through the Wireless Expert, your AirCard is set up and ready to use. When you want to establish a connection with your carrier, you will run the AirCard Watcher software. This software can be conveniently set up to appear on your Today page (discussed in Chapter 2) and allow you to tap over to connect or disconnect sessions easily.

FIGURE 9-3   Four green checkmarks indicate that your wireless connection is correctly set up.

The AirCard Watcher dialog box, shown in Figure 9-4, shows you the strength of the signal in your present location by displaying a blue bar in the Signal Strength box. The longer the bar, the stronger the signal. The box immediately to the right tells you what the specific signal strength is in decibels or shows Scan (if seeking a channel) or Sleep (if the card is sleeping waiting for traffic). The Status box shows whether you are currently connected, or if an error occurs in your connection, what went wrong. The Channel box indicates the channel you are currently connected on. Data Transfer shows you the total amount of data sent and received. You can tap the Connect/Disconnect button at the bottom of the window to initiate connection to or disconnection from the network.

FIGURE 9-4   The AirCard Watcher dialog box is where you will initiate or terminate a wireless session.

You are now ready to use your wireless card to send and receive e-mail, surf the Internet, or run connected applications.

Setting Up a Novatel Wireless Merlin G100: GSM/GPRS

The Novatel Wireless Merlin G100 is a Type II PCMCIA card. This means that you will need an expansion sleeve for your iPAQ that supports PCMCIA cards. Either the single or the dual sleeve will work. If you have all the equipment, then follow these steps:

1. Slide your iPAQ into the sleeve until it is firmly seated. You should see a window with the message "Initializing Expansion Pack" on the screen for a brief moment while your iPAQ and your sleeve set up their communication. DO NOT insert the wireless modem until after you have installed the drivers.

2. Connect your iPAQ to your PC with your ActiveSync cable, and make sure there is an active connection. Once this is established you are ready to install the drivers onto your iPAQ.

3. Install the necessary drivers for your Merlin. These likely came on a CD-ROM with your card, but if not, you can download the latest drivers from the Novatel Wireless website (**www.novatelwireless.com**). Once you have the install program, run it, and the install should initiate through your ActiveSync connection to your iPAQ.

NOTE   *The software for the Merlin G100 that we have is still beta, so the actual steps in the installation may vary with the final release. Any additional requirements will be displayed on your screen for you to follow.*

4. Insert your SIM (Subscriber Identity Module) chip into your Merlin G100. The SIM chip is a very small piece of plastic (smaller than a postage stamp) that identifies you to the network. It will have been provided to you by your carrier. This automates communication method setup.

Once you are all set up, you just need to connect to your network. The GPRS modem manager, shown in Figure 9-5, should launch by default, but if it doesn't, you can launch it from the Programs folder. The status window will enable you to see whose network you are going to connect to, or are already on, what the service type is, who the carrier is that is managing your signal, and the strength of the signal in your location.

At the bottom of the dialog box is a menu. You can use this menu to initiate a connection or disconnection, or to see the properties of the modem, as shown in Figure 9-6.

The Roaming tab will give you the option to set the modem to automatically roam onto any GPRS network when you are away from your home network, or to require manual network selection where it will find all the available networks, and then let you select from the list of networks to connect to one.

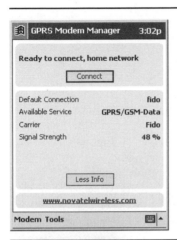

FIGURE 9-5   Use the GPRS Modem Manager dialog box to establish a connection with your GPRS network.

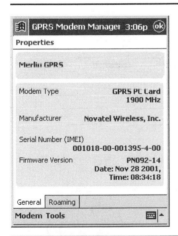

FIGURE 9-6   The modem properties will tell you all the specific attributes of the modem you are using.

Use the Tools menu to get a detailed history of activity on the modem and find out useful statistical information such as the percentage of errors encountered. You can set modem options and also configure the connection manager in case you have multiple GPRS accounts. For example, I might be using the AT&T network in North America, but have a separate account with MMo2 when I am in the United Kingdom. I can configure the connection manager with the relevant information on both networks. By having the two, I will likely reduce my overall costs by paying fewer roaming charges.

Sending and Receiving E-mail Wirelessly

By far the most useful thing that the average user can do today with a wireless connection is send and receive e-mail from their iPAQ in real time. This does not happen from the ActiveSync folder on your handheld where we worked with e-mail in Chapter 5. You will need to set up a standard Internet e-mail service (or set up an enterprise Internet replication strategy with IIS) to send and receive real-time e-mail. For myself, I have stopped using the ActiveSync e-mail sync and instead use only an Internet connection. When my iPAQ is connected with the sync cable, it updates my mail using the Internet pass-through feature discussed earlier in Chapter 2 and works as well as the ActiveSync feature, but also updates through a wireless connection. For details on how to specifically set up a new e-mail service, refer to Chapter 5, which explains the correct process in detail.

Tapping the send and receive e-mail icon at the middle right of the toolbar at the bottom of the window, or the check new mail icon, will cause the Inbox application to update your mailbox through the wireless connection. If you have composed messages that are sitting in your Outbox, they will be sent through the same process.

We recommend using the IMAP4 protocol wherever possible because it is a much more efficient protocol than POP3, meaning it will perform better across your low-bandwidth wireless connection. IMAP4 also enables you to replicate and synchronize the folder structure of your e-mail.

Surfing Wirelessly with Pocket Internet Explorer

Your iPAQ will come preloaded with Pocket Internet Explorer. This is to allow you to browse web pages and surf the Internet while connected (either wirelessly or wired) to an Internet source. You may find surfing on your Pocket PC to be a less than satisfactory experience. This is largely due to three factors:

Low bandwidth   The wireless modems that we are surfing the Internet with are very low bandwidth. Even the latest GPRS and CDMA 1xRTT modems only provide a 53.6 Kbps connection, which is about the same as the best dial-up modem you can buy for your PC. Most websites you will want to visit are optimized for the high-bandwidth connections that many of us now have at home and at the office. Maximizing the user experience on the desktop has resulted in a very poor user experience on the handheld.

Small screen   Our iPAQs have very small screens, only a fraction of the size of the usual desktops, resulting in the need to do a lot of scrolling to try to see what comes up on the web page. Even with scrolling, many pages still come up formatted in an irregular fashion.

We are early in the adoption cycle   We are still very early in the adoption cycle of Pocket PCs. As more and more people get these devices, organizations with websites will begin building multiple front ends to their website. In such a setup, the website can automatically detect when you connect from your desktop, and provide a broadband-rich media user experience, and when you connect from a handheld, and send you a stripped-down page with fewer graphics, formatted to fit your screen. Although this technology exists today, very few websites have taken advantage of it. Expect to see this capability become much more common as time goes by, and for your handheld surfing experience to improve.

When you first start up Pocket IE (by selecting it from the Start menu), it will take you to the default home page. This is a local page, not actually pulled from the Internet with links to PocketPC.Com, Compaq, MSN Mobile, and AvantGo. The interface of Pocket IE has a number of similar features to the full version of IE, as shown in Figure 9-7.

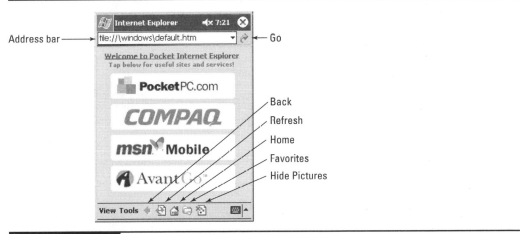

FIGURE 9-7   The Pocket IE interface has a number of features in common with the desktop version of IE.

You can type any address you like in the Address bar and then tap the Go button to be taken to that site. The Back button will back you up to the last site you visited. By default, if you have been to a site before, Pocket IE will try to reuse the page from memory to save the download time. This can cause you to not get the most up-to-date information from sites that change frequently. Tapping the Refresh button will download the latest version of a page that you are viewing. The Home button will take you to your home page (you can designate your home page in the Options dialog box, discussed later in this section). The Hide Pictures button is very useful for sites that use a lot of graphics. Tapping this button will toggle between hiding or showing the graphics on a page. If they are hidden, they will not be downloaded, causing the page to be loaded much more quickly. If you are operating this way but find that you want to see a particular graphic, you can tap and hold on the graphic and then choose Download from the shortcut menu to bring that one graphic down to your device. This gives you the power of choice to only view those graphics that are important to you.

The Favorites button will open the Favorites folder allowing you to jump to any sites you have bookmarked (you can synchronize these with your desktop IE through the ActiveSync settings, as discussed in Chapter 2). The Favorites folder is shown in Figure 9-8.

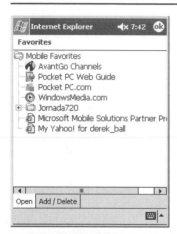

FIGURE 9-8 Tapping the Favorites button will open your folder of favorite sites to visit. Tapping any of these sites will take you directly to that site.

Tapping the Add/Delete tab at the bottom of the window will take you to a similar window where you can organize your favorites into folders, add new favorites, or delete ones that you no longer wish to keep in your list.

The View menu in the main Pocket IE window includes commands that enable you to change how the window appears:

- You can choose to hide or show the Address bar.

- You can also turn the Fit To Screen option on or off. By default this option is on, and IE will wrap text onto the next line to make it fit into the screen. If this option is off, IE will not try to make lines fit the screen, and you will have to use the horizontal scroll bar to move back and forth across the window.

- There are five commands under the View menu that enable you to select five different text sizes. This will allow you to display more or less text in the window. The more text you show, the less scrolling you will have to do, but the harder it will be to read.

- The History command opens a list of the previous pages you've visited in case you want to return to one of them.

- The Properties command opens a window that displays the properties of the web page you are currently viewing, as shown next.

The Tools menu contains the following commands:

Send Link Via E-mail   Sends the current URL link by composing a new message in the Inbox application.

Cut   Cuts any selected text and places it on the clipboard.

Copy   Copies any selected text to the clipboard.

Paste   Pastes text from the clipboard into the document where the insertion point is currently positioned.

Select All Text   Selects all the text on the page for you to copy onto the clipboard.

Options   Enables you to configure options for Pocket IE, as described next.

Selecting the Options command opens the options dialog box, where you can set how you want Pocket IE to behave. This dialog box contains two tabs; one for general options and one for advanced options, as shown in Figure 9-9.

The General tab, shown in Figure 9-9, includes options for the following:

Home Page   You can set which page you want to come up by default when you open Pocket Internet Explorer. In order to do this, you must surf to the page you want as your home page, then open the options dialog box and select Use Current.

History   You can set how many days of past links you want saved to the History list and also enables you to clear the history list with a click of a button.

Temporary Internet Files   You can delete any stored temporary Internet files from memory.

The Advanced tab, shown in Figure 9-10, enables you to set options for the following:

Cookies   You can choose whether to allow or deny cookies and to clear cookies currently stored on your iPAQ.

Security Settings   You can set the option to warn you when you are shifting from a secure page to a page that is not secure.

Language   You can set the default character set used by Pocket IE.

FIGURE 9-9   Use the General tab of the options dialog box to set home page, history, and temporary file options.

FIGURE 9-10   The Advanced tab of the options dialog box enables you to set your preferences for cookies, security warnings, and default language.

Instant Messaging and Chatting with Your iPAQ

If you are one of the many individuals who is part of the massive online chatting craze, you will be happy to know that most online chat utilities have versions that will run on your wireless iPAQ, enabling you to chat while waiting in line at the grocery store, sitting in a dull meeting, or anywhere your wireless connection works!

Here are some of the commonly used chat programs that you can use on your Pocket PC:

MSN Messenger   This is built right into the full Pocket PC 2002 install, so you don't even have to install anything. We will show you how to access and set this up next.

AIM (AOL Instant Messenger)   This application was designed for Pocket PC 2000, not 2002, but appears to work fine in PPC 2002. For more information and to download the application, go to **http://www.aim.com/get_aim/win_ce/latest_wince.adp**.

ICQ   There is a client for the ICQ instant messenger; it can be downloaded from ICQ at **http://www.icq.com/download/ftp-pocketpc.html**.

Yahoo Instant Messenger   There is a full Pocket PC client that can be downloaded at **http://messenger.yahoo.com/messenger/ce/downloads_ce_msgr.html**.

With MSN Messenger, start the program by tapping on the MSN Messenger link in the Programs folder. This will open a prompt where you will enter your sign in name and password, as shown in the illustration:

You can choose to save the password by selecting the Save Password check box, saving you the step of signing in each time you launch Messenger. Tapping Sign In will take you to the main MSN Messenger window, as shown in Figure 9-11.

FIGURE 9-11   The MSN Messenger window lets you see who is online that you can chat with.

You can initiate a chat with another person by tapping on his or her name. You can respond to a request to chat as they pop up on your screen. If you enter a chat, you will be taken to the chat window, as shown in Figure 9-12.

FIGURE 9-12   The chat window lets you talk with one or more of your friends who are online.

The chat window includes three menus at the bottom of the screen; Tools, Chats, and My Text. The Tools menu includes the following commands:

Sign In / Sign Out   Signs you in or out of Messenger.

My Status   Allows you to change your status to Online, Busy, Be Right Back, Away, On The Phone, Out To Lunch, or Appear Offline.

Add A Contact   Takes you to a window to enter the information for a new contact to add to your list.

Edit My Text Messages   Allows you to create your own custom messages, which will then be available in the My Text menu.

Invite   Invites an additional person into your chat.

Block   Stops you from receiving any chat requests from a blocked user.

Chat Members   Gives you a list of all the contacts currently involved in your chat session.

Options   Opens the MSN Messenger Options dialog box. Here you can designate your screen name (the name that appears to others online), set the program to open automatically upon connection to a network, manage your Allow or Block lists, and configure Passport and Exchange accounts.

The Chats menu enables you to switch between multiple chats that you have underway. The My Text menu enables you to insert one of your My Text strings into the chat (My Text strings are discussed in Chapter 5).

Choosing 802.11 or a Wired Connection

When working in your office or anywhere else with access to a local area network, you can choose to connect your iPAQ to the LAN with either a wireless or wired LAN card. The standard for wireless LAN at present is 802.11b. You can find a variety of manufacturers that make a card that will fit your iPAQ. In order to make any of the cards work, you will need to set up a wireless access point. A number of other facilities are also setting up wireless 802.11b networks that you will be able to access while moving around. Starbucks Coffee, for example, is installing 802.11b wireless access points into their stores so you will be able to check your e-mail and surf the Web while sipping your morning espresso!

In this section, we will not go through the setup of each wireless card because each vendor is slightly different. We will look at the setup of one type of wireless card and provide a listing of the various wireless cards that we have tested and where to get more information on them.

> **TIP** *Although wireless access with 802.11b or other wireless protocols is extremely convenient, you need to be cautious on the security front because there are many well-known ways to crack through the native encryption on these wireless devices. You should make sure that any software you implement for business purposes has adequate built-in security in the software layer, or you should take advantage of third-party virtual private network (VPN) technology. Security and your iPAQ is discussed in more detail in Chapter 8.*

Setting Up a Cisco Aironet 802.11b Wireless LAN Card

The Cisco Aironet card is a Type II PCMCIA card. This means that you will need an expansion sleeve for your iPAQ that supports PCMCIA cards. Either the single or the dual sleeve will work. If you have all the equipment, then follow these steps:

1. Slide your iPAQ into the sleeve until it is firmly seated. You should see a window with the message "Initializing Expansion Pack" on the screen for a brief moment while your iPAQ and your sleeve set up their communication. DO NOT insert the Aironet card until after you have installed the drivers.

2. Connect your iPAQ to your PC with your ActiveSync cable, and make sure there is an active connection. Once this is established you are ready to install the drivers onto your iPAQ.

3. Install the necessary drivers for your card. These likely came on a CD-ROM with your card, but if not, you can download the latest drivers from Cisco's website (**www.cisco.com**). Once you have installed the program, run it, and the install should initiate through your ActiveSync connection to your iPAQ.

4. Review the onscreen instructions and follow them as indicated. You may be asked to soft reboot your iPAQ.

5. Now you may insert your Cisco Aironet card into the slot in the expansion sleeve.

The drivers are installed, but the card is still not quite ready to go. You must first configure the card so it knows how to talk. You will need to know some basic information about your network to continue, including the following:

SSID   This is the unique ID for the wireless network that the card will connect to, similar to the name of a domain on a local area network.

Client Name   This is the name for this client device.

Do you use DHCP?   Dynamic Host Configuration Protocol is where an IP address is assigned to each card as it accesses the network. The alternative is static IP addressing, in which case you will need to know which IP address you should use.

Do you have Wireless Equivalent Protocol (WEP) encryption turned on?   You can choose to use WEP or not use WEP, however, keep in mind that WEP has been shown to be very insecure, so you shouldn't count on WEP to protect your sensitive information.

Authentication Mode   Here you indicate whether you are using Open or Shared key authentication.

You might need other settings depending on which brand of card you are using. If you encounter settings you are not familiar with, contact your network administrator.

With this information in hand, you are ready to configure your card. With the Cisco card, you run the Aironet Client Setup utility located in the Cisco folder, which is in the Programs folder. The dialog box shown in Figure 9-13 appears.

FIGURE 9-13   The Aironet Client Setup utility allows you to set all the necessary options for the Aironet card.

For each property in the box on the left, you will need to configure the appropriate value in the box on the right. Once this is done, tap the OK button to save the settings. Once these settings are in place, you should be able to connect to your wireless access point. Note that there are other Cisco utilities for monitoring the quality of your 802.11b link, setting up your encryption keys if you are using WEP, and loading new firmware onto your card.

Setting up 802.11b cards is not as straightforward as setting up a CDPD or GPRS card and often requires a little trial and error before you get it right.

Wireless LAN Cards We Have Used Successfully

Table 9-3 contains a list of cards that we have successfully configured on our iPAQs.

Vendor and Model	Type	Information Site
Compaq WL100 & WL110	PCMCIA Type II	http://www.compaq.com/products/wireless/wlan
Linksys Wireless PC Card	PCMCIA Type II	http://www.linksys.com/products/product.asp?grid=22&prid=156
Linksys Wireless CF Card	CF Type II	http://www.compaq.com/products/wireless/wlan
Symbol CF Card	CF Type I	http://www.symbol.com/products/wireless/flash_card.html
Symbol PC Card	PCMCIA Type II	http://www.symbol.com/products/wireless/pc_card.html
Socket CF Card	CF Type I	http://www.socketcom.com
Intel PC Card	PCMCIA Type II	http://www.intel.com/network/connectivity/products/wlan_family.htm
Cisco Aironet	PCMCIA Type II	http://www.cisco.com/warp/public/cc/pd/witc/ao340ap

TABLE 9-3   Wireless LAN Cards We Have Used Successfully

Using a Wired Ethernet Connection

In addition to using a wireless 802.11b card, you can certainly use a wired Ethernet connection, although this will remove the single biggest advantage of your Pocket PC—its portability.

You can insert any standard PCMCIA or CF card (using the appropriate sleeve) as long as the appropriate Pocket PC drivers exist for the card. Using the same instructions for the Cisco Aironet card given earlier, install your drivers, insert your card, plug it into a LAN cable, and you should be in business!

Performing Advanced Network Diagnostics

In addition to e-mail, surfing, and chatting, there are useful third-party applications that can add value to having your iPAQ wirelessly enabled. Check out these products as examples:

Cambridge Computer Corporation (**www.cam.com/vxutil.html**)   Produces a product called vxUtil that is invaluable for troubleshooting your wireless network and contains very useful tools for a network and system administrator. The tool set includes DNS Lookup, Finger, Get HTML, Info, Ping, Port Scanner, Trace Route, Whois, and more.

Sonic Mobility Inc (**www.sonicmobility.com**)   Produces a tool that allows network and systems support personnel to securely connect into their back-end network and servers and diagnose and repair mission-critical problems from their wireless iPAQ from anywhere at any time. Start and stop services and processes; change user passwords and properties; reboot frozen servers; get command line access to NT, Win2000, Unix, Linux, and VMS servers; and more.

As time goes by, you will begin to see even more tools emerging for wirelessly enabled iPAQs. This is truly the wave of the future for these devices.

Chapter 10

Take Your Presentations on the Road with Your iPAQ Pocket PC

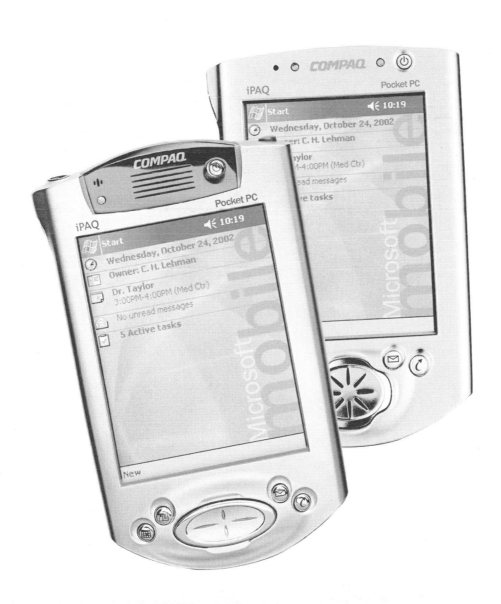

How to...

■ Convert and transfer your PowerPoint or other presentations to the iPAQ

■ Display the iPAQ screen on an external monitor or projector

■ Manage and edit your presentations on the iPAQ

■ Convert PowerPoint presentations to Pocket PC formats

This chapter introduces you to the power of the iPAQ as a presentation tool. Many business people today use applications such as Microsoft's PowerPoint to get their ideas across. Until recently, the only way to present such a presentation was with a laptop. With the speed and power of the iPAQ, these presentations can be not only stored on and presented from an iPAQ, but also edited on it.

To enable the iPAQ to manage and display these presentations on a monitor or through a projector, specialized hardware is necessary. The chapter will begin with the description of these hardware add-ons. The presentation tools can be divided into two categories: PowerPoint presentation tools (hardware and software) and remote desktop tools. Both of these categories will be covered within the chapter.

It is important to note that the hardware currently available for displaying presentations via iPAQ has some limitations. If your presentation has video or audio in it, the software or hardware will not support it. The Voyager CF card, for example, will only do about 4 frames per second (fps), which is too slow for video, never mind the fact that there's no audio support. Another product, iPresentation Mobile Client LE, is a little bit of a mystery in this area—we don't think it will convert a PowerPoint presentation with an embedded MPEG clip. To convert the video to their presentation format, you must use their special software.

Presentation Hardware

To use the iPAQ to display your presentations, you will need some additional hardware. The presentation hardware add-ons available today use the following technologies:

■ PC card

■ CompactFlash (CF) card

■ Expansion sleeve

Some manufacturers offer multiple formats for their presentation hardware, others are exclusive. The following products are currently available:

■ MARGI Presenter-to-Go

■ The Presenter-to-Go Infrared Remote Control

■ ColorGraphic Voyager VGA Adapter

■ FlyJacket i3800

The next sections discuss these products and the technology they use.

Presenter-to-Go

MARGI System's Presenter-to-Go (**www.presenter-to-go.com**) is an all-in-one solution. It not only includes the necessary hardware (in either a PC card or a CF card format), but the necessary software. Because Presenter-to-Go falls into both the software and hardware categories, this section will only discuss the hardware side of their equation.

The Presenter-to-Go system ships with different hardware depending on which of the two versions is used. The following is included with the PC card version:

- Presenter-to-Go PC card
- 12-inch VGA adapter cable with power port
- 14-button infrared remote control
- AC adapter power supply
- Gender adapter for direct connection to projectors

The following hardware is included with the CF card version:

- Presenter-to-Go CF card (Type II)
- VGA adapter cable
- 14-button infrared remote control
- Male-to-male VGA cable for direct connection to projectors

Both versions of the card ship with the software necessary to not only convert and display your PowerPoint presentations, but the software drivers needed for the iPAQ to recognize and run the card itself. Two software packages ship on the CD-ROM as well, MARGI's Mirror application and Presenter-to-Go. Both of these products are covered in the software section of this chapter.

Although the PC card version ships with an external AC power adapter, the CF card version does not and can only run off either the internal iPAQ battery or through the iPAQ AC adapter.

The Presenter-to-Go Infrared Remote Control

Both the Presenter-to-Go cards have the same infrared remote control. The remote control has a complete numeric pad (numbers 1 through 0) and a Return button. This enables you to quickly jump to any slide in your presentation by choosing the slide number and pressing the Return button.

Three other buttons are located on the top to move forward and backward in the presentation and to set the presentation to auto (which will automatically advance slides).

10

As mentioned, an application called MARGI Mirror is also installed during the installation procedure. This application simply echoes or mirrors what is displayed on the iPAQ screen directly to the Presenter-to-Go card. This allows the PowerPoint viewer application (discussed in more detail in the software section of this chapter) to display the presentations on the screen even though they do not support the video cards themselves.

As Figure 10-1 illustrates, the MARGI Mirror application allows you to manually enable the VGA card. By doing this, everything that is displayed on the iPAQ will be mirrored through the display card to the projector or monitor. You can also double the size of the screen and rotate it. As you will see with the PowerPoint viewer applications, this will enable you to use them to display your presentations on a monitor or projector.

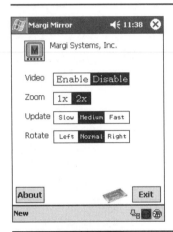

FIGURE 10-1 The Margi Mirror application is used to mirror your iPAQ screen to the VGA card.

Voyager VGA Adapter

ColorGraphic's Voyager VGA adapter (**www.ColorGraphic.net**) is another product used to display the iPAQ screen on an external monitor or projector. Although the Voyager VGA adapter used to be sold in a PC card version, only the CompactFlash version is now available. It does, however, ship with a PC card adapter, which allows for the CF version to be used in the PC card expansion sleeve.

The Voyager VGA CF adapter will handle analog VGA and composite/S-video TV outputs and ships with a three-foot cable for connecting to these outputs. It also ships with Voyager Shadow, the driver and control application. As shown in Figure 10-2, with Voyager Shadow you can:

- Set the screen update to either real time or timed (with the timed interval configurable)

- Choose the desired output (VGA, composite, or S-video)

- Specify the presentation orientation (portrait or landscape) with options to center the output and stretch the image to fit the screen resolution

■ Choose whether a background is to be displayed (and its color)

■ Select the video mode (resolution and refresh rate) at which to display the presentation

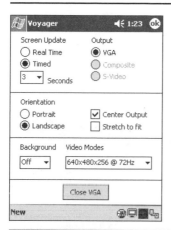

FIGURE 10-2   Voyager Shadow controls the output of the Voyager VGA adapter.

FlyJacket i3800

FlyJacket i3800 by Lifeview Animation Technologies (**www.lifeview.com**) is different from
the other presentation hardware products discussed so far. Instead of consisting of a video
display card, Lifeview Animation Technologies decided to create an expansion sleeve to house
all the hardware for their system. Therefore, instead of requiring the purchase of a separate
expansion sleeve (either the CF or the PC card expansion sleeve), all you need is this one
solution. FlyJacket is smaller than Compaq's dual PC card expansion sleeve and is about the
same size as the PC card expansion sleeve. Another thing that sets it apart is the fact that it has
an internal battery (for supplying power to FlyJacket itself and to a CF slot). Other features
include the following:

■ Video input and output

■ AV cable (composite video)

■ S cable (S-video)

■ NTSC/PAL auto scan

■ Infrared remote control

■ Laser pointer

Along with the hardware, FlyJacket ships with several software packages. These include the
drivers (LifeView Shadow), presentation software (LifeView PowerShow), and a third-party
presentation suite, which is partially covered in "IA Presenter," later in this chapter.

10

LifeView Shadow contains both the drivers for the expansion sleeve and the configuration software. As Figures 10-3 and 10-4 illustrate, LifeView Shadow enables you to configure the following:

- The position of the display
- The size ratio of the screen
- The resolution to be used
- The type of output used (VGA, NTSC, or PAL)
- The display position of the screen

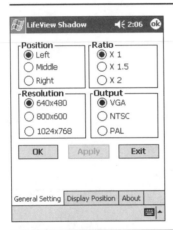

FIGURE 10-3   Controlling the LifeJacket using the LifeView Shadow application

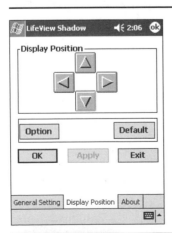

FIGURE 10-4   Changing the position of the displayed screen

Presentation Software

Now that we have seen the presentation hardware available for the iPAQ, it is time to look at the software. Unfortunately, there does not seem to be much standardization between the different players in this category. We will therefore cover each of the applications separately and discuss what you need to do to get your PowerPoint or other presentations to be displayed by them. It is important to note that some of these applications support VGA themselves, whereas others require applications such as MARGI Mirror or Voyager Shadow to drive the VGA cards. The applications that require a secondary application to drive the display card are really just PowerPoint viewer applications, rather than PowerPoint presentation applications. Note that we are using the term *PowerPoint* as a generic word to mean a projected visual presentation.

Therefore, we will break these software packages into two distinct categories: VGA-enabled and PowerPoint viewers. This section discusses the following VGA-enabled software packages:

- Presenter-to-Go
- IA Presenter
- Pocket Slides
- Pocket SlideShow
- iPresentation Mobile Client LE

The PowerPoint viewer applications covered in this section arc thc following:

- AlbatrosSlides
- ClearVue Presentation

A third type of application exists that is in a class all their own; both Periscope and Slide Show Commander fall into this category. This type of application is used more to control the presentation than to actually display it. We will cover this application last.

Presenter-to-Go

MARGI System's Presenter-to-Go (**www.presenter-to-go.com**) kit ships with either the CF or the PC card video adapter. The installation process includes installing the following:

- The Presenter-to-Go Printer
- The Presenter-to-Go icon in PowerPoint
- The Presenter-to-Go desktop application
- The Pocket PC Presenter-to-Go application
- The Pocket PC MARGI Mirror application

The Presenter-to-Go suite of applications makes it easy for you to convert and transfer not only PowerPoint files, but information from any printer-aware application (that is, any application that can send information to a printer). This is done through the Presenter-to-Go Printer. For example, if you wanted to take a simple Microsoft Word document and present it as a PowerPoint presentation, all you have to do is print it to the Presenter-to-Go Printer (as illustrated in Figure 10-5), which generates a presentation that contain slides of the Word document.

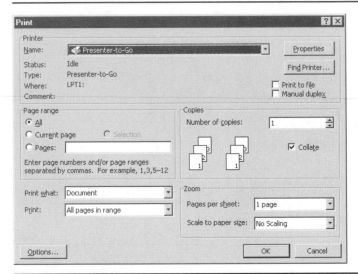

FIGURE 10-5   Printing a Word document to the Presenter-to-Go Printer

Once you click the OK button, Microsoft Word will "print" the document to the printer, which will begin converting the document into a PDB file (the format used by Presenter-to-Go). A PDB file is more compact than the original file and is automatically recognized by the iPAQ as a Presenter-to-Go file. While the files are being converted, Presenter-to-Go displays a status window, shown in Figure 10-6.

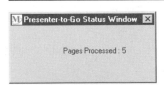

FIGURE 10-6   Status window for conversion to the PDB file format

Once the document is printed, it is forwarded to the Presenter-to-Go Creator utility (shown in Figure 10-7). It is within this utility that you can decide whether to generate the presentation or append it to an existing presentation. You can also look at the previous presentations converted by the Presenter-to-Go system, but more on that later in this section.

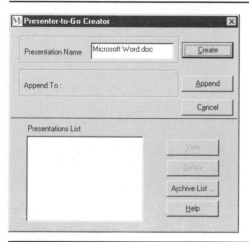

FIGURE 10-7   Create presentations from most documents quickly and easily with Presenter-to-Go Creator.

When the Create button is clicked in the Presenter-to-Go Creator dialog box, the utility generates the presentation and forwards it to the Presenter-to-Go desktop application. It is this program that actually transfers the presentation (the PDB file) to the iPAQ. Simply click the Transfer button in the Presenter-to-Go Desktop dialog box (shown in Figure 10-8), and the file will be transferred. This dialog box also enables you to install the Presenter-to-Go Pocket PC application to the iPAQ (should you prefer to do this from here rather than from ActiveSync).

10

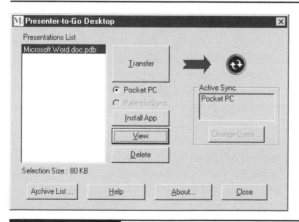

FIGURE 10-8   Transfer your presentations to your iPAQ using the Presenter-to-Go desktop application.

The presentation can also be viewed (both in a low-resolution preview and in a full-screen presentation) before the transfer is performed. The size of the presentation is displayed on the screen and the option to delete the presentation before transfer is available. Finally, you can view all the previous presentations that were created and transferred to the iPAQ by clicking the Archive List button—a nice feature, if you need access to a large number of presentations but don't want them to use precious storage space on the iPAQ.

Presenter-to-Go also creates a new icon within PowerPoint. This allows you to quickly convert and transfer your presentation to the iPAQ while maintaining the graphics, color schemes, notes, and animations. After you click the Presenter-to-Go button, you follow the same process as that of the Presenter-to-Go Printer.

On the iPAQ, there are two ways to view your presentations. You can either run Presenter-to-Go from the Programs menu or navigate to a PDB file with File Explorer and tap it. Both methods are equally easy to use and both launch the Presenter-to-Go application. The only real difference is that when you navigate to a specific presentation, that presentation will be the one opened. When the presentations are transferred to the iPAQ, they are stored in the My Documents\Presenter-to-Go folder.

Once within the Presenter-to-Go application, you have a few choices. If this is a real presentation, you cannot only view a list, but also the notes for each frame, and a preview of the presentation. Figure 10-9 shows the three different views: from left to right, List, Notes, and Preview.

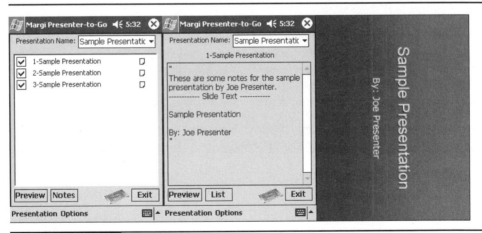

FIGURE 10-9   Presenter-to-Go's List, Notes, and Preview views

You can also hide and display different slides in your presentations by simply clearing or selecting the check box to the left of the slide. From the Presentation menu, you can choose to hide or select all the slides, generate an Auto Slide Show, or delete the presentation. Finally, from the Options menu, you can specify the Preferences for the slide show. These include the delay between slides in the Auto Slide Show, whether to loop the presentation continuously, and an option to preview the presentations in a Left Hand Mode (rotated 180 degrees).

One major drawback of Presenter-to-Go is its inability to support shapes or animations. If your presentations contain these features, then you may want to look at some of the other products mentioned in this chapter.

IA Presenter

IA Presenter from IA Style (**www.iastyle.com**) is an advanced application for not only viewing your presentations, but also for making some modifications to them once they are on the iPAQ. A version of IA Presenter ships with both the Colorgraphic Voyager card and the FlyJacket i3800 discussed earlier in this chapter.

Once the application is installed, it installs a desktop component (for setting the ActiveSync conversion options), the iPAQ application, and an ActiveSync converter for converting the file from PowerPoint file format to IA Presenter's IAP format. As you may have already noticed, to convert a PowerPoint file to the IAP file format, you simply have to drag it from your desktop to your iPAQ by navigating to it through ActiveSync. When you drag and drop a PowerPoint file, ActiveSync detects the .ppt extension and launches the IA Presenter – ActiveSync Converter application (shown in Figure 10-10). All you need to do now is choose the resolution at which the presentation is to be saved and click the OK button. The presentation will then be converted and copied to the iPAQ.

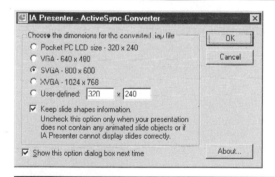

FIGURE 10-10   Transfer your presentations to your iPAQ using the IA Presenter – ActiveSync Converter.

Like other applications, IA Presenter can be launched in one of two ways. You can either navigate to the presentation file (the .iap file) through File Explorer and tap it, or through the Programs folder in the Start menu of the iPAQ. Again, if you tap a presentation file's icon, IA Presenter will open that file, whereas if you launch the IA Presenter application, you will be presented with a list of presentation files stored on the iPAQ from which you can choose.

IA Presenter enables you to look at your presentation in one of three ways: Normal view (displays the current slide and thumbnails), Slide Sorter view (displays thumbnails only), and Notes Page view (displays the current slide and notes), as shown in Figure 10-11 (from left to right, respectively). These same views can be selected from the View menu at the bottom of the IA Presenter window.

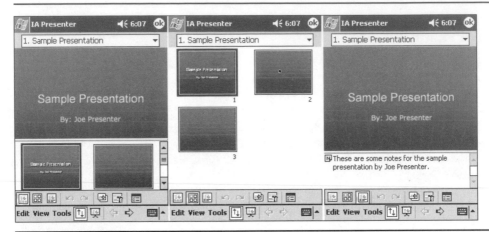

FIGURE 10-11   View your slides in the Normal, Slide Sorter, and Note Page views.

As we mentioned earlier in this section, IA Presenter enables you not only to view your presentations, but to make some basic changes to them. You can modify the speaker notes and the slide transitions. To modify the slide transition, you can either click the Slide Transition button on the toolbar (the icon of a slide with an arrow on it) or choose Slide Transition from the Edit menu.

Pocket Slides

Another advanced PowerPoint presentation application is Pocket Slides from Conduits Technologies (**www.conduits.com**). It is similar in many ways to IA Presenter, in its ability to convert presentations on-the-fly through ActiveSync, hide and show slides, view slide thumbnails, and control slide transitions. Where it greatly differs is in its ability to not only edit the speaker notes, but the text, images, and animations of the slides themselves.

As Figure 10-12 illustrates, Pocket Slides enables you to select text or graphic objects and control how they enter or exit the slide. This includes the order and timing and the effects that are performed on these objects. This application includes many of the features for the creation and modification of slides that are found in Microsoft's PowerPoint.

Much like IA Presenter, Pocket Slides gives the presenter full control over the presentation from the iPAQ before and during the presentation. The speaker notes can be displayed (as shown on the left in Figure 10-13), and the stylus can be used as a pen to highlight information onscreen (refer to the right in Figure 10-13).

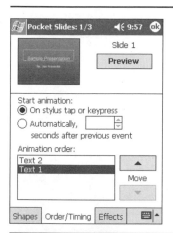

FIGURE 10-12   Modifying the order or timing of a slide

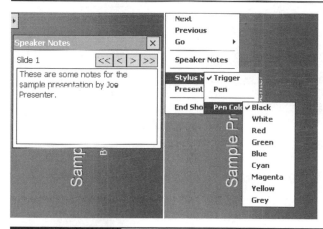

FIGURE 10-13   Controlling the presentation from the Slide Show screen

Pocket Slides uses the .cpt extension on its converted PowerPoint files and has the ability to not only automatically convert PowerPoint presentations to the CPT file format automatically through ActiveSync, but going in the other direction by using ActiveSync to convert CPT files to PowerPoint files automatically. To do this, simply drag the CPT file from the iPAQ to the desktop system. At this point, you will be presented with a wizard in which you choose the conversion options for the presentation. This enables you to modify your presentations on either the iPAQ or on your desktop and then move it from one location to the other.

Though we cannot cover all the features of this product, it is by far the most advanced on the market today. It is truly a presentation application. You can create and edit presentations that are almost as complex as PowerPoint presentations.

Pocket SlideShow

Much like the other PowerPoint presentation applications covered in this chapter, Pocket SlideShow from CNetX (**www.cnetx.com**) has several different viewing options, can support VGA cards, and enables you to configure slide transitions. Again, it can display the Slide Preview view with either a notes pane or a thumbnail pane (as Figure 10-14 illustrates). A nifty feature is its ability to swap the panes, moving either the notes or thumbnail pane to the top and the preview pane to the bottom.

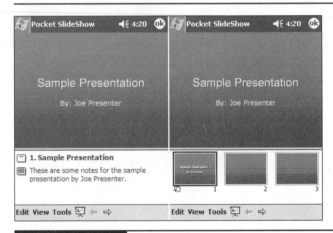

FIGURE 10-14   The different views of the Pocket SlideShow application

Pocket SlideShow uses ActiveSync to convert PowerPoint presentations into its own format, using a .pss extension. When a document is copied from the desktop to the iPAQ, a slide conversion wizard will launch, allowing you to choose the resolution at which to convert the presentation. Like some of the other applications covered here, Pocket SlideShow presents a list of all the PSS files on the iPAQ when you first launch the program.

iPresentation Mobile Client LE

iPresentation Mobile Client LE from Presenter (**www.presenter.com**) is a PowerPoint presentation application that requires approximately 2.2MB of memory on the iPAQ. Once you install the product, however, you will quickly realize why it is so large. It supports not only PowerPoint presentations, but also video presentations. This program was designed for the Pocket PC 2000 OS and works very well on it. However, when we tried it, it would only run sporadically on the Pocket PC 2002 operating system, so if you have one of the new 37*xx* or 38*xx* series iPAQs, you may be out of luck for now.

As Figure 10-15 illustrates, the application offers four different views (from left to right): Video/Slide Title view, Video/Slide Thumbnail view, Thumbnail view, and Preview view. iPresentation Mobile Client LE also enables you to add sound and video to existing presentations, control the timing, and send the presentation directly to the video card.

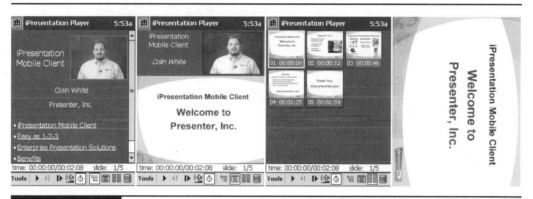

FIGURE 10-15   The iPresentation Mobile Client LE application in action

Converting PowerPoint files to iPresentation Mobile Client format is simple. Again, this application uses an ActiveSync filter to convert from the PowerPoint PPT file format to an IPF file. The first thing you will notice when you copy a PPT file over to the iPAQ is that PowerPoint is launched, the presentation is converted, and PowerPoint is then closed.

AlbatrosSlides

AlbatrosSlides from Albatros (**www.albatros-development.com**) is a simple application for displaying PowerPoint presentations. It is not as powerful as some of the other applications listed here, but is still a good product. Unlike IA Presenter and Pocket Slides, it does not use ActiveSync to convert the presentations. Nor does it use a printer-type conversion process like that of Presenter-to-Go.

It does, however, have a utility, AlbatrosPPConverter, for converting the applications. This utility, shown in Figure 10-16, allows you to choose the existing presentation, the location to store the converted presentation, and the resolution to use during the conversion.

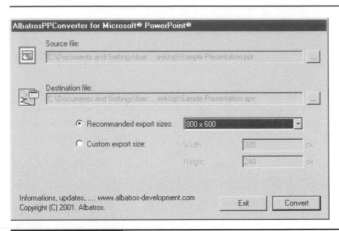

FIGURE 10-16   You can convert your presentations so that they work with AlbatrosSlides with the AlbatrosPPConverter.

AlbatrosSlides uses the .apv extension for its converted slide presentations and will automatically detect all presentations on the iPAQ when the application is started. As shown in Figure 10-17, AlbatrosSlides has three views (from left to right): Thumbnail view (the number of thumbnails in this view can be controlled from the Tools | Setting menu), Slide/Speaker Notes view, and Presentation view. Although you can zoom in and out of the presentation, you cannot edit the presentation.

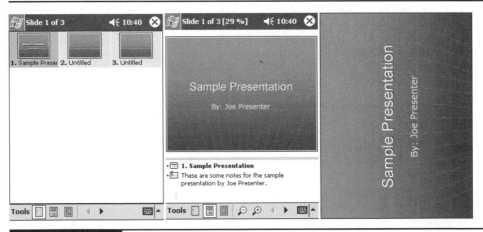

FIGURE 10-17   AlbatrosSlides also provides multiple ways to view your presentation— Thumbnail, Slide/Speaker Notes, and Presentation.

ClearVue Presentation

ClearVue Presentation from Westtek (**www.westtek.com**) is a PowerPoint viewer. It requires a secondary application, such as MARGI Mirror or Voyager Shadow, to allow it to display a full presentation. It allows you to do some basic editing, including modifying slide order and the timing between slides. One thing that sets ClearVue Presentation apart from the rest is the fact that it does not require any conversion of the PowerPoint files. This is both a blessing and a curse. Not needing a conversion ensures that the presentation is the same as it is on the desktop computer. However, this usually means that the presentations are not optimized for the iPAQ and can be quite large in size—especially if they contain graphics. Being able to view a PowerPoint presentation that was sent to you via e-mail, however, is a real bonus.

ClearVue Presentation has three views, shown in Figure 10-18 (from left to right): Normal, Slide Sorter, and Slide Show. The Setup Show command on the Setup menu enables you to choose either a manual presentation or an automated one and gives you the option to configure the timings between slides.

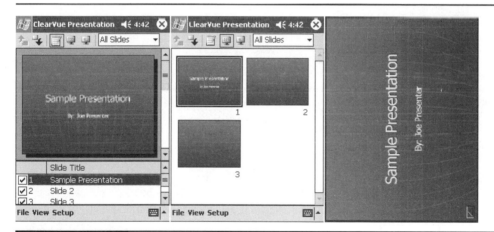

FIGURE 10-18   Viewing your presentations with the three ClearVue Presentation views

Periscope

Periscope from Pocket PC Creations (**www.pocketpccreations.com**) is actually two applications in one. It is really the only application covered here that performs both PowerPoint tasks and remote desktop tasks. For this reason, it will be covered in both sections. It is not, however, a PowerPoint presentation application nor is it a PowerPoint viewer application. What is it then? It is a PowerPoint presentation remote control application.

So what does Periscope do? It enables you to control a PowerPoint presentation running on either a desktop or a laptop system. You can do this either through the serial/USB port or wirelessly. If it is the wireless solution that you desire, you simply need a wireless network card (covered in Chapter 9) and a network connection (to the same network) on the desktop or laptop system.

As Figure 10-19 shows, once the presentation is launched on the desktop or laptop system, it will be displayed on the iPAQ and can be controlled from there.

FIGURE 10-19   Using the Periscope application controlling a PowerPoint presentation

Slide Show Commander

Similar to Periscope is SlideShow Commander from Synergy Solutions. Slide Show Commander (downloadable from **www.Synsolutions.com**) allows you to, either wired or wirelessly, connect to your desktop or laptop system and control the presentation from the iPAQ.

It is a freeware application and therefore does not install as easily or nicely as some of the other commercial products covered so far. If, however, you read the Readme file that comes with the application, you should have no problem installing it. There are two listings for this software in Handango. One is for the freeware application and one is for a purchased version by Synergy Solutions (**www.synsolutions.com/software/slideshowcommander/PPC.html**).

Remote Desktop Software

Now that we have looked at the presentation applications, it is time to look at some of the remote desktop applications that are out there for the iPAQ. Why is this in the same chapter as the presentation applications, you may ask? Well, taking your presentation on the road may also include presenting software on the iPAQ. For example, you may want to view a web page or another application during the presentation. These tools enable you to display the iPAQ screen on your desktop computer.

Remote desktop applications can be divided into two groups. In one group, the applications simply transfer the iPAQ screen at the same resolution as the iPAQ. Anything you do on the iPAQ is echoed on the desktop. And in some instances, the reverse is true, anything that is done on the desktop (within the iPAQ screen) is done on the iPAQ. The following applications fall into this category:

- Remote Display Control
- Virtual CE and Virtual CE Pro
- Pocket Controller Professional
- Periscope

The second group consists of applications that are used to display the iPAQ screen at just about any desired size. You can then use the desktop's keyboard and mouse to navigate and control the iPAQ. Only one application is in this second group: Handheld Handler.

Remote Display Control

Microsoft's Remote Display Control is part of their PowerToys for the Pocket PC suite of software (**www.microsoft.com/mobile/pocketpc/downloads/powertoys.asp**). It is a free application and consists of two components, a desktop Host and an iPAQ client. Remote Display Control can be used over an ActiveSync connection or via a network (wired or wireless). The application is basic and does not have many configuration options. Figure 10-20 illustrates both the host application (left) and the client application (right). You will notice that there is little difference between the two, except for the window and the menu bar at the top.

10

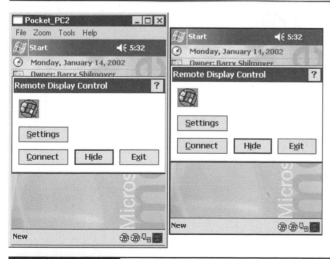

FIGURE 10-20   Controlling your iPAQ from your desktop using Microsoft's Remote Display Control

Virtual CE and Virtual CE Pro

Virtual CE and Virtual CE Pro from BitBank (**www.bitbanksoftware.com/ce**) are remote desktop applications that run over USB, serial, infrared, LAN, WAN/Internet, and ActiveSync connections. Both applications allow you to use your desktop's keyboard and mouse to enter information on the iPAQ, although the Pro version gives you more remote control options and features.

There are two components to the program, a host and a client. The host gives you the ability to not only view the iPAQ's desktop, but to generate a "skin" so that it looks like your iPAQ, as shown in Figure 10-21. You can also specify the color depth to be used, which speeds up the refresh rate if you are connecting over a slow link. Finally, you can record and play back a session.

FIGURE 10-21   An iPAQ under the control of the Virtual CE host application

The client application, shown in Figure 10-22, is simple to use. When you first run it, the window is minimized (the application is running in the background). When you switch to it a second time, you can choose one of the connection methods discussed above. However, you may run into a problem when you try to connect over a USB or serial port. If ActiveSync is already running and using that port, you will be presented with an error informing you that the port is in use. Simply disable ActiveSync, choose a different port, or free the port in the Connection Setting section of ActiveSync.

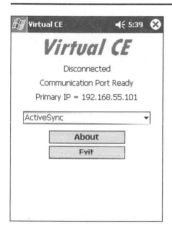

| FIGURE 10-22 | The Virtual CE client application |

The following is a list of features found only in the Pro version of Virtual CE:

- Record/play session as key/mouse clicks or AVI video
- Create custom skins to display in the window
- Single-click screen capture to BMP files for convenient and rapid captures of multiple screens
- Toggle toolbar and always-on-top window settings

Pocket Controller Professional

Pocket Controller Professional from SOTI (**www.soti.net**) differs from the others covered here in that it does more than provide remote desktop capability. It also enables you to open an emulated DOS window to the iPAQ (which you can use to copy, delete, and modify files) and a Pocket Manager application (which you can use to view and kill processes and applications running on the iPAQ, as well as look at system information).

As with the other applications, there is a host and a client component to Pocket Controller Professional, although the client component is simply a driver that cannot be configured. The host application, however, has several options, including the ability to automatically start when the iPAQ is connected via ActiveSync, different skins (sorry, not iPAQ 38xx series yet), and the DOS window mentioned previously. Figure 10-23 shows the desktop side of the application.

| FIGURE 10-23 | Controlling your iPAQ with Pocket Controller Professional |

Periscope

As mentioned in the presentation software section of this chapter, the Periscope application consists of two parts. The first is a remote control application for PowerPoint presentations. The second is the ability to view and control the iPAQ from your desktop.

Periscope not only has the ability to connect to the desktop wirelessly, it does it almost in real time. The protocols used by Periscope make it appear as though the messages are sent instantly between the iPAQ and the desktop.

Handheld Handler

The final application covered in this chapter is Handheld Handler from Snowshoe Technologies
(**www.snowshoetech.com**). Like the other remote desktop applications, Handheld Handler
enables you to view and manage the iPAQ from your desktop, but it also enables you to create
a virtual screen that is much larger than that of the iPAQ. In fact, it can simulate screens the
size of your desktop screen for applications, such as Internet Explorer and Pocket Word, that
benefit from a larger screen.

Handheld Handler not only creates this virtual screen on the desktop, but on the iPAQ as
well. As you can imagine, viewing a 640×480 screen (or worse, a 800×600 or 1024×769 screen)
on the iPAQ's small screen can be painful, but you have the ability to zoom in at any point and
navigate the screen with a nifty "compass-like" interface.

Figure 10-24 shows the enlarged iPAQ screen. Notice that the screen is considerably larger
than what you would see on the iPAQ and that you have the ability to capture the screen or
rotate it as required.

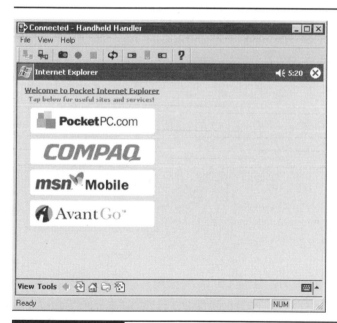

FIGURE 10-24   The Handheld Handler host application runs on your desktop.

10

The client application, on the other hand, gives you the ability to select the size of the virtual screen, as shown in Figure 10-25. Be aware that a reset is required whenever you modify the screen resolution, so make sure that you save any data before you make such a change (a warning message will be displayed to alert you).

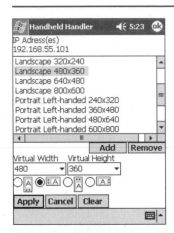

FIGURE 10-25   The Handheld Handler client application executes on the iPAQ.

*There are two other applications that perform similar tasks to those managed by Handheld Handler: JS Landscape from Jimmy Software (**www.jimmysoftware.com**) and Nyditot Virtual Display from Nyditot (**www.nyditot.com**). The main reason that they are not covered in detail here is that they cannot be used to display information on a desktop screen. Instead, they only modify the iPAQ screen so that it can display more information. They do this by "bumping" up the screen resolution to desktop-like resolutions (640×480 and higher).*

Chapter 11

Have Fun and Play Games with Your iPAQ Pocket PC

How to...

- Use your iPAQ's power for games
- Find and download games for you iPAQ

This is the chapter most of you have been waiting for. The games chapter. Nothing really shows the power of the iPAQ like the games. The graphics, the sound, the experience.

Although we cannot cover all the games in this chapter, we cover some of the most visually stunning and amazing games. At the end of the chapter, we also introduce you to a few websites that list all the games for the Pocket PC and allow you to purchase them. So, sit back, download the demos, and enjoy.

Games, Games, Games

As we mentioned previously, we could not even come close to covering all the games in this chapter. There are just too many of them. In fact, an entire book could be dedicated to games on the Pocket PC.

Each of the games mentioned here are listed with the web address and some of their features. Some are free, whereas others carry a small price tag.

Astro Blaster

www.pocketpcgames.info
Astro Blaster, by Rupp Technology, is a space game. Your base is being attacked by an alien force, and the only thing to protect you is a single gun turret, as shown in Figure 11-1. It takes skill to blast away the incoming wave of fighters. Be careful, they could slowly wear down your base's armor. Begin the game with a three-shot maximum, but don't fret, your turret can be upgraded to double the power. If your gun is destroyed, you are built a new one with only a one-shot blaster. Great sound effects too and very addictive.

Batty

www.danieljackson.co.uk/pocketpc
Batty is one of the first games we look at from the mind of Daniel Jackson. He offers four different games that are free of charge and are quite well made. Although he does not offer his games for download off his site, he has an agreement with Applian Technologies to host them on their site.

Batty is an Arkanoid/Breakout–based game, as shown in Figure 11-2. The idea behind the game is to clear all the blocks by bouncing a ball off a moving platform. You control the platform's movements from right to left, attempting to stop the ball from "falling" off the bottom of the screen. As the ball stays in play, it speeds up and becomes harder to control.

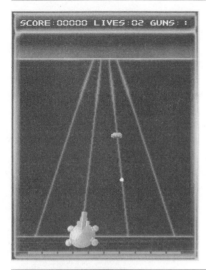

FIGURE 11-1   Astro Blaster   a space shoot-em-up game

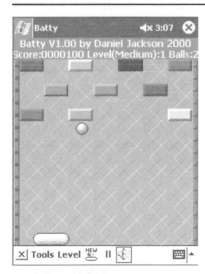

FIGURE 11-2   Batty is the first of several Arkanoid/Breakout games available for the iPAQ.

Blaster

www.geoff.org.uk/fognog/blaster.htm

Blaster, by FogNog, is another shoot-em-up game. You are a pilot of a ship and need to defeat your enemies, as shown in Figure 11-3. There are four different levels with a "boss" to be destroyed at the end of each of those levels. As you advance through the levels, you are presented with different "power ups". These "power ups" give your ship better weapons and shielding.

FIGURE 11-3   Blaster—a four-level, high-paced space shoot-em-up game

Bob the Pipe Fitter

www.hexacto.com/game_bob.php

Bob the Pipe Fitter, by Hexacto, is a game loosely based on the immensely popular Tetris game. Instead of using differently shaped objects to complete straight lines, as in Tetris, Bob the Pipe Fitter uses differently shaped "pipes" to connect pipes with four or more pieces. There are six different pipe types in the game: a straight horizontal piece, a straight vertical piece, and four different elbows.

The more pipe pieces you connect, the more points you get, as shown in Figure 11-4. A nifty feature occurs when you connect a four-piece loop (one of each of the elbow pieces to make a square pipe). At this point, a pipe bomb is created, which blows away the surrounding pipes.

FIGURE 11-4   Bob the Pipe Fitter   a Tetris like game with a twist

Overall, Bob the Pipe Fitter is a highly enjoyable and addictive game, much in the same way that Tetris was. This game won second place in *Pocket PC* magazine's Top 10 Puzzle Games.

Bounty Hunter 2099 Pinball

www.hexacto.com/game_bounty.php
The premise behind this futuristic pinball game from Hexacto, shown in Figure 11-5, is that Earth's criminals have escaped to the stars and it is your job, as a member of the Fugitive Retrieval Agency, to retrieve them and bring them to earth for justice.

Features include:

- Realistic physics
- Story-based, multiple-screen design
- Scrolling backgrounds
- Tons of targets, secrets, and skill shots
- Multichannel sound
- Many speech samples
- Customizable button configuration

11

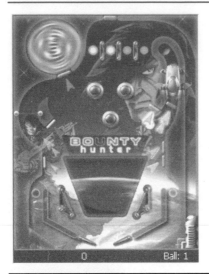

FIGURE 11-5   Bounty Hunter 2099 Pinball—a futuristic pinball game

Boyan

www.jimmysoftware.com/Software/Boyan

Boya, from Jimmy Software, is based on an old arcade game. The idea behind it is that Boyan is in a ship and aliens (known as Xenophobes) are invading. It is up to Boyan to save his world. The aliens use balloons to descend from the top of the screen to the bottom. You move Boyan up and down and try to shoot the aliens or their balloons.

Should an alien make it to the bottom of the screen without being stopped, it will climb the ladder behind you and try to push your ship off, as shown in Figure 11-6. The aliens also throw rocks at you. If two of these rocks hit your ship, it is knocked off and you lose a turn.

Also available is a Gas Tank. The Gas Tank appears at the top of your screen. Simply move the ship to that level and Boyan will pick up the Gas Tank. You can then throw it at an attacking hoard of aliens. Remember, however, that the tank is heavier and therefore can't be thrown very far.

The end of each level has a "boss" alien, one that is more powerful than the regular aliens and the previous bosses. Should you fail to stop one of these boss aliens, the level resets and more aliens attack. All and all Boyan is a very fun and addictive game.

FIGURE 11-6   Stop the attacking aliens and save your world in Boyan.

Boyan's Crystal

www.jimmysoftware.com/software/crystal
The same aliens that appear in Boyan, also from Jimmy Software, star in this game. The idea behind the game is a simple one. Crystal balls of different colors appear from the top of your screen. You and the aliens control a cannon that shoots out crystal balls of different colors as well. You can burst any of the crystal balls on the screen by hitting them with a crystal ball from your canon of the same color. If crystals of different colors touch one another, they stick together.

Any three crystals of the same color will fall off the bottom of the screen. You can rotate the cannon right or left and can bounce the crystal balls off the walls. Every few seconds the crystals on the screen drop a notch, as shown in Figure 11-7. When the descending crystals come too close to the cannon for you to shoot your crystals at them, the game is over.

Casino–Full Hand

www.hexacto.com/game_casino.php
Casino–Full Hand, by Hexacto Games, is actually four casino games in one. As shown in Figure 11-8, the package includes Blackjack, Roulette, Slot Machine, and Video Poker.

11

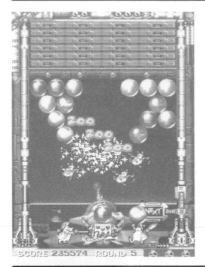

FIGURE 11-7   Burst the crystal balls before they drop to the bottom of the screen in Boyan's Crystal.

FIGURE 11-8   Casino–Full Hand offers four different casino games.

It also gives you the following options:

- Sophisticated graphics
- Sleek integrated interface
- Persistent wallet (allowing you to exit the game and return with the same wallet)
- Ability to synch with compatible online casinos
- Authentic casino rules

With this game you can enjoy very realistic Casino games without breaking the bank should you lose.

CECraft Pinball

Cecraft's Pinball is a pinball game with three different versions—Angel Egg, Dark Paladin, and Young Paladin. A nice feature about the Angel Egg and Dark Paladin versions of the game is a technology called iScore, which allows you to upload your score to the Internet and compare it to other players' ranking.

Angel Egg

www.cecraft.com/product/pinball/default.asp
The idea behind the game is as follows: Each of the seven players is an Archangel that is on probation. God is creating Earth and needs to summon these angels by collecting the angel's eggs. Once the eggs are collected, the Spirits of Fire, Water, Earth, and Wind are summoned. Together with the seven Archangels, the player completes the mission and creates Earth. The seven Archangels are Michael, Gabriel, Raguel, Raphael, Uriel, Sariel, and Akrasiel.

Dark Paladin

www.cecraft.com/product/pinball/paladin.asp
The idea behind this game is that a person by the name of Kariel Lightbringer decides to destroy the existing rules of the world and re-create the world. He does this to release the people of the world from the suffering that they have had to endure throughout the years.

To accomplish this, he changes his name to Kariel Darkbringer and attempts to master the most powerful black magic arts in the world. In this game, you take the role of Kariel Darkbringer and you need to use the Dark Elves' power to destroy the world. You need to get five Minotaur Gems to get this dark power.

Young Paladin

www.cecraft.com/product/pinball/paladin.asp
This version of the game follows the same character as Dark Paladin, only as a younger person. More than 1,000 years ago two races, the Humans and the Demons, fought for the survival on the Pangaea continent. The Humans lost and were enslaved by a number of Demons. They live in the hope that a person known as St. Paladin will restore the human race.

You are St. Paladin as Kariel Lightbringer and must complete five tasks (called virtues) and repel the Demons with the help of the Elves. Once these virtues are completed, you need to pass a final test from the Crono-Dragon.

11

Chopper Alley

www.ziosoft.com/html/pocketpc/chopperalley.html
Chopper Alley, from ZIO SOftware, is an incredible 3D graphics game for the iPAQ, as is
evident in Figure 11-9. In the game, you are a helicopter pilot that needs to complete some
missions. You can choose from 6 choppers, 8 weapons, 25 missions, and 5 unique locations.

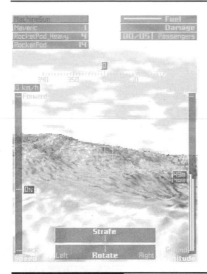

FIGURE 11-9   Chopper Alley is one of the most impressive games out there.

The weapons available to you include Sidewinder air-to-air missiles, Maverick air-to-
surface missiles, rapid machine guns, and weapon pods. The graphics on this game are
incredible, and you will quickly become addicted to it. The multiple locations and missions
provide many hours of unique play.

Christmas Rush

www.ndl.com/news/xmas.html
This game was originally released as a Happy Holiday greeting from NDL software. The idea
behind it is a simple one. Santa is in trouble and behind schedule. It is up to you to help him
out. You fly the sled on your iPAQ through quaint cities and villages, as shown in Figure 11-10.
Drop the presents on the houses and make people happy while helping Santa out.

This game is cute and has some great 3D graphics. You can bank the sled, send it up or
down, and drop presents at will.

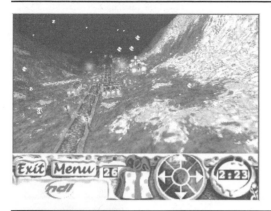

FIGURE 11-10   Help Santa Claus save Christmas in Christmas Rush.

Cubicle Chaos

www.microsoft.com/mobile/pocketpc/downloads/cubiclechaos.asp

Cubicle Chaos is another Arkanoid/Breakaway–type game. This one is available from Microsoft and has a bit of a twist. Instead of just having a ball and a platform and knocking down blocks, you sit behind a desk (the platform) and shoot balls at other cubicles in your office, as shown in Figure 11-11. Each level has different types of cubicles. Some are indestructible, others require you to hit them once, and others require multiple hits.

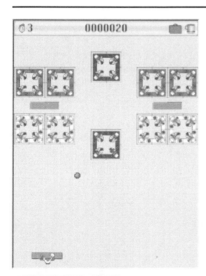

FIGURE 11-11   Destroy cubicles at work in Cubicle Chaos.

11

When some of the cubicles are destroyed, phones or memos are thrown towards you. If you catch these items with your desk, you get different "powers," such as sticky desk, multiple balls, small or large desk, and so forth.

Deep Down Race

www.geocities.com/bonelyfish/ddr.html
Deep Down Race, from Bonelyfish, is a game based on the old Dig Dug arcade game. The premise behind the game is that you are a digger. You have in your possession a high-powered drill and an oxygen tank, as shown in Figure 11-12. You need to loosen blocks and dig to 5,000 feet before you run out of air.

FIGURE 11-12   Dig to 5,000 feet in Deep Down Race.

Be careful, though, some blocks are solid and cannot be dug through and if you dig below a block, it and the blocks above it will fall. Same colored blocks will stick together and if more than four are connected, they will burst. Throughout the dig, there are oxygen capsules so that you can replenish your air supply. A nice feature is that you can create and edit your own levels.

Defender

www.ioboxgames.com
Defender is a port from the classic Defender arcade game. iobox Games have ported several of these games over to the Pocket PC, and they are true to the original. Same graphics, same sounds, and same games. If you remember the originals from the 1980s, then you are in for a lot of fun.

Doom4CE

www.jimmysoftware.com/software/doom4ce

No game platform would be complete without a port of the classic Doom game. This version, ported by Jimmy Software, is true to the original PC version with the same levels, sounds, graphics, and performance. Except for the small screen size, you would not be able to tell the difference, as you can see in Figure 11-13.

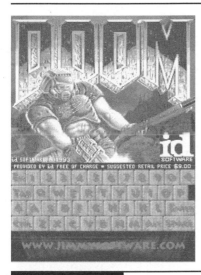

FIGURE 11-13   The classic original now on the iPAQ in Doom4CE

As with the original PC version, the Pocket PC version has support for multiple\and customized WAD files (the files that are used to create the levels and characters). Original Doom, Ultimate Doom, and Final Doom are all supported.

Expresso Run

www.ziosoft.com/html/pocketpc/expresso.html

Expresso Run, from ZIO Software, is a fun game. You race across multiple distant planets on an extremely important mission. In the future, the human race has been spread throughout the galaxy. All of these humans on these remote and distant planets rely on a regular shipment of one of the most crucial products: coffee.

You are a Java Jockey. You drive a state-of-the-art hover truck and are hauling several tons of fresh coffee beans to these distant planets through alien landscapes, as shown in Figure 11-14. Be careful, many obstacles are in your way—from the coffee-loving local alien life forms to rock falls, blizzards, and attack vegetation. As you pass each level, your assigned routes will become tougher and your cargo more precious.

11

FIGURE 11-14   Bring coffee to the galaxy in Expresso Run.

Fade

www.fade-team.com

Fade, by Fade-Team, is an incredible first-player adventure game. You play the role of Louis. He lives happily with his wife, Anne, in a small village. Louis has a secret behind his quiet life. Every night he has a strange dream, he is in financial difficulties, and he follows a treatment for his daily headaches. One of his customers offers him a job that he has no choice but to take. You must solve the mysteries in this game.

This game has incredible computer graphics in 65,000 colors, as illustrated in Figure 11-15. There are more than 450 of these screens. You need to help Louis solve mysteries and puzzles, talk to people, and visit incredible places. This game has more than 20 hours of play.

Fun2Link

www.ziosoft.com/html/pocketpc/fun2link.html

This is a highly addictive puzzle game from ZIO Software. The object of the game is to connect two points on the screen with a variety of different links. These links can consist of pipes, road, or crystal. As you pass each level, the higher levels give you faster flowing water, which increases the difficulty of the game.

There are several levels with special themes in which you will:

- Raise water through a dry well
- Transfer oil via pipe over a desert
- Transfer light beams through crystal
- Build roads on a desert

FIGURE 11-15   Solve an intriguing mystery in full color in Fade.

Hot Hoops

www.ioboxgames.com

Hot hoops, from iobox, is a game for all you basketball fans. You need to sink as many hoops as you can before your time runs out. If you sink three in a row, you arc on fire and the basket catches on fire, as shown in Figure 11-16. It is a race against the clock and your skill. A fun little game.

FIGURE 11-16   Sink hoops against the clock in Hot Hoops.

11

Hyperspace Delivery Boy

www.monkeystone.com/products/hdb
You are a mail courier for the Hyperspace Delivery Service in this Monkeystone Games game.
Your name is Guy Carrington, and you take your job very seriously. You need to get mail and
packages to their destinations no matter where they are. If only the job were that easy! You
will face robots and dangerous environments in your quest to deliver these packages, as shown
in Figure 11-17.

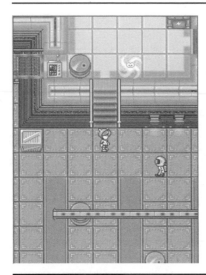

FIGURE 11-17   Neither rain, nor sleet, nor evil alien robots will keep Hyperspace
Delivery Boy from completing his rounds.

Some of the features of this game are:

- 30 levels
- Your choice of puzzle or action-puzzle modes
- Three completely different environments to choose from
- Hidden bonus items

ICBM II

www.geoff.org.uk/fognog/icbm_ii.htm
ICBM II, from FogNog, is a port from the classic arcade game. You are the protector of several
cities during a nuclear attack. As missiles bear down on your cities, you must protect them by

launching counterstrikes with your own missiles, as shown in Figure 11-18. Don't forget to protect your bases as well. If they are destroyed, you will not have a way to protect your cities from utter destruction.

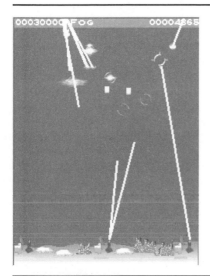

FIGURE 11-18   Protect your cities from missile attack in ICBM II.

iGolf

www.cecraft.com/product/igolf/default.asp

iGolf from Cecraft is a great golf simulation game, as shown in Figure 11-19. It has several built-in courses as well as add-on courses that can be downloaded right from the Internet. Features include:

- Real field environment-like wind, various sound support, undulation of ground
- Various views (Normal, Top, Far, Target view)
- Landscape mode
- Swing speed and power control function
- Convenient interface (available to control the club selection, swing direction, power, and spin on one screen)
- Various player types
- Support swing tutorial mode
- Statistical data and Internet ranking system

11

| FIGURE 11-19 | Play golf without leaving your seat. |

J-Five

www.jimmysoftware.com/software/jfive

J-Five, from Jimmy Software, is a shoot-em-up space adventure. The most valuable mineral in the universe is an energy source called "Paragon." The most abundant source of Paragon is the Planet Jakra. In order to control Paragon, the Bavog Empire has invaded the planet. Their people have tried to withstand the attack but failed. Because the Bavog Empire now controls all the Paragon mines, they are quickly becoming the richest and most powerful group in the universe.

You are part of a space pirate group (made up of Jakra people) who are stealing Paragon and selling it on the black market. You need the money to buy better weapons to fight the Bavog.

What makes this game amazing is not just the great graphics and sound but the fact that it is a true 3D game, as shown in Figure 11-20. With the ChromaDepth 3D glasses you will be able to view the game in true 3D.

JimmyARK2

www.jimmysoftware.com/software/jimmyark2

JimmyARK2 is another Arkanoid clone, as shown in Figure 11-21. It is similar to the other games of its type mentioned here. You control a platform that bounces a ball into blocks. Blocks of different colors react differently to being hit and may return power up options.

FIGURE 11-20   Fight the evil Bavog in 3D in J-Five.

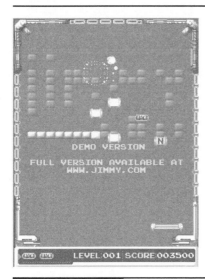

FIGURE 11-21   An Arkanoid clone from Jimmy Software

11

Lemonade Inc.

www.hexacto.com/news.php?nwid=11
Lemonade Inc., from Hexacto, is more then just a game. It is a business simulation. In the game you need to set up a successful lemonade stand, as shown in Figure 11-22.

FIGURE 11-22   Start your own lemonade business.

Check the latest weather forecast and try to pick the best location for your stand, tweak your lemonade recipe, set your prices, and manage your inventory. Re-invest your profits and streamline your production methods to earn the best margins out of every workday. Make the wrong decisions and you'll be on your way to bankruptcy faster than you think...
Features include:

■ Five maps with different characteristics and attributes

■ Multiple customer types with distinctive personalities

■ Three lemonade stands with tons of equipment and upgrade possibilities

■ Complex game system based on realistic parameters allowing the player to choose his or her own business strategy providing close to infinite re-playability

■ Watch your company results and value on LSX (Lemonade Stock Exchange)

Leo's Flight Simulator

web.jet.es/leobueno/leo_flight_sim.htm
This is the best flight simulator available for the iPAQ today. It allows you to fly on different missions, including take offs and landings. Excellent 3D graphics, realistic controls, and play add to the enjoyability of this game, as shown in Figure 11-23.

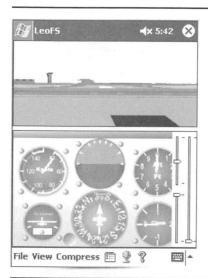

FIGURE 11-23   Fly a plane on your iPAQ in Leo's Flight Simulator.

Marble Madness

www.ioboxgames.com

Marble Madness, from iobox, is an exact port of the popular arcade game. It features the same sound effects, music, and levels as the original. You control a marble that needs to follow a course to the finish line. You have a limited amount of time and many obstacles—from the black marbles that block your way to the acid pools to the narrow bridges you must traverse, as shown in Figure 11-24.

This game is a hoot. You will enjoy it, as it is challenging as well as fun. Don't forget about that time limit. Finish under the time and you receive bonus points.

Marble Mania

www.pocketpcgames.info

Marble Mania is very similar to Marble Madness. Where Marble Madness has a single screen that scrolls with the action, Marble Mania has multiple screens. As you leave one screen, you appear on the next, as shown in Figure 11-25. Although it takes a bit to get used to it, it is an extremely fun game.

11

FIGURE 11-24   Control your marble through the obstacle courses.

FIGURE 11-25   Huge mazes await your marble in Marble Mania.

Metalion

www.ziosoft.com/html/pocketpc/metalion.html

Metalion is another great game from ZIO. The premise is this: The year is A.D. 2252. Facing extreme overpopulation and lack of food, the world leaders assemble a group of top scientists and engineers known as the Universal Federation to research the conversion of dead planets to living ones, better known as terraforming. After nearly 100 years, the group of scientists successfully terraformed Mars and began colonization. Venus, Jupiter, and Saturn are transformed and colonized 50 years later.

Unfortunately, the transformation of Jupiter was not as successful as the others. Jupiter's new atmosphere and environment began to deteriorate after only 15 years. The colony on Jupiter rebels against the Federation. Due to this renegade colony of Jupiter, the leaders on Earth form the "Universal Federation Corps" to serve and protect the Federal colonies. The colony of Jupiter claims its independence from the Federation, and the self-proclaimed Emperor of Jupiter creates his own army called the "Red Galaxy Knights." For 50 years, the Red Galaxy Knights wreak widespread havoc and destruction on the peaceful colonies of the Federation.

On September 21, 2710, the Red Galaxy Knights launch a full-scale attack on Earth. Millions of lives are lost. Four days later, the Federation declares war on Jupiter.

After four long years of war, the Federation has finally developed a new weapon called "Metalion." This robotic weapon, piloted by a single human being, was developed specifically for interplanetary travel and battle. It is the Federation's last hope for peace.

Because of the enormous size of the Red Galaxy Knights' army, the Federation begins to recruit pilots for the Metalion. You have just received a letter from the Federation stating your enlistment into the Universal Federation Corps as a Metalion Pilot.

This is an amazing game with amazing sound and graphics, as illustrated in Figure 11-26. Each level ends with a boss ship that must be destroyed. Power up pods appear regularly to give you more firepower and smartbombs.

Need for Speed

www.ziosoft.com/html/pocketpc/nfs.html

Need for Speed, from ZIO Software, is a great 3D racing game for the Pocket PC. It features 60 different racing events, full 3D graphics, and real world reflections, as shown in Figure 11-27. It will have you playing again and again (once you master the controls).

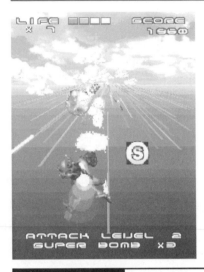

FIGURE 11-26   Metalion has great graphics, sounds, and play.

FIGURE 11-27   Need for Speed—an incredible 3D racing game

You can choose from one of 12 racing cars:

■ BMW Z3 and M5

■ Chevrolet Corvette

■ CLK-GTR

- Ferrari 550 Maranello
- Ferrari F50
- Jaguar XKR
- Lamborghini Diablo SV
- McLaren F1 GTR
- Mercedes SLK 230
- Pontiac Firebird
- Porsche 911

Pocket Bass Pro

www.ziosoft.com/html/pocketpc/bass.html

Pocket Bass Pro is a fishing game that offers the world's eight best fishing spots, overflowing with 17 species of your favorite game fish. You can cast, reel, jerk, hook, and retrieve (see Figure 11-28).

FIGURE 11-28   Fish to your heart's content without getting wet with Pocket Bass Pro.

Enjoy the breathtaking scenery from Lake Delaware, U.S.A. to Lake Turkana, Kenya, all displayed in amazingly detailed 3D graphics.

11

You can fish for Large Mouth Bass, Lake Trout, Walleyes, Pikes, Perches, and many more. You can fish in solitude, waiting for your catch-of-the-day, or you can test your skills by competing with other anglers in Tournament Mode.

Pocket Hexen

www.oke-e-doke.com/PocketHexen
Pocket Hexen is a port of the original PC game by Raven Software (**www.raven-games.com**). If you liked the original, you will love the Pocket PC version, which is shown in Figure 11-29. This port features:

- Six-channel stereo sound with pitch bend
- Special compressed WAD support that does not slow down the game
- Compressed save games to save valuable space
- Soft keyboard for entering cheat codes
- Shareware or full retail mode
- Support for custom levels

FIGURE 11-29   Cause mayhem on your iPAQ with Pocket Hexen.

Pocket Runner

www.jimmysoftware.com/software/pocketrunner

PocketRunner by Jimmy Software is a game based on the original LodeRunner game for the PC, as you can see in Figure 11-30. The goal of this game is to collect the diskettes on the screen and exit the level at the top of the screen. There are some protectors, and you must not be caught by them. You can slow them down by trapping them in a hole.

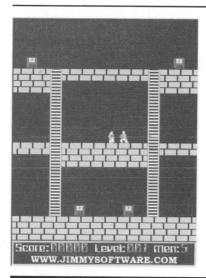

FIGURE 11-30   Pocket Runner—a port of the original LodeRunner

11

PocketSlay!

windowsgames.co.uk/slayCE.html

Slay, by Sean O'Connor, is an extremely addictive game based on the Warcraft/Age of Empires–type games. Slay is a simple to learn game of strategy and cunning set in medieval times. The island is divided up between the six players, and you must try to capture your enemies' land and link up your own territories to create larger and stronger ones, as shown in Figure 11-31. You begin capturing land by attacking with your peasants. Once your territories become richer you can combine peasants to make stronger and stronger people (Spearmen, Knights, and then Barons), who can kill weaker enemy troops, or knock down their castles. Just be careful that you don't create too many expensive men or the territory will go bankrupt!

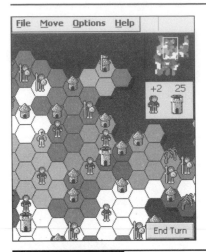

FIGURE 11-31   PocketSlay!—a medieval game for conquering your opponents

Make sure that your iPAQ is fully charged before you start. Play this game for a bit and you will be hooked.

Pow Wow

www.ziosoft.com/html/pocketpc/powwow.html
Pow Wow is a shooting game. You are presented with one of 10 themes and 28 scenarios, so you will never be bored. You get to shoot at different objects from targets to fish, as shown in Figure 11-32. Don't forget to reload, as you will quickly run out of ammo.

A nice feature about this game is that you simply need to tap on the screen with your stylus for shooting. No need to aim. Just tap. Reloading is easy too, just tap on one of the corners. You pass stages by beating a minimum number of hits.

QTris

www.danieljackson.co.uk/pocketpc
QTris, shown in Figure 11-33, is another game from Daniel Jackson that is available through Applian Technology. It is a great Tetris-like game, and best of all, it is free! You will be addicted to this game in no time and will find yourself spending all your available time on it.

FIGURE 11-32   Shoot the different targets in Pow Wow.

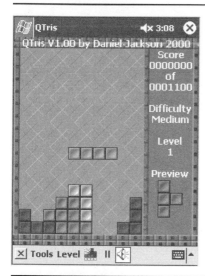

FIGURE 11-33   QTris—a great Tetris game

11

Rayman

www.raymanpocket.com
Rayman is a game that has been available on a variety of platforms including the PC, PlayStation, Dreamcast, N64, and Game Boy, with more than 9 million copies sold. Rayman has no arms or legs. The game consists of 31 levels in eight different worlds, with more than 20 characters.

It is based on the Rayman body and its magical abilities. It's a great cartoon game with lots of action, as shown in Figure 11-34. Another nice feature is the ability for two players to confront each other using special turn-based races.

FIGURE 11-34   Our arm-less, leg-less hero, Rayman

Robotron 2084

www.ioboxgames.com
Robotron 2084, by iobox, is an incredible port of the original arcade hit. The idea behind the game is simple. The year is 2084 and we have perfected the Robotron, a race of robots so advanced that humans are now inferior. It is your role to protect the last of the humans from the mutant army of robots.

This game is very true to the original in both graphics and sound. Playing the game makes you feel like you are playing the real arcade game, although on a much smaller device with much more power than the original.

SimCity 2000

www.ziosoft.com/html/pocketpc/simcity.html

SimCity 2000, from ZIO Software, is the Pocket PC version of the popular PC game. Become the undisputed ruler of a sophisticated real-time simulated city. Become the master of existing ones or get creative and start building your own dream city from the ground up. Whether you take over an existing city or decide to build your own, you are the Mayor and City Planner with complete autonomy. Your city is populated by Sims (Simulated Citizens). Like their human counterparts, they build houses, condos, churches, stores, and factories, as shown in Figure 11-35. And, also like humans, they complain about things like taxes, mayors, and city planners. If they get too unhappy, they move out, you collect less taxes, and the city deteriorates.

FIGURE 11-35   Rule your city or be dethroned in SimCity 2000.

Slurp

www.hexacto.com/game_slurp.php

Slurp, from Hexacto, won a spot in *Pocket PC* magazine's Top 10 Puzzle Games. A wonderfully addictive game, your goal is to grab your pen, slurp up the colored drops, and clear the board. As you slurp, the remaining drops reform into different shapes. Bigger drops are worth more points, so the challenge is to slurp up the big ones, but also think about how the slurp will cause the drops to reform, as shown in Figure 11-36. Make big drops and slurp up big points!

11

FIGURE 11-36	Hours of "Slurping" fun

After you clear all the big drops a new board appears, but this one is smaller because any uncleared drops from the previous board turn solid at the bottom! As you continue, the new boards get smaller and the game goes faster until you can't go any further. But don't worry; the next game is only a tap away!

The concept is easy, but so addictive. Keep your battery charged; because once you start playing you won't be able to put it down. What seems like a simple clicking game at first quickly becomes as challenging as any game of strategy. The more you play, the more puzzling it becomes, and the more you find ways to increase your score! If it becomes too easy you can increase the game's difficultly by choosing more colors (up to seven).

Soccer Addict

www.hexacto.com/game_soccer.php

Soccer Addict 2002 International Cup, from Hexacto, brings one of the most popular sports in the world to the iPAQ. Combining great graphics, simple yet realistic controls, and addictive gameplay, Soccer Addict offers an exciting, fast, and challenging soccer experience for casual and hardcore soccer fans alike, as illustrated in Figure 11-37.

Soccer Addict 2002 International Cup brings game play elements and immersive atmosphere usually found only on console games to your handheld device. Featuring insanely crowded stadiums, immersive sound FX, and active team strategies, everything in Soccer Addict aims at reproducing the excitement of world-class soccer games and getting your adrenaline pumping.

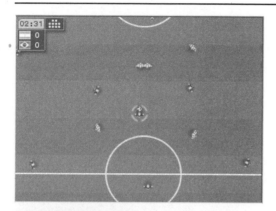

FIGURE 11-37   Incredible soccer action in Soccer Addict

Soccer Addict features 18 teams, each with specific strengths and weaknesses. Tackle a single computer opponent in exhibition mode for a quick soccer fix. Work your way up to the top of the soccer world by challenging the greatest international teams in tournament mode. Or simply battle for survival in the dramatic penalty shot mode.

Squirmy

www.danieljackson.co.uk/pocketpc
Squirmy, by Daniel Jackson, is a fun Snake/Worms–type game, as shown in Figure 11-38. Your goal is to eat the fruit on the playing field without running into the walls. The game becomes more challenging as you eat the fruit. The more fruit you eat, the longer squirmy gets, and the harder the game becomes.

Tennis Addict

www.hexacto.com/game_tennis.php
Tennis Addict, also from Hexacto, is sure to please even the most demanding sports fan. The intuitive interface and realistic ball physics make it easy to play, even for beginners, as illustrated in Figure 11-39. No fumbling with buttons, as all game input is through the iPAQ's stylus. The more you play, the better your skills at controlling ball speed and placement become.

Choose from 16 different opponents and four court types, each with their own unique characteristics and challenges. Play a quick game using the "Quick Match" option, or play an entire tournament where you have to climb your way to the top, match by match. The game keeps track of your progress, even when you stop for a break. You can even synch your results with others online, at the Tennis Addict Web Lobby.

11

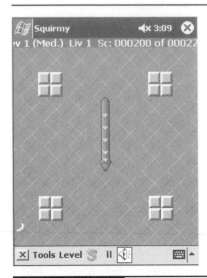

FIGURE 11-38   Eat the fruit without running into the obstacles in Squirmy.

FIGURE 11-39   Tennis Addict—an incredibly realistic tennis game

Features include:

■ Select from four different court types: indoor carpet, outdoor clay, and real or synthetic grass

■ Get rewarded for high scores with better performing racquets and tougher players to beat.

■ Win experience points that increase your strength, stamina, and speed in order to compete at a higher level.

- Play a quick game using the Quick Match option, practice in the training mode, or play an entire tournament where you have to climb your way to the top, match by match.

- Choose from 16 different 3D-rendered opponents with fully animated and realistic strokes, serves, volleys, smashes, and dives. Each opponent has their own unique characteristics and challenges.

- Hear the crowd cheer and the referee call the play.

- See your ranking and compare your scores with other players at the Tennis Addict Web Lobby.

Turjah

www.jimmysoftware.com/software/turjah
Turjah, from Jimmy Software, is a Galaga-type game. It is a scrolling game where you need to destroy the enemy. You get several weapons at your disposal including different guns and smartbombs. As you destroy the different enemies, they drop power ups to allow you to increase the power of your ship, shown in Figure 11-40.

FIGURE 11-40   Turjah—a space shooting and flying game

Every level ends with a boss ship that requires a lot of firepower and skill to destroy. A great game with excellent graphics and amazing sound.

11

Ultima Underworld

www.ziosoft.com/html/pocketpc/ultima.html

Ultima Underworld by ZIO Software, shown in Figure 11-41, is a game in a long line of PC-based Ultima games. This is a Dungeons and Dragons–type game. In this ultimate underworld, there is no up—just down, all the way down! Explore the Stygian Abyss, a tremendous cavern fraught with peril, where the only way out is to go deeper into the abyss. Then travel to a mysterious maze where dark magic has opened rifts that lead to eight dangerous new worlds!

FIGURE 11-41   Incredible graphics make Ultima Underworld an enjoyable game.

Your quest is to prove your innocence. You have been implicated as an accomplice for the kidnapping of Arial, Baron Almric's daughter who has been kidnapped by a troll. Your punishment—your head for the taking. To prove your innocence you must find and rescue a maiden from the deep, dark underworld known as the Stygian Abyss!

Ultima Underworld for Pocket PC will give you all the mystery and excitement you're venturing for.

ZIOGolf 2

www.ziosoft.com/html/pocketpc/ziogolf2.html

ZIOGolf 2, shown in Figure 11-42, is another incredible golf game for the iPAQ. It features:

- Full 3D graphic representation of real golf courses
- Undulation and sloping
- Graphically enhanced grid mode for accurate putting on the green
- Skins mode option
- Wagering an amount of money

- Practice, Normal, and Professional modes

- Provides Mulligan for normal level

- Choice of multiple players

- Choice of screen, portrait, or landscape view

- Personal record statistics

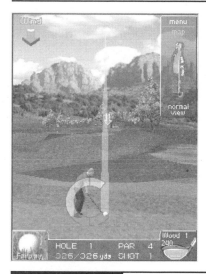

FIGURE 11-42   An amazing golf simulation program

11

Game Sites

As promised, this section will cover a few websites that you should be aware of if you are an avid gamer on the Pocket PC (or if you would like to become one).

By far, the most popular and unbiased website for Pocket PC games is the PocketGamer site, found at **www.pocketgamer.org**. This site contains not only a database of games, but introduces you to new ones, reviews existing games, and maintains a forum where you can discuss your games and their secrets with other fans.

A couple of the websites that offer Pocket PC games for download and trial are PocketGear (**www.pocketgear.com**) and Handango (**www.handango.com**). Both sites offer more then just games, but separate the games into their own section.

Chapter 12

Navigate with GPS on Your iPAQ Pocket PC

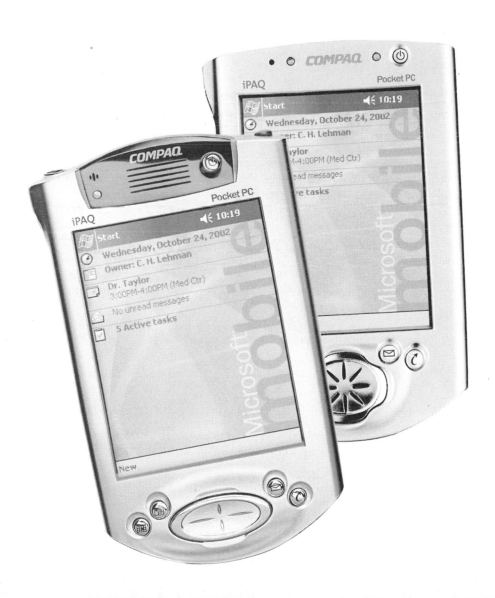

How to...

- Use your iPAQ as a GPS receiver
- Never get lost again
- Map out your destinations

At the title states, this chapter covers the different GPS systems for the iPAQ. We will begin the chapter with a quick introduction to GPS and what you should expect as an end user of the system. We will then cover the different hardware solutions that are currently available for the iPAQ, as well as the software that ships with those hardware add-ons. Finally, the GPS add-in software (software that does not ship with GPS units) will be covered.

An Introduction to GPS

GPS (Global Positioning System) devices rely on dozens of satellites that orbit the Earth. The U.S. military has placed these satellites in space and maintains them on a regular basis. Each one of these satellites has a unique radio frequency, which it emits toward the Earth. GPS devices "listen" for these frequencies and recognize which satellite is emitting the detected frequency. A GPS device can locate four different satellites and use the information about the satellites' frequencies and the GPS software to calculate your exact position, your elevation, your direction and speed of travel, and your current time.

A GPS device itself is nothing without the software that powers it. With these software packages, a GPS device can help you establish the fastest route from one location to another, provide you with turn-by-turn directions while you are driving, and help you recalculate a route should you miss an exit or intersection.

One of the nicest features of GPS is that the service is free. The U.S. Department of Defense sent up and maintains 24 satellites that enable your GPS receiver to pinpoint your location.

This chapter is divided into two sections: the hardware and the software. The first section introduces you to some of the GPS receivers that are currently available for the iPAQ, whereas the software section lists and discusses some of the GPS software packages and their features.

GPS Hardware

Before we look at the actual hardware GPS receivers, we need to talk about the different types of hardware available. Currently, you can get GPS receivers in one of five formats:

CompactFlash card   CompactFlash (CF) card units simply connect into the iPAQ via either a CF card expansion sleeve or a PC card expansion sleeve with a CF card adapter.

The CF versions tend to be a bit bulkier than some of their serial port counterparts because the actual receiving antenna must be attached to the CF card itself. Power is usually drawn directly from the iPAQ to power the unit; however, external power sources such as car adapters are available for many models.

PC card   PC card GPS receivers are similar in size to the CF units except that they require either the PC card or the dual-slot PC card expansion sleeve to connect to the iPAQ. As with the CF versions, they normally draw power directly from the iPAQ, although adapters are usually available.

Expansion sleeve   This type of GPS receiver does not require the addition of an extra expansion sleeve. Instead, the receiver is the expansion sleeve. Although these allow for a nice, compact unit, they do not allow you to use any other expansion sleeves at the same time. Another nice feature about the expansion sleeve form factor is the fact that it will work with any iPAQ device on the market today. Though Compaq changed the serial interface at the bottom of the iPAQ, they did not modify the expansion slot at the back. This means that all existing expansion sleeves can function in the newest iPAQ models (assuming that any required drivers are supported in Pocket PC 2002).

Serial port   Probably the most popular type of GPS unit is the serial port version. This version simply clips into the serial interface at the bottom of the iPAQ. If you decide that this is the type of unit for you, make sure that you purchase the correct version. With the 38*xx* series of the iPAQ, Compaq changed the bottom connector so that it is no longer compatible with the previous iPAQ form factor (including the 37*xx* series).

Standalone   Standalone GPS receivers are just that. They are receivers that can function with or without the iPAQ (although the iPAQ usually extends the receiver's functionality and usability). These receivers tend to connect to the iPAQ through the bottom serial port. Therefore you need to know whether it is compatible with the 38*xx* series (it should not be long before an adapter is available that enables devices designed for the older model's port to connect to the 38*xx* port). One nice feature about this type of receiver is that you can use it alone, with an iPAQ, or with a laptop.

We will be looking at six of the leaders in the GPS/iPAQ market:

- NAVMAN GPS 3000i
- Pharos iGPS
- TeleType WorldNavigator
- PowerLOC Destinator
- TravRoute CoPilot
- Pretec CompactGPS

12

NAVMAN GPS 3000i

The NAVMAN GPS 3000i receiver (**www.navman-mobile.co.uk**) falls into the expansion sleeve category. It replaces any other expansion sleeve that you may have, which can be a problem if you have some peripherals that you need to connect to your iPAQ. To solve this problem, a Type I and II CompactFlash slot is included on the back of the expansion sleeve. This feature enables you to connect a network card, a modem, or a storage card to your iPAQ while still using the GPS receiver.

The NAVMAN GPS3000i kit includes the following:

- ■ GPS satellite receiver for the 36*xx*, 37*xx*, and 38*xx* series iPAQ
- ■ SmartPath City GPS-enabled software
- ■ SmartPath Trip GPS-enabled software
- ■ Suction mount and Power Cable for in-car use
- ■ Instruction manual
- ■ Type I and II CompactFlash slot

As with many of the GPS receivers covered in this chapter, the NAVMAN 3000i receiver ships with several pieces of software. To allow you to compare the bundled software with some of the other third-party software available for GPS receivers, we will cover this software in the GPS software section of this chapter.

Pharos iGPS

Pharos (**www.pharosgps.com**) decided to sell their GPS hardware and software either separately or together in a kit. There are two kits available for purchase; the Compaq iGPS Receiver PocketPak and Compaq iPAQ Pocket GPS Navigator Kit.

The PocketPak contains both the iGPS-180 receiver and the cable assembly. The cable assembly is customized to fit your Compaq iPAQ (make sure you mention whether you have a 36*xx*/37*xx* series or a 38*xx* series iPAQ, because the connectors for the two types of units are different), and it utilizes an integrated 12-volt car lighter adapter to power the iGPS, making it ideal for in-vehicle use. Be aware that you can purchase the cable assembly separately, which is ideal if you have multiple vehicles or if you own more than one type of iPAQ.

The Compaq iPAQ Pocket GPS Navigator Kit contains all the components in the PocketPak plus Pharos's Ostia for Pocket PC software (covered in the software section of this chapter).

One limitation of the iGPS-180 receiver is that it needs to be connected to power (via the 12-volt car lighter adapter) in order for it to function. Should you require a truly mobile iPAQ GPS solution, this may not be the one for you.

NOTE *Before making a decision about which GPS receiver to purchase, make sure that you check with the vendor. In the case of the iGPS-180, check to see if it has changed to draw power from the iPAQ rather than from the car lighter adapter before making your final decision.*

The iGPS-180 receiver is extremely compact and includes the following features:

- Instant positioning—track your vehicle in real time as it moves down streets and highways

- Accurate turn-by-turn mapping

- Low power consumption

- 12-channel satellites

- Integrated receiver with built-in patch antenna

- Water-resistant enclosure (for use in marine environments, such as on a boat)

- Connection to all PDA applications and laptop

- Accuracy of 7 to 8 yards

The GPS-180 uses the serial connector at the bottom of the iPAQ. This enables you to use expansion sleeves for peripherals such as memory storage cards (covered in Chapter 14) to store your GPS maps and other applications. Another nice feature of this receiver is its ability to connect to a laptop by simply adding a USB connector to the unit.

TeleType WorldNavigator

The TeleType (**www.teletype.com**) family of GPS receivers comes in many different flavors. In fact, there are five different versions of their GPS receivers:

- WorldNavigator CompactFlash Wireless GPS

- Mini-Auto GPS

- Handheld Traveller

- Serial PCMCIA GPS

Their most popular GPS unit is the WorldNavigator, and even it comes in two different versions: the regular and the rugged version. The normal version, shown in Figure 12-1, uses the CompactFlash form factor and includes an external antenna for faster lock-in and best reception in particularly difficult areas. Although the rugged version is, as the name implies, made to stand up to rugged outdoor field operations, it is also of interest to anyone using Compaq's dual-slot CompactFlash expansion sleeve or a laptop. The back of the rugged

12

version is completely flat, allowing a PC card such as a modem or storage card to be used concurrently with the GPS receiver.

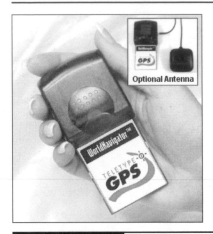

FIGURE 12-1   The WorldNavigator GPS uses the CF form factor.

The rugged version of the WorldNavigator GPS includes:

■ Optional booster antenna plug

■ 12-channel GPS receiver with integrated antenna

■ Rugged Type II adapter

The Handheld Traveller is a bundle of TeleType's GPS software and maps, Windows CE 9-pin connector, Garmin's Etrex 12-channel GPS receiver, GPS serial cable, and 2 AA batteries. It is a standalone GPS receiver that can be used either with the iPAQ or by itself. The final GPS receiver that TeleType offers is the Serial PCMCIA receiver. The only real difference between this unit and the others is that it uses the PC card (formerly known as the PCMCIA type) form factor.

When deciding which TeleType GPS unit to purchase, make sure that you check out their compatibility chart. The chart can be found online at **www.teletype.com/pages/gps/compatibility.html**.

PowerLOC Destinator

One of the most technologically advanced GPS units is the Destinator from PowerLOC Technology (**www.destinator1.com**). What sets this product apart from its competitors is not just the hardware, but mostly the Destinator software. So much so, in fact, that PowerLOC is releasing the software as a standalone product to enable you to use this product with any other GPS receiver.

The Destinator hardware, shown in Figure 12-2, is a serial connection–based receiver. It ships with the necessary cables to connect to the iPAQ and the 12-volt car lighter adapter. You will also notice the receiver and a suction cup to attach the antenna to the vehicle windshield.

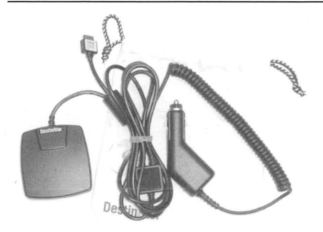

FIGURE 12-2   The PowerLOC Destinator GPS comes with all the necessary connectors and a carrying bag.

Included with the Destinator package are these items:

- GPS antenna-receiver, car lighter adapter/charger, and cables
- CD-ROM containing the following:
    - Destinator software
    - All NAVTECH North American maps
    - User manual
    - Tutorial
    - Destinator movie
- Durable canvas travel pouch for Destinator hardware

NOTE   *When this book was written, the serial connector of the Destinator was only available for the 36xx/37xx series iPAQ. We were informed that the 38xx series version was being tested and approved by Compaq and should be available shortly. Check with PowerLOC to ensure that the 38xx series serial cable set is available.*

12

TravRoute CoPilot

TravRoute's (**www.travroute.com**) GPS solutions are a little different from the other products mentioned here. The company mostly sells the GPS software, but they bundle it with one of two different GPS receivers.

The first, the Pocket CoPilot 2.0, is a serial connection–based GPS receiver. As with the other serial connection–based GPS solutions, make sure that you purchase the one that will work with your iPAQ. Once again, the cable system connects to the serial port on the iPAQ and to the 12-volt car lighter adapter in your vehicle. This allows you to charge the iPAQ while the vehicle is running but does not allow the GPS unit to function when removed from the vehicle.

The second GPS receiver available from TravRoute uses the NAVMAN GPS 3000i receiver. It allows you to run the GPS receiver on battery while disconnected from the vehicle, but also ships with a charging cable to allow you to recharge the iPAQ's internal battery while the car is running.

Pretec CompactGPS

Another CF GPS receiver is the CompactGPS unit from Pretec (**www.pretec.com**). CompactGPS includes the following features:

- CompactFlash form factor
- 12 parallel satellite-tracking channels for fast acquisition and reacquisition
- Support for true NMEA (National Marine Electronics Association) 0183 v2.2 data protocol
- Enhanced algorithms, which provide superior navigation performance in urban canyon and foliage environments
- Maximum navigation accuracy with the Standard Positioning Service (SPS)
- Enhanced TIFF upon power-up when in a keep-alive power condition before startup
- Automatic altitude hold mode from three-dimensional to two-dimensional navigation
- Built-in antenna
- Power saving mode with trickle power
- LED indication for navigation update
- Data retention with Li-Ion battery inside

GPS Software

This section covers some of the software available for the iPAQ to enable you to use GPS navigation systems. We will first cover the software packages that ship with the GPS units covered in the first section of the chapter, followed by the packages that are GPS independent. It is important to note that some of the GPS manufacturers' software will function with the different GPS receivers. Make sure, however, that you double check with both the hardware and software vendor on compatibility before purchasing the products.

The software packages are:

- NAVMAN SmartPath

- Pharos Ostia for Pocket PC

- TeleType WorldNavigator GPS software

- PowerLOC Destinator

- TravRoute Pocket CoPilot

- Microsoft Pocket Streets

- ESRI ArcPad

- TomTom CityMaps

NAVMAN SmartPath

Because NAVMAN is located in the United Kingdom, they specialize in European maps. Currently, their SmartPath software includes maps for 90,000 towns and cities in 12 European countries. The countries currently supported are:

Austria	Luxembourg
Belgium	Netherlands
Czech Republic & Slovakia	Norway
Denmark	Portugal
Ireland	Scandinavia
Finland	Spain
France	Sweden
Germany	Switzerland
Italy	United Kingdom (excluding Ulster)

12

SmartPath is actually made up of two different products: SmartPath Trip, shown in Figure 12-3, and SmartPath City, shown in Figure 12-4. SmartPath Trip is used to manage maps on a town-to-town or city-to-city basis. It generates maps based on the trip between the cities or towns without going into street-level detail. SmartPath City, on the other hand, generates the maps needed within cities and to plan trips from one city location to another.

FIGURE 12-3   Navigating with NAVMAN's SmartPath Trip software

FIGURE 12-4   Navigating with NAVMAN's SmartPath City software

Both SmartPath Trip and SmartPath City include the following features:

- Route planning from point to point to point
- Trip planning from city to city or across city
- Ability to plan the quickest route
- Turn-by-turn instructions
- Split view instruction and map display option

- Route summary display-only option

- Display road and city names

- Go to street/road or place names

- Go to latitude/longitude coordinates

- Zoom to route

- Variable map scale

- Store favorite locations

- Variable map display and color style

- Metric or English distances

- Route and borders graphics options

- Set road speeds

- Map and Font zoom and details levels

- Keep GPS position on screen

Pharos Ostia for Pocket PC

Ostia is Pharos's software product. Much like the other products available today, it allows you to plan your trips and get turn-by-turn directions (both text-based and voice-prompted). As Figure 12-5 illustrates, Ostia is not as colorful or data-rich as some of its competitors. The software, however, is extremely useable and stable.

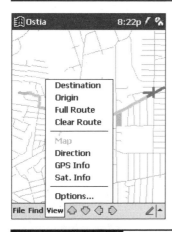

12

FIGURE 12-5   Pharos' Ostia software is lacking in that it only offers U.S. maps.

Ostia includes the following features:

- Real-time tracking and detailed street maps
- Route computation with turn restrictions
- Voice-prompted driving directions
- Turn-by-turn directions
- Addresses, intersections, and points of interest
- Point-to-point routing

One drawback of the Ostia software is that it cannot generate a re-route. This means that if there is an obstruction on the path, it cannot calculate another route.

TeleType WorldNavigator GPS Software

The WorldNavigator software, shown in Figure 12-6, has many of the features of its competitors. Although the feature list is too long to list here (go to **www.teletype.com/pages/gps/street.html** for the complete feature list), we have included some of the more powerful features:

- GPS moving map software and maps
- Ability to display lakes and rivers
- Highly compressed map format
- Turn-by-turn directions
- Route and re-route selections
- Door-to-door routing, with voice and visual alerts, and re-route
- Voice and visual alerts
- Trip route recording and replaying
- Metric and English scale units
- Supports any NMEA (National Marine Electronics Association)–based GPS receiver
- 12 satellite tracking channels
- Voice alerts available for turn-by-turn directions in Italian, French, German, Dutch, and English spoken with female French accent

WorldNavigator is compatible with other, non-TeleType GPS receivers. A table listing these receivers can be found at **www.teletype.com/pages/gps/compatibility2.html**.

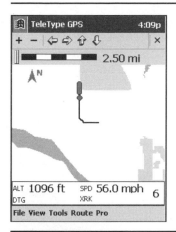

FIGURE 12-6   The WorldNavigator software is simple, yet effective.

PowerLOC Destinator

PowerLOC's Destinator, shown in Figure 12-7, is one of the most powerful GPS software products covered in this chapter. It uses NAVTECH maps (**www.navtech.com**), which are some of the most trusted and used maps for GPS navigation.

Destinator includes the following features:

- Easy input of destination or select from address list
- Turn-by-turn voice prompts guide you to your destination
- Shortest or quickest route
- Dynamic and interactive maps throughout your trip
- Automatic recalculation of alternate route if a turn is missed
- Fully featured menus and audio-visual navigation
- English, French, and Spanish voice
- Ability to store up to 4000 destinations in its address book
- Instant recall of last 15 destinations
- Completely portable
- Detailed street maps of the United States and Canada

- NAVTECH mapping technology
- No activation or monthly user fees
- Manual use of maps including off-line routing
- Advanced points of interest database

Destinator's interface is unique and allows very intuitive access to all the desired information. There are currently 12,769 cities in Destinator's database (**www.destinator1. com/maps.emb?tl=products**).

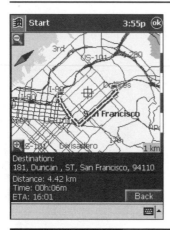

FIGURE 12-7   PowerLOC's Destinator is one of the most advanced GPS mapping software.

TravRoute Pocket CoPilot

When we first used Pocket CoPilot 2.0, we knew that it was designed with both the Pocket PC and the auto driver in mind. It has two display modes, a driver and a passenger mode. The first allows you to enter your destination, at which point it will simply give you all the information you need without cluttering the screen with colorful maps and information that may distract you from your driving. With the voice prompts, this product is top-notch. The information on the Driver screen includes the following:

- Detailed text directions
- Distance to next turn
- Next turn arrow
- Distance to destination

- GPS signal strength
- Current location

Pocket CoPilot's other features include:

- A human voice rather than a robotic voice
- Spoken turn-by-turn directions that guide you to any address nationwide
- Automatic updated directions within seconds of going off route
- Real-time dynamic routing on the Pocket PC device
- Large buttons for easier touch-screen operation
- Clear and concise navigation information to the lone driver on the screen with a map that automatically appears as you approach each turn
- Passenger screen that presents both navigation information and a map at all times
- Large turn arrow that indicates direction of next turn
- Quick and easy access to your 25 most frequently visited addresses
- Address-to-address trip planning on your Pocket PC that enables you to view complete turn-by-turn directions and maps of your trip before you get on the road

Microsoft Pocket Streets

Microsoft's Pocket Streets (**www.microsoft.com/pocketstreets**) is simply an extension of their Streets application. It is actually not a product that can be purchased separately; instead it comes with Streets & Trips 2002 (**www.microsoft.com/streets**). As Figure 12-8 shows, Pocket Streets enables you to view your maps with any number of points of interest. You can zoom into any level of detail that you require.

A couple of nice features of Pocket Streets is its ability to export user-generated maps from Microsoft MapPoint, Streets & Trips 2002, and AutoRoute 2002 and the availability of almost 600 cities in North America and Europe. To download Pocket Streets maps, navigate to **www.microsoft.com/pocketstreets/mapdownload/MapDownload_EN.html**.

 *Pocket Streets includes GPS support. To get this support, however, you will need to install the Pocket Streets 2002 Update from **www.microsoft.com/pocketstreets/ using/download.htm**.*

ESRI ArcPad

ArcPad from ESRI (**www.esri.com**) is not a GPS solution in the true sense of the term. Instead, it is a Geographic Information Systems (GIS) package. It enables the operator to collect, use, and review geographic data in the field. It is very specialized and will not help you get from one location to another.

12

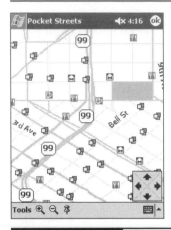

FIGURE 12-8 Microsoft Pocket Streets uses icons to illustrate general categories.

One warning about this product is that the maps use a huge amount of memory. If software such as this is something that you need, then consider getting a GPS receiver that does not use the PC or CF expansion sleeve. Also notice that the user interface seems to be flipped upside down with the start menu at the bottom. This is because this software was written for the older palm-sized PC devices. No Pocket PC version has been released yet. Figure 12-9 shows an ArcPad view of a map of San Diego.

FIGURE 12-9 ESRI's ArcPad displaying a map of San Diego

ArcPad offers many of the features provided by the other products as well as some unique capabilities, including the following:

- Provides wireless support for ESRI's ArcIMS image services

- Offers feature and attribute identification

- Provides hyperlinks to external files (photographs, documents, and videos)

- Lets users measure distance, area, and direction

- Lets users save personal map layer and style settings

- Offers scale-dependent layer display

- Allows users to create, edit, and locate shapefile (files used for GIS mapping) data

- Supports user-defined input forms

- Supports NMEA (National Marine Electronics Association) and TSIP (Trimble Standard Interface Protocol) GPS protocols and will operate in two-dimensional, three-dimensional, and differential modes

- Provides for integration with ESRI's ArcView GIS 3.2 software

TomTom CityMaps

One of the biggest complaints about using GPS systems is that the maps available tend to cover only Canada and the United States. TomTom's CityMaps (**www.palmtop.nl**) solves that problem. CityMaps has a database of more than 100,000 cities across Europe, which ships on a CD-ROM. A select number of cities (Amsterdam, Barcelona, Berlin, London, Madrid, Milan, Munich, Paris, Rome, and Vienna) are available for download electronically.

CityMaps also uses an ingenious slide bar to zoom in and out of the map quickly and easily, as Figure 12-10 illustrates.

FIGURE 12-10   TomTom's CityMaps gives non–North American users GPS maps.

12

Part III

Select Hardware and Accessories for Your iPAQ Pocket PC

Chapter 13

Go Further with Expansion Sleeves

How to...

- Support PCMCIA cards
- Support CompactFlash expansion cards
- Use an expansion sleeve to connect to a GPRS/GSM network
- Use an expansion sleeve to connect to a Bluetooth network
- Use expansion sleeves for medical, multimedia, GPS, and digital photography

Another great feature of the iPAQ is the ability to expand the "naked" iPAQ by adding expansion sleeves to it. An iPAQ fits snugly into the front of an expansion sleeve and interfaces with it to provide new and expanded functionality for GPS location, wireless networking, digital photography, external storage, printing, bar code scanning, and much more. The primary manufacturer of expansion sleeves is Compaq, but recently a number of other hardware vendors have gotten into the game, and the list is growing. For the most up-to-date list of iPAQ expansion sleeves, check out **www.pocketpctools.com**.

In this chapter, we will look at all the Compaq expansion sleeves and discuss what they can do for you. In addition we will look at some of the third-party expansion sleeves that you can get for your iPAQ.

 *Are you an electronics wizard? Would you like to try making your own expansion sleeve? Compaq provides all the specs for building an expansion sleeve on their website at http://csa.compaq.com/CSA_For_iPAQ_Developers_CD.shtml.*

Compaq CompactFlash Sleeve

The standard Compaq CompactFlash (CF) expansion sleeve, shown in Figure 13-1, is an essential tool for iPAQ expansion if you like to store files on removable media, or want to use any of the dozens of CF-based tools that are on the market. A CF slot can be a lot more than just storage; it can be used for modems, wireless and wired LAN cards, digital cameras, printers, and much more. The expansion sleeve slides onto your iPAQ from the bottom, where it will link into the expansion port on the bottom of your iPAQ. Once connected, it will automatically initialize and get ready to work with your iPAQ. Then you can connect any CF card you like by plugging it into the top of the expansion sleeve.

This sleeve enables you to insert any standard Type I or Type II CF card into your iPAQ, but check to make sure that drivers are available for the version of Pocket PC that you run on your iPAQ. This sleeve is much thicker than it needs to be, but does the job well and is reasonably inexpensive. It is available from anyone who sells Compaq products. The Compaq part number is 170339-B21, and it is compatible with all models of iPAQ.

| FIGURE 13-1 | The CompactFlash sleeve from Compact allows you to use almost any standard CompactFlash card with your iPAQ. |

Compaq PC Card Expansion Sleeve

The Compaq PC card expansion sleeve, shown in Figure 13-2, is the add-on accessory that we use more than any other. It enables you to insert any standard Type II PCMCIA PC card that is compatible with Pocket PC. These are the same cards that we insert into our laptop computers, which enables us to use the same cards in both our iPAQs and our laptops. We use these sleeves extensively for our wireless modem cards and our 802.11b networking cards, giving us real-time access to information while fully mobile. The range of PC cards that are available is tremendous. Toshiba makes a 5GB (no, that is not a typo) hard drive that fits into this slot that allows you to store an incredible amount of data. You can also use the expansion sleeve to insert wired or wireless modems and network cards. You can output presentations to a monitor or projector with a VGA card, and much more.

This sleeve also contains an extended battery pack, which is very important; otherwise the power drawn by the PC card would quickly run down your iPAQ battery. The Compaq part number for this sleeve is 170338-B21. The battery roughly doubles the run-time of the iPAQ. Users who primarily use CF cards often use the PC card expansion sleeve with a CompactFlash adaptor instead of the CF sleeve in order to have access to this extra battery power.

13

FIGURE 13-2   The PC Card expansion sleeve from Compaq is the expansion sleeve that we use more than any other.

Compaq Dual PC Card Expansion Sleeve

The Compaq dual PC card sleeve, shown in Figure 13-3, is basically the same as the standard single PC card expansion sleeve except that it holds two cards simultaneously. This is useful for activities that require two cards at the same time, such as maintaining a wireless connection while showing presentation slides on a projector.

FIGURE 13-3   The Dual PC Card expansion sleeve is invaluable if you need to run two cards frequently, but otherwise is very bulky.

This unit is, however, thick as a brick and will probably only be used by people who *must* have two cards running at the same time as an essential business activity. In addition to the business person who needs to connect wirelessly while simultaneously making a presentation, a medical technician might need a wireless card to connect to the hospital WLAN and another card to plug in a medical device. The dual PC card is made thicker to accommodate the two slots as well as a battery that is twice as big as the single card sleeve to enable it to power two cards for an extended period of time. The Compaq part number for this sleeve is 216198-B21.

Compaq Bluetooth Wireless Sleeve with CompactFlash Slot

This sleeve is brand new to the market and is very useful (and this usefulness will increase over time as more Bluetooth-enabled devices come out). Bluetooth is a wireless communications protocol that allows any Bluetooth-enabled devices within range of each other (usually less than 50 feet) to communicate wirelessly without complicated configuration exchanges. The kinds of things that you can do today with this sleeve include:

Wireless Internet/e-mail/network access   If you have a Bluetooth-enabled cell phone, your iPAQ can surf the Web, get e-mail, and run TCP/IP applications by using your cell phone as the data modem.

Printing   You can automatically print documents to printers equipped with this technology.

File and information sharing   Transfer information to any other Bluetooth device, such as another iPAQ for transferring files, meeting notes, contact information, and more.

ActiveSync   You can synchronize your iPAQ with a Bluetooth-equipped PC.

This sleeve looks identical to the standard CF sleeve and also offers a standard CF card in addition to its Bluetooth capabilities. Although Bluetooth is new to the technology space, it promises a whole new set of mobile wireless functionality that we have never experienced before. For example, if you have a Bluetooth-equipped GPRS cell phone in your pocket, your iPAQ can connect to it at any time and surf the Internet, or pull down your latest e-mail. If you are in a meeting in someone else's office, but they have a Bluetooth-enabled printer, you can send your documents to the printer from your iPAQ through the Bluetooth connection without having to make any special adjustments for their network. Perhaps at some point in the future you will walk past a Bluetooth-enabled vending machine and be able to use your iPAQ to make a purchase from the machine without physical money.

13

Compaq Wireless Pack for GSM/GPRS Networks

The Compaq Wireless Pack for GSM/GPRS networks, shown in Figure 13-4, is also a brand-new unit that will be available by the time this book hits the shelves, so watch **www.pocketpctools.com** for a full review. This amazing sleeve turns your iPAQ into a cell phone. It is a tri-band (900,

1800, and 1900 MHz) GSM phone, which means that it will work on any GSM network in the world (and GSM is the most widely used cell phone network protocol in the world). In addition, it supports GPRS data (it is a multi-slot Class 10 GPRS device), which means that you can use it as your wireless modem to surf the Internet, send and receive e-mail, and anything else that you need to do via the Internet.

FIGURE 13-4   Compaq provides you with full device convergence by turning your iPAQ into both a cell phone and wireless data device with the GSM/GPRS Wireless Pack.

This sleeve features "always-on" capability, which is what enables it to receive a cell phone call, or notify you of a new e-mail message, even when it is powered off. You can use the iPAQ speaker and microphone, or use an ear-bud style microphone and earpiece plug-in. We can't wait for this device so that we won't have to carry our cell phone and our iPAQ everywhere we go (combine this with the iHolster discussed in Chapter 15, and you have a very functional telephone and data device). This sleeve is still significantly bulkier than your current line of cell phones, but if you are already carrying an iPAQ, why not combine them?

Silver Slider CompactFlash Expansion Sleeve

The Silver Slider CF sleeve, shown in Figure 13-5, is a modified Compaq CF sleeve. The manufacturer has removed a lot of the excess plastic to make it much more streamlined (lighter and thinner) and has painted the card a metallic silver to match the iPAQ for the fashion-conscious user!

FIGURE 13-5   The Sliver Slider is essentially a modified standard CompactFlash sleeve that is lighter and more retro looking.

This unit is available from the Silver Slider website at **http://ss2andmore.homestead. com/G1.html** or through a second provider, PDAmotion, at **www.pdamotion.com**. If you send in your existing CF sleeve, there is a significant discount. There are three different varieties of the CF Silver Slider, in addition to one now available for both the single and dual PC card sleeve.

NAVMAN GPS Expansion Sleeve

The NAVMAN GPS unit was discussed in detail in Chapter 12. It is mentioned here because it is an excellent example of a third-party expansion sleeve for the iPAQ.

With the NAVMAN GPS you can find exactly where you are within a distance of 6.8 meters. In conjunction with navigation software you can use it to locate and get driving directions to services and points of interest in your area, such as restaurants, gas stations, theaters, and more. You can learn more about the NAVMAN GPS sleeve at **www.navman-mobile.com**.

FlyJacket i3800 (CompactFlash and Multimedia Monitor Output)

The FlyJacket i3800 is a complete multimedia expansion sleeve that also features a CF slot. A multimedia expansion sleeve is one that enables you to send your output to a projector, television, or monitor directly from your iPAQ. You can view full-motion video on the iPAQ. It comes with a pen-sized remote control to advance and back up a PowerPoint slide show running on your iPAQ. The FlyJacket is discussed in more detail in Chapter 10.

13

The FlyJacket features video input, as well, allowing for full-frame video capture from an input source (TV, camcorder, or other). It also includes an additional battery to make all of this activity possible without draining the main battery. More information can be found on the LifeView website at **www.lifeview.com.tw/web_english/fly_jacket.html**.

Nexian NexiCam Digital Camera Expansion Sleeve

The NexiCam is a new device from Nexian, which should be available by the time this book is on the shelves. It is a digital camera that will record pictures on its CF card slot or in the iPAQ memory. You can take 800×600–resolution photos, or capture up to 45 seconds of full-motion video. It won't match the most up-to-date digital cameras in quality or functionality, but for mobile workers who use their iPAQs to enter data and also need to take photos (insurance adjusters and real estate appraisers, for example), this product's all-in-one capabilities make it a great choice. Not only that, but with a wireless modem, you could immediately send the photos to the person who needs them, speeding up the claims process in an insurance case, for example. Watch for information directly from Nexian at **www.nexian.com** or at **www.PocketPCTools.com**.

Nexian NexiPak Dual CF Sleeve

The NexiPak sleeve from Nexian allows for the insertion of two CF cards at the same time, allowing you to run, for example, a wireless 802.11b LAN card and a storage card at the same time. This is similar to the Dual PCMCIA sleeve from Compaq, but it is CF instead of PCMCIA.

MicroMedical Pocket ECG/EKG Unit

IPAQs are beginning to appear more and more in medical fields, where they are used for patient charting, prescriptions, and much more. This interesting sleeve, shown in Figure 13-6, is made by an Australian company called MicroMedical. It enables you to run a real-time electrocardiogram on a patient. More information can be found at **www.micromed.com. au/08_products/20_pocketview**.

This sleeve could have an interesting impact on the field of telemedicine (providing medical services in remote locations by having a less-skilled assistant who is on site transmit medical information to a doctor or specialist in another location). The iPAQ can store multiple ECG readings, and can e-mail them with a wireless modem or transfer them to a PC through an ActiveSync connection.

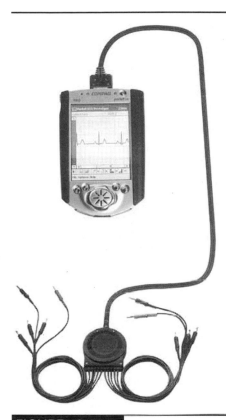

FIGURE 13-6   The MicroMedical Pocket ECG/EKG unit is just one example of the potential of expanding your iPAQ with expansion sleeves.

Chapter 14

Store Your iPAQ Pocket PC's Information Externally

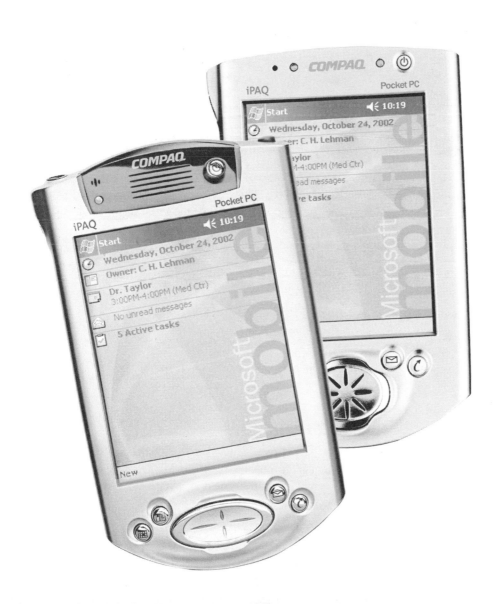

How to...

- Choose a storage medium that makes sense for you
- Understand the difference between the storage mediums available today

In this chapter we will look into some of the products that are available for the iPAQ for external storage. Because we cannot cover all the different products, we have included the ones that we found to be easily available and that we know work with the iPAQ.

We've divided these products into four categories and will discuss each in the sections that follow:

- Storage cards
- Hard drives
- Iomega Clik!/PocketZip
- Storage peripherals

Storage Cards

A storage card is a device that uses solid state technology to store information. It has no moving parts and is non-volatile (that is, it does not require power to retain its information). Although many of the hard drives that we discuss later in the chapter have the same form factor as the storage cards, they are not the same.

Four different types of storage cards are currently on the market:

- MultiMediaCard (MMC)
- Secure Digital (SD) card
- CompactFlash (CF) card
- PC card

In the next sections we will cover the different storage card solutions and some of the vendors that sell them.

MultiMediaCards (MMC Cards)

The MultiMediaCard standard was introduced in November 1997 and was a joint development between SanDisk Corporation and Siemens AG/Infineon Technologies AG. It is very small (24 mm × 32 mm × 1.4 mm) and weighs less than 2 grams. It is designed to store data for portable devices, such as cameras, MP3 players, and PDAs.

 *For more information on the MMC standard visit the MultiMediaCard Association website at* **www.mmca.org**.

The iPAQ 38*xx* series contains a Secure Digital/MMC slot at the top of the unit. The iPAQ will simply recognize the MMC as another storage card and allow you to store information (applications and data) on it. When you first install a new MMC card (or any other storage card, for that matter), you will be presented with a dialog box, shown in the following illustration, asking whether you would like to format the card. Once formatting is complete (which is an extremely quick process) you will be able to not only transfer files to it, but read these cards on a desktop or laptop computer using a special card reader. The card readers are covered later in this chapter.

Be aware that the MMC standard is designed for the connection of storage cards only. As we will see in the next section, Secure Digital (SD) technology allows you to not only read and write to MMC cards, but also to SD cards, which include non-storage cards, such as network cards or modem cards. Currently, the MMC standard only supports memory cards up to 64MB in size.

Following is a partial list of companies that offer MMC memory cards:

- Delkin Devices (**www.delkin.com/eFilmProducts/eFilmMemoryCards.htm**)
- Kingston Technology (**www.kingston.com/products/cf.asp**)
- Lexar Media (**www.digitalfilm.com**)
- SanDisk (**www.sandisk.com**)
- Simple Tech (**www.simpletech.com**)
- Viking Components (**www.vikingcomponents.com**)

14

Secure Digital (SD) Cards

A newer technology that uses the same form factor as MMC cards is Secure Digital. Secure Digital cards have the distinction of not only storing information, but having the ability to secure the data from unauthorized access (hence the name). Be aware, however, that the iPAQ currently does not support the security features of SD. If you lose an SD card with sensitive information on it, that information will be secure. SD cards also have a locking read-only switch to protect the data from being erased accidentally. Another nifty feature of SD cards is their ability to support not only storage cards, but also multifunction cards such as Bluetooth and network cards.

NOTE   *For more information on the SD standard visit the Secure Digital Association website at* **www.sdcard.org***.*

Like MMC, the SD card is about the size of a postage stamp and has the same dimensions. In fact, you can easily use MMC cards in the SD slot of your 38*xx* series iPAQ (or in a 36*xx* or 37*xx* series iPAQ with an adapter). Be aware that MMC tends to be considerably slower than SD (although they run at the same speed on the iPAQ).

As with MMC, SD cards are non-volatile and are solid-state. Currently, you can purchase SD cards that are up to 256MB in size. Following is a partial list of SD storage card suppliers:

- Compaq Corporation (**www.compaq.com/products/handhelds/pocketpc/options/memory_storage.html**)
- Delkin Devices (**www.delkin.co/eFilmProducts/eFilmMemoryCards.htm**)
- Kingston Technology (**www.delkin.com/eFilmProducts/eFilmMemoryCards.htm**)
- Kodak (**www.kodak.com**)
- Lexar Media (**www.digitalfilm.com**)
- SanDisk (**www.sandisk.com**)
- Simple Tech (**www.simpletech.com**)
- Viking Components (**www.vikingcomponents.com**)

CompactFlash (CF) Cards

One of the most common and popular storage cards on the market today is the CompactFlash card. These cards were made popular by digital cameras, since most of the digital cameras on the market today support their form factor.

It is important to note the different form factors of CF cards. Currently there are two CF card types; Type I and Type II. Both CF card types have the same dimensions when you look at the flat side, approximately 1 inch square. Where they differ is in their width. A Type I CF card is about $^1/_8$ inch thick whereas the Type II CF card is slightly thicker. Although they are very similar, that little bit of extra width can make all the difference in the world. A Type I CF card will fit into a Type II connector, but the reverse is not true.

As mentioned in Chapter 13, Compaq offers a CF card sleeve for the iPAQ. This expansion sleeve has a CF Type II slot, which allows you to connect any CF device to it. If you are purchasing a non-Compaq expansion sleeve, make sure that it supports Type II. You might be surprised as to what types of sleeves have CF slots in them. These can include GPS sleeves, camera sleeves, and sleeves with bar code readers. CompactFlash cards are quickly becoming a hit with iPAQ users because of their small size, low cost, and high capacity. Several vendors recently announced 1GB CF storage cards. With these storage capacities, CF cards are quickly catching up to their hard drive brothers for huge storage. As you will see, however, the hard drives that are compatible with iPAQ are getting quite large as well.

PC Cards

The last solid-state, non-volatile storage card that we will look at is the PC card. These are becoming less and less popular because of their storage size and the storage capacity versus price of the CF cards. The PC card, formerly known as the PCMCIA card, has a large form factor (about the size of a credit card, but much thicker) and is available on just about every laptop around. Although PC cards are not that popular, it is interesting to note that one of the reasons the iPAQ was such a big hit when it was first introduced was because it was one of the only devices available with a PC card expansion pack. This allowed people to not only connect storage devices to them, but full-sized network cards, modems, and other peripherals (such as video cards).

NOTE *Although there are a few other storage card technologies, namely Sony's Memory Stick and SmartMedia (SM) cards, they are not covered in this chapter because they are not really popular for the iPAQ. Having said that, however, be aware that several adapters (covered at the end of the chapter) enable you to connect and use these devices on your iPAQ with a PC card expansion pack.*

You may also notice that PC card memory is known as ATA memory. Although the terms can be used interchangeably, ATA memory seems to be the more common.

14

Hard Drives

As technology gets better, smaller, and faster, truly amazing products make it on the market, including the small hard drives available today that work with the iPAQ. These drives are great for storage since they can store large amounts of information (with 20GB on the way) and they can also be moved into desktops and laptops very easily. In this section we look at two hard drive form factors: the CF card form factor and the PC card form factor.

IBM Microdrive

IBM's Microdrive is the smallest hard drive available today. It measures about 1 inch square and is currently available in three storage capacities: 340MB, 512MB, and 1GB. IBM has also invented a new hard disk technology called "Pixie Dust." This may enable future Microdrives to grow to 6GB in size with the same form factor as the current drives.

Although several vendors (such as Iomega) resell the IBM Microdrive as their own, only the IBM version is covered here. Table 14-1 lists the specifications of the Microdrive (for models IBM 1GB Microdrive/IBM 512MB Microdrive/IBM 340MB Microdrive, and DSCM-11000/DSCM-10512/DSCM-10340). For further information, see IBM's Microdrive website at **www.storage.ibm.com/hdd/micro/overvw.htm**.

Configuration	
Interface	CF+ (ATA and PCMCIA compatible)
Capacity	1000 / 512 / 340
Sector size	512
Disk	1
Areal density (max Gb/in.^{2})	15.2
Recording density (max Kbpi)	435
Track density (TPI)	35,000
Performance	
Data buffer (KB)	128
Rotational speed (rpm)	3600
Latency (average ms)	8.33
Media transfer rate (Mbps)	38.8 to 59.9
Interface transfer rate (Mbps)	11.1 (PIO mode 3); 13.3 (DMA mode 1)
Sustained data rate, typical read or write (Mbps)	2.6 (min); 4.2 (max)
Seek Time (Read)	
Average (ms)	12
Track-to-track (ms)	1
Full-track (ms)	19

TABLE 14-1   IBM Microdrive Specifications

Reliability		
Error rate (nonrecoverable)	< 1 per 1.0 e 13 bits transferred	
Load/unload cycles	300,000	

Power	+3.3 V Power Supply	+5 V Power Supply
Voltage requirement (auto-detect)	+3.3 VDC, ±5%	+5 VDC, ±5%
Current (write)	250 mA	260 mA
Current (standby)	20 mA	20 mA
Power consumption efficiency (watts/MB)	0.000495/0.000967	0.00085/0.00166

Physical Size		
Height (mm)	5 +0 / –0.10	
Width (mm)	42.80/ ±0.10	
Depth (mm)	36.40/ ±0.15	
Weight (g)	16 (max)	

Environmental Characteristics	Operating	Nonoperating
Ambient temperature	0 to 65°C (measured at unit)	–40 to 65°C
Relative humidity (noncondensing)	8% to 90%	5% to 95%
Shock (half sine wave)	175 G (2 ms)	1500 G (1 ms)
Vibration (random [RMS])	0.67 G (5 to 500 Hz)	3.01G (5 to 500 Hz)
Vibration (swept sine)	1 G 0-peak (5 to 500 Hz)	5G 0-peak (10 to 500 Hz)

TABLE 14-1   IBM Microdrive Specifications *(continued)*

14

The IBM Microdrive is available either by itself (with the model numbers listed below) or in the Travel Kit. The Travel Kit includes the Microdrive, a PC card adapter, and a rugged field case for storing the PC card adapter and the drive. The Microdrive also ships in its own little plastic case.

- IBM 1GB Microdrive (Model DSCM-11000)
- IBM 512MB Microdrive (Model DSCM-10512)
- IBM 340MB Microdrive (Model DMDM-10340)
- IBM 170MB Microdrive (Model DMDM-10170)

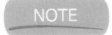 *If you are having problems getting your iPAQ to recognize the IBM Microdrive, go to the Compaq Handhelds Software & Drivers page (**www.compaq.com/support/ files/handhelds/us/index.html**) and check to see if your model and operating system require any updates. Some of the older Pocket PC 2000 iPAQs required an update to make the drives function.*

PC Card Hard Drives

The PC card hard drive is becoming more and more popular with PDA and laptop users. The reasons for this are simple. The form factor (a full PC card) allows you to easily transfer the drive from a laptop to your iPAQ to a desktop (assuming that the desktop is equipped with a PC card reader). Before you can use a PC card hard drive in your iPAQ, you will need the Compaq PC Card Expansion Pack (or Dual PC Card Expansion Pack).

Once the PC card hard drive is installed in your iPAQ, you will be able to format the drive, at which point it will be recognized by the iPAQ as just another storage card, as shown in Figure 14-1.

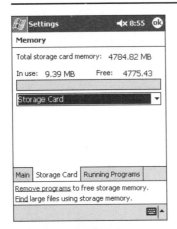

FIGURE 14-1   A 5GB PC card hard drive installed in an iPAQ

Currently, two different PC card hard drives are being sold on the market from two different companies. PC card hard drives are available in either a 2GB or a 5GB format and are available from the following companies:

- Kingston Technology (**www.kingston.com/products/pccard.asp**)
- Toshiba (**www.toshiba.com/taissdd/products/features/MK5002mpl-Over.shtml**)

The Kingston DataPak is a PC Card-based hard drive. It can be used in either the iPAQ or Laptops. Table 14-2 lists its specifications.

Kingston Part Number	5GB	2GB
	DP-PCM2	DP-PCM2
Configuration and Capacity		
Technology	1.8 inch Winchester hard disk drive	
Storage capacity	5GB or 2GB	
Number of disks	1	
Data heads	2	
Cylinders (logical)	3,900	
Data heads (logical)	16	
Sectors per track (logical)	63	
Rotational Speed	**2GB**	**5GB**
	4,200 rpm	3,990 rpm
Seek Times		
Track to track	3 ms	
Average	15 ms	
Maximum	26 ms	
Average latency	7.14 ms	
Data Transfer Rate		
Internal transfer rate	16.25 Mbps (max)	
Start time	3 sec	
Buffer size	256KB	

TABLE 14-2   Kingston DataPak Specifications

14

Power	
Voltage	3 V ±5% or 5 V ±5%
Spinup current	370 mA (3.3 V) or 380 mA (5.0 V)
Active read current	360 mA (3.3 V) or 370 mA (5.0 V)
Active write current	390 mA (3.3 V) or 400 mA (5.0 V)
Idle current	150 mA (3.3 V) or 160 mA (5.0 V)
Standby current	70 mA (3.3 V) or 75 mA (5.0 V)
Sleep current	15 mA (3.3 V) or 20 mA (5.0 V)

Physical Size	
Height	0.20 in. (5 mm)
Length	3.37 in. (85.6 mm)
Width	2.13 in. (54 mm)
Weight	1.93 oz (55 g)

Environmental Characteristics	
Operating temperature	5°C to 55°C (41°F to 131°F)
Nonoperating temperature	–20°C to 60°C (–4°F to 140°F)
Relative humidity	5% to 90% noncondensing
Operating shock	200G
Nonoperating shock	1000G
MTBF	> 300,000 hours
Data reliability	1 nonrecoverable error in 10^{13} bits read

TABLE 14-2   Kingston DataPak Specifications *(continued)*

NOTE   *Toshiba recently announced plans for a 10GB and a 20GB PC card hard drive.*

Iomega Clik!/PocketZip

This section introduces the Iomega Clik!. This solution is actually made up of a couple of components. The first is the Clik! PC card drive, whereas the second is the PocketZip disk.

The Clik! PC card drive is simply a PC card that works with the Dual PC Card Expansion Packs only on the iPAQ. It is the size of a Type II PC card and simply acts as the interface between the iPAQ and the PocketZip disk.

The PocketZip disk is a small disk (similar to a Zip disk) that stores up to 40MB of information. It can only be read in the Clik! adapter.

Before Clik! and PocketZip can be used on your iPAQ, you need to download and install the Iomega Tools for the Pocket PC, which can be found at **www.iomega.com/software/pocketpc.html**.

Storage Peripherals

Various peripherals are available to connect the storage cards discussed in this chapter to your iPAQ and your desktop computer, including the following:

- CF adapters
- SD/MMC adapters
- Memory Stick adapters
- Multifunction adapters
- USB adapters

These adapters are fairly self-explanatory. The CF adapters enable you to connect a CF card to a PC card slot. It simply acts as a connector to change the size of the storage card so that it fits into the PC card form factor. The nice thing about this is that you can purchase a PC card expansion pack and use most memory products in that form factor. The SD/MMC and Memory Stick adapters are the same except that they enable you to connect either SD or MMC storage cards via the PC card slot.

The multifunction adapters are fairly new on the market and enable you to use a single adapter to connect a variety of memory cards using the same hardware. An interesting one is the CompactTrio from Pretec. This three-in-one adapter enables you to convert MMC/SD/Memory Stick to CompactFlash. For more information, check out **www.pretec.com/index2/product/ digital_imaging/Digital_imaging_main.htm**.

14

Chapter 15

Explore Peripherals and Add Functionality to Your iPAQ Pocket PC

How to...

- Choose a peripheral to attach your iPAQ to a network
- Find the right case for your iPAQ
- Select a keyboard for external input
- Run longer with external power options
- Sync on the road with third-party sync cables

The iPAQ by itself is a powerful and useful tool, but it was also designed to be adaptable and expandable. Many companies are creating products to enable you to get even more out of your iPAQ, and new items are appearing on the market all the time. In this chapter we will examine some of the products that we have experience with and will give you our impressions of their value to you, the iPAQ user.

Modems, Wireless Cards, and Connection and Sync Accessories

Connecting your iPAQ to an external network (dial-up, Internet, LAN, or other) is very important for practical management of information. A sync cable is essential to connect it to your PC to sync your contacts, calendar appointments, and more. A network card will give you access to network resources such as printers and file servers. A wireless modem will enable you to connect in real time to run software, send and receive e-mail, surf the Web, and more. The tools in this section are designed to help keep you connected and synchronized.

We will be looking at the following products on the market:

- Symbol Wireless Networker
- D-LinkAir DCF-650W
- Sierra Wireless AirCard
- Other Sierra Wireless AirCards
- Novatel Merlin Wireless Cards
- Pocket Spider Wireless CDPD modem
- Socket Digital Phone Card
- Socket Low Power Ethernet Card
- Pretec CompactModem
- Pharos CompactFlash 10/100 Mbps Fast Ethernet Adapter
- Pharos 56K modem
- RoadWired Auto-Retract Network Cord

- Belkin Power Charger and Sync Cable Combo
- PDAmotion PowerSync Autosync/Charger Cable

Symbol Wireless Networker

Much smaller in size than other wireless card options, the Wireless Networker from Symbol (**www.symbol.com/products/wireless/la4137.html**), shown in Figure 15-1, trades small size for reduced speed and range. However, don't let that fool you into thinking this card is anything less than awesome! With advanced power management features, it will consume almost no power when not transmitting or receiving data. The card can support up to 11 Mbps when close to the wireless access point and will scale down to 1 Mbps as it gets close to the limits of its 300-foot range. The software is feature-rich and will let you monitor signal strength and transmission speed, let you change channels, enable WEP (Wired Equivalency Protocol) security features, and even perform pings against known IP addresses. The Type I nature of this card also makes it compatible with the HP Jornada Pocket PC, letting you share hardware with other Pocket PCs.

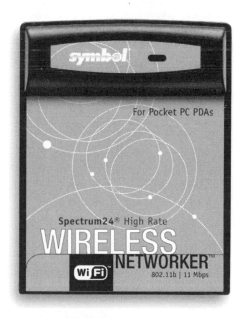

FIGURE 15-1   The Symbol Wireless Networker is an ultra compact 802.11b card.

15

As long as the 300-foot range doesn't bother you, the Symbol Wireless Networker is the best 802.11b CompactFlash card on the market today. It offers a superb blend of features and performance, and we wouldn't hesitate in recommending this card to anyone.

D-LinkAir DCF-650W

NOTE   *802.11b access is becoming more and more widely available—you can go into many cafes across the United States and surf wirelessly. Also known as "WiFi," 802.11b has some known security issues and shouldn't be used to transmit sensitive information without special precautions.*

This Type II 802.11b CompactFlash card from D-Link, shown in Figure 15-2, isn't the smallest one on the market, but its solid performance characteristics make it a winner in our book. Rated for 11 Mbps speed within 460 feet of the access point, the DF-650W (**www.dlink.com/products/ DigitalHome/Mobile/dcf650w**) will sacrifice speed in order to maintain the connection over distance. From 1,311 feet away, the card can still remain connected at 1 Mbps. I did a few distance tests, and though I never took measurements, I was able to stay connected over 500 feet away from home—I was impressed! This performance comes at a cost however: The card is fairly power-hungry. Consuming 380 mA while transmitting, 280 mA receiving, and 170 mA while in idle mode, your battery life in a standard iPAQ with a CF card sleeve will be significantly reduced. If you plan on extended use of the DCF-650W, we recommend using the PCMCIA sleeve for extended battery life.

FIGURE 15-2   The D-Link 802.11b card will provide you with access to your wireless LAN.

The software for the card lets you change channels and SSID information, as well as monitor your signal strength. Setting up the card to work with my WiFi access point was remarkably easy—it was as simple as installing the drivers on my iPAQ, inserting the card, and clicking OK once.

Sierra Wireless AirCard 300

The Sierra Wireless AirCard 300 (**www.sierrawireless.com/ProductsOrdering/300.html**), shown in Figure 15-3, is a Type II PCMCIA card that allows for wireless CDPD data access with your iPAQ Pocket PC. You'll need a PCMCIA sleeve for your iPAQ, and an account with a service provider. The modem itself uses roughly 15 percent of the battery life on an iPAQ, which is quite good for a PCMCIA card. In terms of speed, CDPD is not fast. Real-world speed hovers somewhere around a 14.4 Kbps modem. The good news is that the Sierra card connects very rapidly to the network—within a few seconds you're fully connected and active. The bandwidth is appropriate for checking e-mail, instant messaging, and web browsing with the graphics turned off. You won't be streaming media at these speeds, but it's fast enough to get most jobs done.

15

FIGURE 15-3   With the Sierra Wireless AirCard 300, you can access the Internet through the wireless cellular network.

I also found that the compatibility with a laptop was useful—when I was traveling and didn't have access to my dial-up ISP, I could pop in the Sierra card and get online within a few seconds to find the local phone number for the ISP. A very useful accessory! Although CDPD will eventually be eclipsed by 2.5 and 3G technologies such as GPRS and CDMA2000, for now it's a fairly widespread method of accessing your data wirelessly in North America.

Other Sierra Wireless AirCards

In addition to the AirCard 300, Sierra Wireless (**www.sierrawireless.com**) also makes several other AirCards for use on different networks. These include the following:

AirCard 750   This is the tri-band card, so it is suitable for use on any GSM/GPRS network worldwide.

AirCard 710   This is the GSM/GPRS card for those who never leave North America. It does not have tri-band support so you cannot roam to European, Asian, or other GSM/GPRS networks outside of North America.

AirCard 555   This is a CDMA 1xRTT card for the Verizon Express network (up to 144 Kbps, the Bell Mobility Network (Canada), and the Telus network (Canada) in North America only.

AirCard 550   This card is the same as the AirCard 555, but for the Sprint PCS CDMA network in North America only.

AirCard 350   This card offers the same functionality as the AirCard 300, but with "ruggedized" construction for more challenging environments. It also has the option to plug in a 3 watt amplifier to boost the signal for those working in fringe areas of limited coverage. This card is ideal for people working in the oil industry, forestry, or other environments that can be hard on equipment.

Novatel Merlin Wireless Cards

Novatel Wireless (**www.novatelwireless.com**) also produces a full line of PC card wireless modems for your iPAQ. Their product line parallels the Sierra Wireless line of modems and includes the following:

Merlin G201   This is a GSM/GPRS dual-band modem for use in Europe, Asia, Africa, and the Middle East. With the right software, your iPAQ can also be your cellular mobile phone through the GSM network.

Merlin G100   This is a GSM/GPRS single-band modem for use in North America. Unfortunately, the antenna design of this card means that you can never fold the antenna down when it is in the iPAQ expansion sleeve, making it awkward to carry around when not in active use.

iStream This card is essentially the G100 specifically tuned and marketed for the Voicestream network in the United States.

Merlin C201 This is a CDMA 1xRTT network card with support up to 153.6 Kbps. This card can be used on the Verizon Express network in the United States or the Bell Mobility or Telus networks in Canada.

Merlin Platinum Special Edition This CDPD card is specifically designed for low power consumption in handheld devices like your iPAQ. It will run on existing low-bandwidth CDPD networks offered by carriers such as Verizon, AT&T, and Telus Mobility.

Pocket Spider Wireless CDPD Modem

This CDPD modem (**www.enfora.com**) is the only one that we have found that works through a CompactFlash slot. Thus it doesn't require the PCMCIA expansion sleeves to operate or can operate in conjunction with other sleeves that only offer CF expansion, such as some of the multimedia sleeves addressed in Chapter 10.

Socket Digital Phone Card

The Socket Digital Phone Card (**www.socketcom.com/product/dpc.htm**), shown in Figure 15-4, is a Type I CompactFlash card that enables iPAQ owners to connect their Pocket PC to a cell phone, giving easy wireless Internet access. Using this product is very simple: drivers are installed on the iPAQ via the desktop or laptop computer, and once the drivers are installed, you simply plug in the Socket Digital Phone Card, enter the phone number of your ISP, and you're set. It's important to understand that this solution for wireless access is different from solutions like the Sierra Wireless AirCard 300. The AirCard 300 requires an account with a WISP (wireless Internet service provider), which means separate monthly service charges. The Socket Digital Phone Card allows you to dial into your local ISP account and use your regular cell phone airtime minutes.

Several brands of phones are supported, including Audiovox, Ericsson, Kyocera, Motorola, Nextel, Nokia, Qualcomm, Samsung, Siemens, and Sprint PCS. Be sure to check the website to confirm that your phone is supported before ordering, and that your network will support data. Some networks will charge a small one-time activation fee to support data transfer on your account, whereas others will charge a monthly fee. I used the Socket Digital Phone card in conjunction with my Samsung phone and iPAQ 3650 on the Sprint PCS network, and it worked wonderfully. The transfer speeds are quite slow (think 14.4Kbps modem), but it worked well for sending and receiving e-mail and connecting to the Web. Instant Messaging also works superbly in low-bandwidth situations. The Socket Digital Phone card is a great way to get online wirelessly without spending a great deal of money.

15

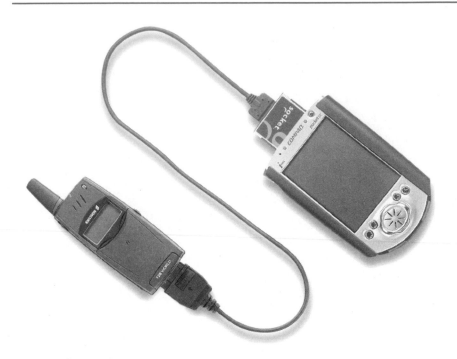

FIGURE 15-4   The Socket Digital Phone Card allows you to access the Internet through your cell phone.

Socket Low Power Ethernet Card

The Socket Low Power Ethernet Card (**www.socketcom.com/product/ethernet.htm**), shown in Figure 15-5, is a great solution for connecting to a wired LAN. It's a Type I CompactFlash card with a short cable that ends in a female dongle and operates at 10 Mbps. Connecting is as simple as plugging in the cable and configuring the software drivers installed using a desktop or laptop. Once installed, the drivers allow you to configure the Socket card to connect on a specific IP or DNS address or have them assigned dynamically via DHCP. What advantages does an Ethernet connection give you? In one word: speed. An Ethernet connection is hundreds of times faster than a serial connection, and dozens of times faster than a USB connection. The Socket software can be configured to launch a specific program upon connection, making it easy to run ActiveSync automatically when the card is inserted.

The "Low Power" moniker isn't just marketing babble—the card draws a meager 19 mA of power, compared to some PCMCIA Ethernet cards that draw more than 300 mA. Compatibility is also a key element with this card: By inserting the card into a PCMCIA adapter, you can use this card with a laptop running Windows 9x, ME, 2000, or XP. Double-duty means you carry less hardware when traveling.

| FIGURE 15-5 | The Socket Low Power Ethernet Card allows you to connect your iPAQ to a wired LAN. |

I've personally used the Socket Low Power Ethernet Card to help diagnose LAN problems. Smaller and lighter than a laptop, it's easy to take your iPAQ on site and plug it in to an Ethernet port to diagnose problems. With third-party software, you can perform ping and tracer tests to test equipment.

Pretec CompactModem

The Pretec CompactModem (**www.pretec.com/index2/product/Mobile_peripherals/CompactModem.htm**) is a Type I CompactFlash 56K modem suitable for data and fax purposes. It supports a wide variety of protocols, including ITU-T V.90 and K56flex, making it compatible with most ISPs. It supports fax transmit and receive at 14,400 bps, and will automatically drop down to 300 bps to maintain the connection if required. Combined with a PCMCIA modem, the Pretec CompactModem can be used in a laptop. Like the Pharos 56K modem (discussed later), the Pretec CompactModem has an integrated RJ-11 phone jack.

15

Pharos CompactFlash 10/100 Mbps Fast Ethernet Adapter

The Pharos CompactFlash 10/100 Fast Ethernet Adapter (**www.pharosgps.com/products/ accessories/ACCESSORIES.htm**) is one of the few 100Mbps Ethernet adapters on the market today, making it a powerful tool for high-speed Ethernet access. Because the Pocket PC is limited in hardware specifications compared to a desktop or laptop PC, you likely won't see true 100Mbps speeds. You will, however, see significantly increased speeds over a 10Mbps card. The Pharos card is a Type I CompactFlash card with an integrated RJ-45 Ethernet port—there's no external cable or dongle to lose or break off. As with the Socket Ethernet card, the software configuration on the iPAQ is easy to do. Pharos hasn't published the power requirements for this card, so it's difficult to compare to the Socket Low Power Ethernet card. However, by it's very nature CompactFlash is power-friendly, so it's unlikely the Pharos card would be hard on the battery life of your iPAQ.

Pharos 56K Modem

The Pharos 56K modem (**www.pharosgps.com/products/accessories/ACCESSORIES.htm**) is designed for mobile professionals who want to plug into a land line in order to access the Internet or use a Microsoft Remote Access Server (RAS) to connect into a network with their Pocket PCs. Setup and operation are simple with this modem—as long as you have an ISP to which you can dial up, you should be connected within minutes. The Pharos 56K modem is a Type I CompactFlash card with an integrated RJ-11 phone jack, so there are no external parts to lose. The speed is about what you'd expect from a 56K modem—fast enough for e-mail and instant messaging, but a little slow for Web browsing. If you're looking for a simple way to get connected, this is it.

RoadWired Auto-Retract Network Cord

If you connect your iPAQ to a network with a modem or an Ethernet card, you'll need a cable to do it. And when it comes to mobility, there's no better cable than the RoadWired Auto-Retract Network Cord (**www.roadwired.com/store/Product.cfm?categoryid=8&Productid=41**). It's a small black case, 4×2.75×0.75 inches in size, that weighs in at 3.5 ounces. The 7-foot CAT 5e cable has a three-piece adapter making it easy to switch the cable from Ethernet to standard phone line use. The pieces to the adapter fit in a housing on the body of the case, making it a compact, all-in-one solution for carrying both Ethernet and standard phone line cable with you.

Belkin Power Charger and Sync Cable Combo

The Belkin USB Sync Charger for iPAQ (**www.belkin.com**) is one of the most useful accessories that I use. It enables me to travel without having to carry my sync cradle and charger, because it replaces both. It will perform full syncing from my USB port and also charge my iPAQ from my laptop battery or AC power supply. In addition to this, it comes with a cigarette lighter adapter, which enables me to charge my iPAQ from my car as I move around. It fits the 31*xx* to 37*xx* series iPAQs, but will not fit the charger on the 38*xx* series units (they are supposed to be bringing one of these to market, but so far, no sign of it).

PDAmotion PowerSync Autosync/Charger Cable

Made for the 31*xx* and 36*xx* series iPAQs (not the newest 37*xx* and 38*xx* series devices), the PowerSync Autosync/Charger Cable from PDAmotion (**www.pdamotion.com**) is a great accessory for the mobile worker. Instead of purchasing a second cradle and power adapter for your iPAQ, you can lighten your load and carry only a single USB cable. This PDAmotion cable enables you to synchronize your Pocket PC with any USB-equipped PC, and it also charges it. It clears up desk clutter and is superb for traveling. The cable is 4 feet long and weighs practically nothing. And remember that you can get power from any USB port—a laptop, a Mac, or even a PC running Linux. Whenever I travel, this cable comes with me—it's a must-have accessory for anyone who travels with an iPAQ and has a notebook they can charge it from. The AC adapter is one less thing to carry!

Expansion Sleeves

Expansion sleeves are essential for anyone who wants to use their iPAQ as more than just an electronic day timer. They allow you to connect a wide variety of accessories and tools such as CompactFlash cards, PCMCIA cards, and the like, or can turn your iPAQ into a digital camera, Global Positioning System or more.

We will cover the following products:

- PDAmotion Silver Slider
- Compaq CompactFlash Sleeve
- Compaq PCMCIA Sleeve
- Compaq Dual PCMCIA Sleeve

PDAmotion Silver Slider

The Compaq iPAQ Pocket PC is one of the slimmest, best-looking Pocket PCs around. But it's also one of the only Pocket PCs without a CompactFlash slot, requiring a CompactFlash sleeve in order to access the cards. The problem? The default CompactFlash sleeve from Compaq is quite bulky and doesn't match the silver hue of your Pocket PC. The solution is the Silver Slider (**www.pdamotion.com**)—a sleek, stylish sleeve made by PDAmotion. It adds a mere 0.18 inches to the thickness of the iPAQ, compared with the 0.43 inches of the regular Compaq CompactFlash sleeve. Weighing only 2.3 ounces, it adds very little to the weight of your iPAQ. It's also compatible with all series of iPAQs. If you routinely use CompactFlash

15

cards with your iPAQ, the Silver Slider is a must-have accessory—it's well-designed, inexpensive, and will make your iPAQ even more useful.

Compaq CompactFlash Sleeve

Out of the box, your iPAQ can't use CompactFlash cards. Why is this a problem you might ask? CompactFlash cards are the most common form of removable storage cards on the market today, found in digital cameras, PDAs, MP3 players, and more. In addition to storage, other communication devices such as modems and wireless LAN cards are in CompactFlash format. If you want to increase the usability of your iPAQ, a CompactFlash sleeve (**www.compaq.com/ products/handhelds/pocketpc/options/expansion_packs.html**) is a must. The question is, should you get the Compaq branded sleeve? At 5.13×3.38×1.0 inches, it's not small. The Silver Slider is a much better option for looks and size, but the Compaq product is more reliable and easier to find.

Compaq PCMCIA Sleeve

PCMCIA cards, sometimes called "PC cards," are an aging format most commonly used with laptops. Pocket PCs have several things in common with laptops, so it wasn't surprising that some companies started writing software drivers for their PCMCIA cards so that Pocket PC owners could use them. Because the iPAQ, like most Pocket PCs, doesn't have a built-in PCMCIA slot, you'll need a PCMCIA sleeve in order to use the cards. The Compaq PCMCIA sleeve (called the PC Card Expansion Pack) is a good solution (**www.compaq.com/products/ handhelds/pocketpc/options/expansion_packs.html**), offering a second battery, which greatly extends the life of your iPAQ when using PCMCIA cards (which are very power-hungry). At 5.13×3.38×1.25 inches, it adds significant bulk to your iPAQ. I tend to use mine only when traveling, because the extra battery lets me listen to more music off my Microdrive.

　　Day to day, I find it far too bulky to bring with me. Yet for some, this is an absolute necessity. Some products, like the Sierra AirCard 300 CDPD wireless modem, haven't yet been released in CompactFlash format. If you absolutely need to use a PCMCIA card, pick up the Compaq PCMCIA sleeve. Otherwise, stick to CompactFlash sleeves and the Silver Slider sleeve.

Compaq Dual PCMCIA Sleeve

Take the Compaq PCMCIA sleeve, add another slot, another battery, add another 3/4 of an inch, and you have the Compaq dual PCMCIA sleeve (called the Dual-Slot PC Card Expansion Pack) (**www.compaq.com/products/handhelds/pocketpc/options/expansion_packs.html**). There's no nice way to say it: This sleeve is huge! Measuring 5.13×3.38×1.8 inches, it makes your iPAQ look and feel like a small brick. But talk about options! With a second battery, this sleeve will massively extend the battery life of your iPAQ. And the ability to use two PCMCIA slots at once is very beneficial in some cases, specifically product demonstrations. With an 802.11b wireless LAN card in one slot, and a VGA output card in another, you'd be able to interact with your device wirelessly while showing it in a demo to others. This is the most common scenario I've seen this sleeve used in—it gives presenters many options when performing a demo. It can also accept one of the more rare Type III PCMCIA cards. Beyond that, the sheer size makes it all but useless in day-to-day life. At nearly 2 inches thick, you'd be hard pressed to carry an iPAQ in this sleeve with any sort of comfort level. Yet for people that rely on functionality more than size, the Compaq Dual PCMCIA Sleeve is an unbeatable option.

Keyboards, Styluses, and Input Accessories

Many accessories have been designed to make it easier to input data into your iPAQ, or to simply add some pizzazz to the way that you do it.

We will discuss the following products:

- Think Outside Stowaway Keyboard
- Snap-N-Type Keyboard
- Compaq Micro Keyboard
- Daughter Judie Silver Stylus

Targus / Think Outside Stowaway Keyboard

If you've used your iPAQ for a while now, you've likely come to realize that it's a very capable device—straight out of the box, it has a flexible set of features that let you do what you need to do. But what about data entry? The handwriting recognition of Transcriber works quite well under most circumstances, but for extended data entry, handwriting recognition is a slow process at best, and a hand-cramping painful one at worst. The keyboard is the standard method of data entry for most of us on our desktop and laptop computers, and anyone who writes more than ten e-mail messages a day will type faster than they can write.

The engineers at Think Outside knew this and developed a type of keyboard that balances the needs of data entry and portability: the Stowaway Keyboard (**www.thinkoutside.com/ products/ipaq-oview.html**), shown in Figure 15-6. Unlike the tiny hunt and peck keyboards on some PDAs with keyboards, when you attach a Stowaway Keyboard to your iPAQ you have a 100 percent, full-sized keyboard. It has great tactile response, and it's easy to type quickly on it, and with no batteries or cables to worry about, it's easy to set up and use. The keyboard folds up into a rectangle roughly the same size as your iPAQ, and weighs less than half a pound. I can't say enough about the construction of the keyboard—it has a metal casing and after more than a year of using various Stowaway keyboards with Pocket PCs, I've never encountered a problem with any of them. If you want to leave your laptop at the office for a business trip, the Stowaway Keyboard is a must-have accessory.

| FIGURE 15-6 | The Stowaway keyboard is invaluable for doing lots of data input on the road. |

TT Tec Snap-N-Type Keyboard

The Snap-N-Type Keyboard from TT Tec (**www.pocketpcfanatic.com/detail.asp?PRODUCT_ID=TT301**) is an innovative accessory for your iPAQ Pocket PC that enhances your ability to input information. For most of us, no matter how good we get with Transcriber, using a keyboard will still be faster. Unlike the Targus Stowaway keyboard, which is designed to be carried with you and set up when you stop moving, the Snap-N-Type keyboard is designed to be kept on your iPAQ while you're on the go. Each has its uses, but if you're looking to make your mobile life easier, the Snap-N-Type keyboard may be the best solution for you.

Like a CompactFlash sleeve, it slides onto your iPAQ to give added functionality. The keyboard slides onto the bottom of the iPAQ, covering the buttons and control pad. It's compatible with some iPAQ sleeves—I found that it slipped over the Compaq CompactFlash card sleeve very easily, but there was too much movement when I put it over the Silver Slider from PDAmotion. It draws power from the iPAQ's main battery, so although it's convenient that it doesn't require batteries, keep this battery drain in mind when you're using it with your iPAQ. The keyboard is compatible with the 36*xx* and 37*xx* series iPAQs, but not the 38*xx* series.

Compaq Micro Keyboard

The Compaq Micro Keyboard (**www.compaq.com/products/handhelds/pocketpc/options/ keyboards.html**), as shown in Figure 15-7, snaps right onto the bottom of your iPAQ, allowing you to type text using the tiny keyboard. This is very convenient and easy to adapt to, although the keyboard itself is arced downward like a smile rather than arced upward like a frown, as the keyboards on the popular Research In Motion Blackberries are. The Blackberry keyboard is much easier to use with the upward arc, but I've learned that they hold a patent on this design, and that is why Compaq's features a downward arc. I am sure that you could adjust to either one, but I find the Compaq keyboard harder to use.

FIGURE 15-7   The Micro Keyboard is useful for entering text without having to resort to the stylus.

Daughter Judie Silver Stylus

Only for the most serious iPAQ aficionados, the Daughter Judie Silver Stylus (**www.styluscentral. com/daugjudsters.html**) is a sterling silver replica of the iPAQ stylus, designed to fit in the stylus slot of your 36*xx* or 37*xx* series iPAQs (it will not work in the 38*xx* series iPAQs). Weighing a hefty 23 grams, the stylus is much heavier than the standard iPAQ stylus. Far from being a hindrance, the added heft of the Silver Stylus improves control of the tool. The craftsmanship is wonderful, and if you're willing to pay the price, this is a great add-on for your iPAQ.

15

Cases

A case is an essential accessory to protect your iPAQ from bumps, dust, scratches, and more while you carry it around. Some cases also have options for snapping the iPAQ onto your belt or briefcase.

We will take a look at the following products:

- iHolster
- Vaja Cases
- PDA Jacket
- HandheldPlanet Flip-top iPAQ 38*xx* Case
- Compaq Rugged Case
- Rhino Skin Aluminum Slider Case

iHolster

We found the iHolster (**www.iproductsonline.net/iHolsterIV.htm**) to be a fantastic case for the iPAQ. It clips onto your belt, and the iPAQ slides easily into its form-fitting molded Kydex sleeve. When you need your iPAQ, you simply "quick draw" it out of the holster, and it is ready to use. The holster stays clipped onto your belt. It provides excellent protection for the screen, and the sturdy construction means that your iPAQ won't get accidentally turned on by applying pressure to the case, which can happen with many other cases. This holster fits all models of the iPAQ with almost any kind of expansion sleeve attached. It is not designed for the "naked" iPAQ because it would be too loose in the holster; however, if you don't use an expansion sleeve, you can use the sleeve blank/port protector that comes with the iPAQ to make it fit the holster properly.

Vaja Cases

Your iPAQ Pocket PC is an investment worth protecting, so having a case is important. And for the best-looking cases, look no further than Argentina-based Vaja (**www.vajacases.com**). They make a wide variety of PDA and cell phone cases, but their iPAQ cases are the most beautiful examples of their craftsmanship. With a variety of choices for both leather and color, Vaja cases look like nothing else on the market. In addition to cow leather, in the past Vaja has offered ostrich, buffalo, alligator, and Dundee. With more than 20 color choices for the custom cases, you can create a truly unique case for your iPAQ.

Vaja has made an assortment of cases designed to work with various iPAQ sleeves, including the PCMCIA sleeve, CompactFlash sleeve, and even the massive dual PCMCIA sleeve. Vaja also has an interesting option for personalization—certain Vaja cases can be ordered with a custom logo, offering companies a great way to extend their corporate branding. Other models include options for belt clips, wallets, Secure Digital (SD) card slots, cushioned covers, and business card holders. Vaja cases are among the most expensive on the market, but they are peerless in both design and quality.

PDA Jacket

Ever felt like spicing up your iPAQ Pocket PC with a little personality? A PDA Jacket (**www.pdajacket.com**) is the solution. Made of a smooth plastic, PDA Jackets are available in 13 different colors ranging from aqua to pink. In addition to being available for the iPAQ Pocket PC itself, you can also purchase PDA Jackets for the iPAQ CompactFlash and PCMCIA sleeves. They even have a PDA Jacket for the Silver Slider sleeve. The purpose of a PDA Jacket is twofold: the first, and most obvious use, is to change the look of your iPAQ. It makes your iPAQ unique, different from the other iPAQs out and about. The jackets are easy to change; you can have a different color iPAQ every week. Second, the PDA Jacket will protect your iPAQ from the minor scratching and body damage that can occur when putting the device in a sleeve. Although the colors are anything but subtle, and might not be appropriate for some business environments, I really enjoyed having an iPAQ that stood out from the rest. The jackets are very affordable, so it's easy to order a few just to experiment with.

HandheldPlanet Flip-top iPAQ 38xx Case

HandheldPlanet is the maker of several iPAQ cases, and its latest creation is made for the 38xx series iPAQ. Similar in design to the Vaja cases, the Flip-top case (**www.handheldplanet.net/detail_compaq_ipaq_38.html**) is an all-leather design with two slots for cards and a larger slot for money or even a memory card or two. It has a snap closure that is very sturdy, and because it contains no magnets, the case is safe for carrying credit cards. An optional belt clip lets you attach the case to your belt for easier carrying. The case is also cut away in various spots, allowing you to charge it, use headphones, and press the voice record button, all without needing to remove the case. The HandheldPlanet cases are well made, and with a retail cost significantly less than that of the Vaja cases, they are a good choice for any iPAQ owner looking for a case that blends style with functionality—as long as you like the color black, because that's your only choice.

NOTE   *Cases are also available for the other models of iPAQs.*

Compaq Rugged Case

The Compaq Rugged Case (**www.compaq.com/products/quickspecs/10971_div/10971_div.HTML**), shown in Figure 15-8, is designed specifically for users who will be putting their iPAQ through environmentally harsh conditions or excessive abuse. It is built to resist damage to the display and resist water and dust contamination. It can enable an iPAQ to withstand an impact from a height of up to 4 feet.

15

FIGURE 15-8   The Compaq Rugged Case will protect your iPAQ from a harsh environment.

This case features a hard cover for the screen that can be raised to expose a clear, soft, plastic membrane allowing you to still interact with the iPAQ touch screen. This membrane is also designed to be replaced; so if it gets damaged during use, you can simply insert a replacement membrane.

This case will fit all versions of the iPAQ, including the most recent models. If you are at all concerned about destroying your iPAQ given your work conditions, this case is a very worthwhile investment.

Rhino Skin Aluminum Slider Case

The Rhino Skin aluminum case (**www.rhinoskin.com/perl-bin/safe-shop?std-00130-16**), shown in Figure 15-9, is designed to protect your iPAQ from the abuse it suffers when you toss it into your briefcase, backpack, or car trunk. It features a neoprene interior to absorb shock if you drop it. It is designed specifically for the iPAQ 36xx and 37xx series and does not accommodate any expansion sleeves. Given the wide usage of sleeves, this unfortunately limits the usability of this model of case.

Rhino Skin also makes a number of other accessories for the iPAQ including leather cases and portfolios. Check their website for their latest product offerings.

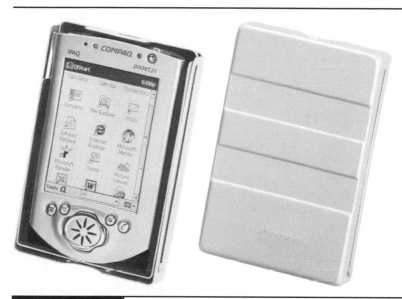

FIGURE 15-9   The Rhino Skin aluminum case is very durable, but unfortunatcly does not accommodate expansion sleeves.

Power Accessories

Although the iPAQ is a wonderful tool, it is a power pig. With its bright color screen, large storage capacity, and other features, the battery isn't as long-lived as we would all like. This section looks at some accessories designed to help with this problem.

We will cover the following products:

■ Electric Fuel Instant Power Batteries

■ DataNation iPowerPak

Electric Fuel Instant Power Batteries

When you're on the go, the last thing you need is for your iPAQ to run out of power. There's not always a power outlet around to plug into, but no matter where you are, there's always one thing: oxygen. The Electric Fuel batteries (**www.instant-power.com/charger/pda/index.shtml**) generate power using oxygen! The innovative zinc-air batteries from Electric Fuel were originally developed for large vehicles like postal vans and transit buses, and even high-powered torpedoes. Nowadays, they focus on mobile devices such as PDAs and cell phones.

15

Operation is simple: you plug the adapter into your iPAQ's power jack, crack the seal on the battery to allow oxygen in, and within seconds you can use your iPAQ while it charges. The powerful 3300 mA batteries will give the iPAQ roughly three full charges before running out of power. These batteries are popular accessories for mobile professionals—toss one in your briefcase just in case, because you never know when you'll need power.

DataNation iPowerPak

No matter how big the battery, at some point it needs to recharge. So, although the 38*xx* series iPAQs have more advanced batteries than the 36*xx* series iPAQs, at some point your battery will run out. For day-to-day recharging you can put the iPAQ in its cradle, but it's a different story when you're sitting in an airport after having used your iPAQ for several hours on the flight. The solution is the iPowerPak (**www.data-nation.com**) from DataNation.

The iPowerPak is a small plastic case that holds four AA batteries. It has a 1-foot long cord that plugs into the power plug of your iPAQ and a simple switch that turns the unit on. While it's plugged in with a fresh set of AA batteries, the battery life of your iPAQ will be roughly doubled. I used this device several times on trips, and it always worked well—until I forgot to bring a screwdriver with me! Swapping in new batteries requires a screwdriver to open the casing, so if you don't have one, you can't put in fresh batteries. That aside, the iPowerPak is a must-have tool for people who do a lot of traveling and are away from power sources.

Storage Accessories

Even with the extensive storage capacity of the iPAQ, for some users it still is not enough! If you want to store several hours of MP3 music, digital photos, design schematics, or perhaps a large set of games for keeping you entertained while traveling, then expanded storage will be essential. In this section we discuss some options for expanded storage.

Let's take a look at the following products:

- Times2 Tech 256MB Internal Memory Expansion
- IBM 1GB Microdrive
- Delkin eFilm 512MB CompactFlash Card
- Addonics Pocket ExDrive

Times2 Tech 256MB Internal Memory Expansion

The 256MB memory upgrade from Times2 Tech (**www.times2tech.com**) is an absolutely amazing upgrade for your iPAQ. This is an internal memory upgrade, so there are no external attachments to worry about. This is done by physically upgrading the memory by "stacking" a new set of memory chips on top of the existing memory on the iPAQ motherboard, as shown in Figure 15-10.

© PCE2000.COM/Times2Tech.COM

FIGURE 15-10   You can upgrade your iPAQ to up to 256MB of internal memory with Times2 Tech.

In order to perform this upgrade, you must send your iPAQ to Times2 Tech, they will perform the upgrade and send the unit back to you. The extra 192MB of memory will show up as an alternative storage location, much like using a CompactFlash card or other external storage.

There is a small cost in terms of battery performance once the upgrade has been carried out. You will lose about 5 percent of the operating time with your current battery, and the suspend time will be reduced from approximately 5 days, to 3–4 days depending on a few external variables.

This upgrade is available for the 36*xx*, 37*xx*, and 38*xx* series iPAQs and is available in the 64MB, 128MB, or 256MB packages.

IBM 1GB Microdrive

Despite its diminutive size, the IBM Microdrive (**www.storage.ibm.com/hdd/micro**) is a real spinning hard drive, rotating at 3600 rpm! Everyone I show this accessory to is amazed that 1GB of data can fit on something so small. The Type II CompactFlash form-factor card will fit in the Compaq CompactFlash sleeve, and it also works in the PDAmotion Silver Slider. The 1GB Microdrive is the cheapest form of storage in the CompactFlash form-factor on a cost-per-megabyte basis, costing around 27 cents per megabyte. It's available in several models: 170, 340, 512, and 1000 MB (1GB). It's worth noting, however, that the 1GB model uses less power than the smaller models, making it the best choice. The Microdrive can be used to store and retrieve any sort of data—after an initial spin-up period of one second or so, the Microdrive functions just like a normal CompactFlash storage card. You can move data to and from it, install programs to it, and play both audio and video files from it. With 1GB of storage, you could fit two entire movies on it!

The downside? Because it has moving parts, the Microdrive is hard on battery life. A fully charged iPAQ 3650 with the screen turned off will play music off the Microdrive for three hours, compared to six hours with standard CompactFlash. Battery life aside, the other issue is fragility—the Microdrive is a spinning hard drive, so while normal use doesn't endanger the

15

Microdrive, dropping it can easily damage it. These issues aside, the IBM 1GB Microdrive is a truly awe-inspiring piece of Pocket PC hardware.

Delkin eFilm 512MB CompactFlash Card

When it comes to Type I cards, the Delkin eFilm 512MB card (**www.delkin.com**) is a great choice. With 512MB of storage, you can store a full two-hour movie, more than 250 songs (over two dozen CDs), or more than a thousand photos. Need to carry huge corporate databases with you? A large CompactFlash card is the answer.

NOTE   *If you're looking for the ultimate in battery-friendly storage, CompactFlash cards are the way to go. With no moving parts, CompactFlash storage is perfect for long battery life on your Pocket PC. There are two kinds of cards: Type I and Type II. Type I cards are thinner than Type II cards, but either size will fit in the CompactFlash sleeves you can get for your iPAQ. For full compatibility with digital cameras and other devices that read the CompactFlash format, it's best to stick with Type I.*

Prices on CompactFlash cards have been falling rapidly this year, making large capacity cards very affordable. There are various brands to choose from—Sandisk, Delkin, Viking, Simple Technologies, and others—but in most cases the performance characteristics are exactly the same. One thing to be aware of is the power consumption: the vast majority of cards function at 3.3 volts, but certain brands (like Mr. Flash) function at 5 volts and will consume your Pocket PC battery much quicker. Stick to 3.3 volts whenever possible. And remember that your memory card can also be used in a digital camera, so buy the biggest size possible—you never know when you're going to need some extra space.

Addonics Pocket ExDrive

Addonics makes a line of innovative external peripherals (**www.addonics.com/products.htm**), from hard drives to external CD writers. The devices that are interesting for iPAQ owners are the external hard drives—would you believe that you can hook up 48GB of storage to your iPAQ Pocket PC? You can! Using the PCMCIA card interface, Addonics has created a very innovative add-on for Pocket PCs. They sell either a casing and cable that allows you to mount your own 2.5-inch hard drive, or a complete package. If you opt for the do-it-yourself route, you can put in any 2.5-inch hard drive, usually found in laptops. An online auction site such as ebay.com is perfect for buying used laptop hard drives. If you purchase their complete package, you'll get either a 20GB or 48GB hard drive, a PCMCIA card with cable, and a driver for your iPAQ. You'll need a PCMCIA sleeve for the iPAQ (sold separately) in order to use this drive.

I have an earlier model, a 6GB drive that also uses the PCMCIA interface. It was a simple matter to install the included drivers, connect it to my iPAQ, and start playing the thousands of MP3s I had put on it. The only drawback to this drive is the power consumption—you can expect to exhaust the battery on the iPAQ PCMCIA sleeve in a few hours, so if you're planning on extended use, consider plugging your iPAQ into the AC charger or getting the Addonics external power supply.

Other Interesting Add-Ons

Many other iPAQ accessories are available that fall outside of the categories we have looked at so far. Here we will examine some other interesting third-party tools.

We'll cover the following products:

- MARGI Presenter-to-Go
- Colorgraphic Voyager VGA
- Microtech MediaVault
- iPocket Bungee
- Kingmax PCMCIA CompactFlash Adapter
- Arkon Multimedia PDA Mount

MARGI Presenter-to-Go

MARGI Presenter-to-Go (**www.margi.com**), shown in Figure 15-11, is a complete end-to-end mobile presentation solution. Although more expensive than competing products, Presenter-to-Go offers a great deal of value for mobile professionals. The software that installs on the desktop computer allows the user to create content from any application easily—you can transfer PowerPoint slides, Word documents, and anything else that supports printing. On the Pocket PC, the presentation software supports displaying speaker notes, easy slide reordering, and a feature that allows everything on the iPAQ to be projected out (which is great for training or demos). Once a slide is created, however, you can't change the contents of the slide—it's important to ensure your slides are perfect before exporting them.

The CompactFlash card is Type I, outputs a VGA signal at 8-bit (256 colors) and 1024×768 resolution. Visually, the quality of the project images and text is impressive. Although 8-bit color would appear to be a significant limitation, MARGI does some interesting things with its software to make the photos look quite good. Text is sharp and easy to read, and images look great. Once the presentation is started, the included infrared remote enables you to advance from slide to slide, or jump to a specific slide. The range of the remote is limited, however, so you need to be close to your Pocket PC in order to use it. Overall, the MARGI Presenter-to-Go solution is perfect for mobile professionals who need to give presentations and would like to leave the laptop behind.

15

FIGURE 15-11   If you need to show PowerPoint slides from your iPAQ, try the
MARGI Presenter-to-Go.

Colorgraphic Voyager VGA

Colorgraphic (**www.colorgraphic.net**) was the first company to have a VGA out solution for
the Pocket PC in the form of its PCMCIA card, and that has evolved into the powerful
CompactFlash VGA out card available today. Unlike the MARGI Presenter-to-Go offering, the
Colorgraphic card, shown in Figure 15-12, doesn't ship with presentation software or a remote
control—the real focus is the card itself. Unlike some other products on the market, the Voyager
card is a Type I CompactFlash card, which means it can work in a greater variety of Pocket
PCs. If you own other Pocket PCs (such as the HP Jornada) or share hardware in your office
with other Pocket PC owners, this is a great advantage. The card offers 16-bit color at 640×480
and 800×600 with an additional 8-bit color setting for 1024×768.

In addition to the VGA out, the Voyager also offers S-video and composite outputs,
making it easy to connect to a television set or VCR. Text and image output look great
with this card, making it a valuable tool when you want to leave that laptop behind for
presentations.

FIGURE 15-12   The Colorgraphic Voyager VGA card will allow you to output your iPAQ screen to any VGA device like a monitor or projector.

Microtech MediaVault

If you've made an investment in CompactFlash and PCMCIA cards, you should protect them. I've seen several types of cases for these cards, but most provide little to no protection. The Microtech MediaVault (**www.microtechint.com/qs-mediavault.html**) is a product that offers superb protection to the cards. With a brushed aluminum casing and shock-absorbing design, the MediaVault looks great as it's protecting your cards. And according to the company's website, the case also protects against airport X-rays, RFI (Radio Frequency Interference), and electromagnetic damage. The model I had would store two CompactFlash cards and a PCMCIA card. I'd typically use it to carry two CompactFlash memory cards, and the Microdrive inserted into the PCMCIA adapter. Because of the form-fitted slots, there's no "slack" space, meaning it won't carry items such as CompactFlash modems that have built-in dongles or jacks. It will, however, carry cards, such as the Socket Communications Bluetooth card, that don't have any exterior add-ons.

Microtech also offers MediaVault models for Secure Digital (SD) or multimedia cards. Overall, the MediaVault is an excellent accessory that enables you to carry your cards in a protected and stylish manner.

iPocket Bungee

Not all good ideas need to be complex: the iPocket Bungee (**www.ipocketbungee.com**) is a remarkably simple concept that, for some, is a very useful tool. The premise behind the

15

iPocket Bungee is simple: it prevents you from dropping your Pocket PC. The implementation is more interesting. The strap goes around your wrist, made up of a stretchy material that has the consistency of spandex. It's attached to a cable that ends in a metal coil. This cable runs down the side of an iPAQ in a normal Compaq sleeve (CompactFlash or PCMCIA sleeves, not Silver Slider), with the metal coil sticking out the bottom. It's held firmly in place by the pressure of the iPAQ in the sleeve, allowing you to drop the iPAQ and have it bounce back at you. Although I personally didn't find this useful in day-to-day life, I can see how it could be a great asset if you have to hold your iPAQ in your hands all day and dropping it is a distinct possibility.

Kingmax PCMCIA CompactFlash Adapter

Although CompactFlash cards are common to devices like Pocket PCs and digital cameras, most laptops and desktops don't have slots included for reading them. And though it's possible to find USB-based external CompactFlash readers, a cheaper and simpler solution for working with laptops is a PCMCIA CompactFlash Adapter. These inexpensive devices sometimes come with CompactFlash cards and are indispensable for moving data from a Pocket PC to a laptop and back again. When you put a CompactFlash card into a PCMCIA adapter, and then insert it into the laptop's PCMCIA slot, your CompactFlash card can be accessed as if it were a normal hard drive. No drivers are required, and the entire process is completely Plug and Play. In fact, when you get right down to it, a CompactFlash card in a PCMCIA adapter can function exactly like an extra-large 3.5-inch floppy drive, enabling you to move data back and forth with ease. Moving data to and from a CompactFlash card in this way is faster than installing ActiveSync on a laptop and connecting your Pocket PC or even communicating via infrared. A great place to purchase PCMCIA CompactFlash adapters is online auctions sites such as ebay.com.

Arkon Multimedia PDA Mount

Using your iPAQ while in your car can be a challenge, not to mention a safety hazard. Arkon (**www.arkon.com/expansionsleeve.html**) has produced a series of mounting brackets for PDAs that enable you to put your PDA into your vehicle so that it doesn't slide around the passenger seat (and slide under) when you take a corner. These brackets also enable you to see your driving directions if you are using a GPS unit. There is even a version that plugs into your iPAQ headphone jack and sends the music signals to your FM radio, enabling you to listen to your MP3 music files on your car radio as you drive! There are versions that will attach to your windshield, your cup holder, your vent, or for extra stability, bolt onto your dash. I have enjoyed using the version that holds both an iPAQ and a cell phone so that they don't slide around while I drive. My only problem with the unit was that in cold weather (like we get up north here) the suction cups on the windshield tend to come unstuck. I am looking forward to trying the latest version with one large suction cup instead of the three to see if that works any better.

Part IV

Appendices

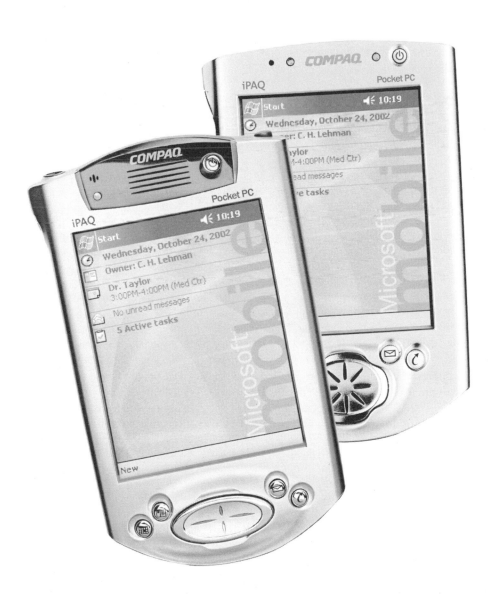

Appendix A

Troubleshooting iPAQ Pocket PC Problems

In this appendix, we will list some of the iPAQ problems that you may encounter and suggest ways to resolve these problems. This list is not a comprehensive. If you encounter an issue that isn't covered here, try the websites listed in Appendix B as resources.

Hardware Problems

Problem	Solution
After a hard reset my iPAQ 38xx does not restore my Contacts and Appointments automatically, even though I have selected both in the Permanent PIM settings.	Unfortunately, the restore of this information after a full reset does not occur automatically on the 38xx series iPAQs. The Permanent PIM check boxes will need to be re-enabled before the restoration of Contacts and Appointments will take place. To re-enable the check boxes, perform the following steps: 1. Tap Start. 2. Tap Settings. 3. Tap System. 4. Tap Permanent PIM. 5. Select both check boxes to restore your Contacts and Appointments.
I plugged the AC power adapter into my cradle while my iPAQ was in it, and now it won't talk to my PC.	This can happen if power is inserted in the middle of an ActiveSync synchronization. Your iPAQ and all other devices on the same USB chain will disconnect from your PC. This usually only occurs on the iPAQ models prior to the 37xx series and can be corrected by installing a driver update available from Compaq at **www.compaq.com/support/ files/handhelds/us/index.html**.
When I tap on the screen, where I tap doesn't produce the results I expect. It is as though I am tapping somewhere else.	Your touch screen is likely out of alignment. From the main drop-down menu, tap Settings. From the Settings folder that appears, select Screen. You will see a button to align the screen. If you are able to, tap the button; if not, press the control disc on the iPAQ, and the align process will begin. If the calibration is so badly out of alignment that you can't get to the alignment screen, install one of the desktop remote control applications mentioned in Chapter 10 and navigate to it from your desktop. As a last resort, you can hard reset the device—the calibration screen is part of the hard reset process.
When I turn my 38xx iPAQ with a Secure Digital card on, it waits before the system starts up.	There is a problem with the SecureDigital slot on the iPAQ. If this problem occurs, eject the SD card and then re-insert it.

ActiveSync Problems

Problem	Solution
After a hard reset, ActiveSync insists on creating a new partnership. What do I do?	Sometimes after a hard reset, ActiveSync thinks you have a new device. Go ahead and create the new partnership. You will need to set up your preferences in ActiveSync on your PC, but after that, everything will behave as normal. If you've changed the name of the device, and you already have a partnership under that name, you'll need to delete the partnership (File | Delete Partnership) before you can create a new partnership under that device name. Remember to select No when prompted to delete your synchronized files!
The ActiveSync connection will not immediately disconnect on the host PC when the Disconnect button is selected from the connection icon on the iPAQ.	This is a known issue with ActiveSync. There is no resolution. Usually the disconnect will occur between 30 seconds and two minutes after you select Disconnect.
ActiveSync does not connect to the iPAQ when it is in the cradle.	Sometimes ActiveSync will not connect to the iPAQ or will not see the iPAQ. The only way to fix this problem is to stop ActiveSync and then restart it. To do this, perform the following steps on your ActiveSync computer: 1. Press CTRL-ALT-DEL on your computer. 2. Click on the Task Manager button. 3. Choose the Processes tab. 4. Find and end the WCESMgr.exe and wcescomm.exe processes. 5. Run ActiveSync again.

Software Problems

Problem	Solution
When I have a voice recording in a note, tapping on the recording doesn't play the recording on my 38xx series iPAQ.	This is a known problem affecting only the 38xx series iPAQs. In order to play this recording, perform the following steps: 1. Tap Edit in the bottom-left corner of the taskbar. 2. Tap the Notes tab. 3. Tap the Recording Icon. This will begin playing the recorded message.

A

Problem	Solution
Duplicate icons appear on the iPAQ after restoring programs from backup.	To remove the duplicate icon, perform the following steps: 1. Tap Start. 2. Tap Programs. 3. Tap File Explorer. 4. Tap the My Documents folder and change the name to My Device folder. 5. Tap the Windows folder. 6. Tap the Start Menu folder. 7. Tap the Settings folder. 8. Delete the duplicate icons by holding the stylus on the duplicate and choosing delete. 9. Exit File Explorer. 10. Perform a normal reset by pressing the stylus into the hole on the bottom of the unit.
I accidentally deleted one of the built-in programs. How do I get it back?	You can recover an accidentally deleted built-in program by performing a hard reset of your device.
I cannot connect to my MSN account to retrieve e-mail.	This problem affects 36*xx* and 31*xx* series iPAQs and occurs because an MSN account requires that a special file be loaded on the iPAQ. This file can be obtained from Microsoft at **www.microsoft.com/mobile/pocketpc/downloads/msnsspc.asp**. Note that if you perform a hard reset of your iPAQ, you will need to reinstall this file. After downloading the file, you will need to install it on your iPAQ by running the file **msnsspc.exe**. Once the file is installed, you will need to provide the following information: 1. The MSN dial-up number: Your local number can be found at **http://supportservices.msn.com/us/phoneaccess.asp**. 2. MSN's POP3 server name: pop3.email.msn.com 3. MSN's SMTP server name: secure.smtp.email.msn.com
I installed a third-party game or application for my iPAQ that requires me to press two or more hardware buttons simultaneously, but it doesn't seem to work.	The iPAQ 36*xx* and 31*xx* series were not designed to allow more than one hardware button to be pressed at the same time, so this function of your game/application will not work on the 36*xx* and 31*xx* iPAQs.

Appendix B

Where to Go for More Information

For the iPAQ owner, there are many sources of interesting information about your device and some of the amazing things (and some not so amazing things) you can do with your device. In this list of references you will find information ranging from the practical, such as troubleshooting tips for when your iPAQ won't power on, to the zany, such as determining how well the iPAQ Bluetooth module communicates when immersed under water in a Ziploc bag.

We have categorized the information sources by type and given a brief description of what you can expect to find at each of these sources. The number of potential information sources is growing so fast that there is no way that we can possibly list them all here. At **www.PocketPCTools.com** we will be hosting an extension to this appendix that will attempt to maintain a comprehensive list of all the information sources where you can get details on your iPAQ and related products.

Websites

The number of websites related to Pocket PCs is becoming incredibly large. A few of the most popular or unique are listed here, along with a brief list at the end of some more sites you may like to check out.

www.pocketpcthoughts.com

Pocket PC Thoughts is a site run by Jason Dunn and a few of his selected contributors. It is one of the most popular websites visited by Pocket PC enthusiasts. It is a day-by-day log of new information or interesting ideas related to the Pocket PC world, rather like an online newsletter for Pocket PC users. The information you will find on this site is usually brief (with links to more detail) and very informative.

www.pocketpcpassion.com

This site is run by Dale Coffing and is also among the most popular of the Pocket PC sites. It also follows a newsletter format with regular postings by Dale of his experiences with the Pocket PC (which are *very* extensive). Dale attends most of the major trade shows and often can be found working in the Microsoft booth. He is not a Microsoft employee, but works closely with Microsoft to ensure that he is on top of all of the latest information for the Pocket PC. This is a very well-presented and informative site for the Pocket PC user.

www.PocketPCTools.com

This site takes a different approach to giving you information on the Pocket PC and aims to be complementary to sites such as the first two on this list. It is a database of tools, software, accessories, and everything that you can possibly attach to your Pocket PC. Many of the products are reviewed so that you can see information on their usability, durability, and so on. You can also find out about books and other sources of information and news on your iPAQ or any Pocket PC.

This site is maintained in part by the two authors of this book, Derek Ball and Barry Shilmover. You may also refer to this site for materials supplementary to this book such as updates to this appendix and other goodies for iPAQ owners.

www.pocketpc.com (www.microsoft.com/mobile/pocketpc)

This site is the official website from Microsoft about the Pocket PC. It has information about the Pocket PC operating system, hardware, software, and accessories. The most useful attributes of this site for the new Pocket PC owner are probably the online tutorials and support (found under the Club Pocket PC section).

www.cewindows.net

Chris De Herrera is the webmaster of this site. He has been working with Windows CE in its various incarnations for more than five years and has a tremendous depth of experience. On his site you will find essays on the different versions of Windows CE, help for the beginning Pocket PC user, reviews and commentary on popular Pocket PC products, as well as lists of known bugs on these platforms.

www.davescompaqipaq.com

Wow! A site dedicated solely to your new iPAQ. In a newsletter format, this site presents new information on software, hardware, and other news that is of specific interest to you, the iPAQ owner. You can find out where to buy the cheapest iPAQ, where to obtain the must-have software for your device, and more. This site is run by Dave Ciccone, who also writes for *Pocket PC* magazine (mentioned below).

www.the-gadgeteer.com

This site is dedicated to reviewing hardware gadgets, mostly but not exclusively, for handheld devices. The site contains a lot of material related to your iPAQ. The reviews are unbiased and usually an interesting read. If you are thinking of acquiring a gizmo for your iPAQ, check the review in *The Gadgeteer*.

www.movilpro.com

A site for the Spanish-speaking Pocket PC user. Neither of us speak Spanish, so we can't tell you much about the site.

B

www.cebeans.com

This site contains a library of unsupported Pocket PC freeware (software that you can use for free!), which you can download for your Pocket PC.

Other Websites

There is a large number of other sites that we wanted to list that have relevant information for the iPAQ owner. They do not get as much traffic, or aren't as well known as the ones we've listed previously, but they are worth checking out just the same.

General, News, and Reviews

This set of websites are focused on general information, news, and product reviews that are relevant for either the Pocket PC world, or the world of mobile computing in general.

www.pocketnow.com	www.pocketpchow2.com
www.pocketpcminds.com	www.ppcsg.com
www.brighthand.com	www.cewire.com
www.pocketpccity.com	www.tekguru.co.uk
www.pocketpclife.co.uk	www.pocketpcpower.net
www.pdagold.com	www.pocketpcwriter.net
www.winceonline.com	www.wiredguy.com
www.pocketpcaddict.com	www.ludipocket.com (French site)

Software

These sites are focused solely on software. Some are for Pocket PCs only, others have software for a variety of handhelds and mobile devices. Most of the sites have a mixture of freeware, shareware, and trial software. Sites like Handango actually sell the software, and Cnet has free downloads.

www.pocketpcsoft.net

www.pocketpcfreedom.com

www.pocketpcfreewares.net (French site)

home.cearchives.com

http://download.cnet.com (select Windows CE applications)

www.handango.com/

http://pda.tucows.com/cesoft.html

www.ppc4all.com

www.pocketgamer.org

www.airgamer.com

Other

This section contains sites that didn't fit into any of the previous categories. They have some information that will be relevant to the iPAQ owner.

www.pocketpcthemes.com

www.pocketthemes.com

www.pocketgear.com

Magazines

There are no magazines focused solely on the iPAQ, but you can find magazines that are focused on either the Pocket PC or on the world of mobile computing. A few of the more popular ones are listed here.

Pocket PC Magazine

Published by Thaddeus Computing, *Pocket PC* magazine is focused purely on the Pocket PC world and is chock full of useful information, news, and reviews of materials that will (usually) run on your iPAQ. They also have a website, but it does not contain the full version of the magazine (although you can buy an online electronic subscription). You can find them at **www.pocketpcmag.com**.

Pen Computing Magazine

Pen Computing is focused on the world of mobile computing in general. It always contains information relevant to the Pocket PC and iPAQ world, but it also deals with Palm and much more. They have a website as well, but it does not contain the full version of the magazine. Look for them at **www.pencomputing.com**.

Conferences

Conferences are always an interesting place where you can get up-to-date information on the Pocket PC world and meet other enthusiasts who use iPAQs and Pocket PCs. They can be a little expensive, but usually the exhibit halls are free if there is one in your general vicinity.

B

Pocket PC Summit

The Pocket PC Summit is an annual conference focused solely on the Pocket PC platform. It features a variety of tracks that might be of interest but is focused largely on the enterprise user of Pocket PC devices. Full information can be found on their website at **www.pocketpcsummit.com**.

Comdex

The main Comdex conference is held annually in Las Vegas. It is a huge conference related to everything in the high-tech industry. It is very broad, but Pocket PCs (and iPAQs) are becoming a larger part of the show every year. There are smaller regional versions of this show held in Vancouver, Toronto, Chicago, and Atlanta. The organizers of this conference have now gone global and are holding Comdexes in Greece, Scandinavia, Australia, Saudi Arabia, China, Egypt, Mexico, Japan, Korea, Switzerland, France, and more. More information can be found at **www.comdex.com**.

Mobile Insights

Mobile Insights, a consulting firm out of Mountain View, California, holds this annual conference, which focuses on the current and future trends in the wireless and mobile computing industries. More information is available at **www.mobileinsights.com/mi2002**.

Pocket PC New York

The Pocket PC New York conference was held in conjunction with the Internet World Wireless conference in New York in 2002. It intends to address the Pocket PC 2002 platform and the devices and applications that will redefine mobile computing in the enterprise market. This dedicated conference provides comprehensive insight, strategies, solutions, vendor support, and development knowledge for the Pocket PC mobile platform. From security, virtual private networking, Windows terminal server, instant messaging, and back-office integration, to advanced development tools, Pocket PC New York addresses all of the important issues driving the adoption of Pocket PC devices and applications within business today. For more information visit **www.pocketpcny.com**.

Hardware Vendors

Many vendors produce hardware for the iPAQ, and the number is increasing daily. For further news on iPAQ compatible hardware, visit **www.PocketPCTools.com,** where we will endeavor to keep an up-to-date database of all the hardware vendors that carry products compatible with your iPAQ.

www.compaq.com

Compaq will of course be an excellent source of information for the iPAQ owner. At the Compaq website you can read any advisories or notices that Compaq feels are of importance to iPAQ owners specifically. You can also elect to have these notices sent to you by e-mail when they are released. You can download drivers, get technical support, and access a whole database of useful information about the iPAQ.

www.sierrawireless.com

Sierra Wireless is the manufacturer of PCMCIA card wireless modems for your iPAQ. You can get information on their AirCard line of modems on their website, as well as download up-to-date drivers for their hardware. Sierra Wireless produces wireless modems for the CDPD, CDMA, and GPRS wireless data networks.

www.novatelwireless.com

Novatel is another manufacturer of PCMCIA card wireless modems for your iPAQ. Their line of modems are known as the Merlin modems. They have modems for CDMA 1xRTT, CDPD, and GSM/GPRS. They have also produced an integrated GSM/GPRS card that can act as a cell phone, allowing a standard iPAQ with a PCMCIA card expansion sleeve to be both your data device and your cellular mobile phone.

Index

N

S

INTERNATIONAL CONTACT INFORMATION

AUSTRALIA
McGraw-Hill Book Company Australia Pty. Ltd.
TEL +61-2-9417-9899
FAX +61-2-9417-5687
http://www.mcgraw-hill.com.au
books-it_sydney@mcgraw-hill.com

CANADA
McGraw-Hill Ryerson Ltd.
TEL +905-430-5000
FAX +905-430-5020
http://www.mcgrawhill.ca

**GREECE, MIDDLE EAST,
NORTHERN AFRICA**
McGraw-Hill Hellas
TEL +30-1-656-0990-3-4
FAX +30-1-654-5525

MEXICO (Also serving Latin America)
McGraw-Hill Interamericana Editores S.A. de C.V.
TEL +525-117-1583
FAX +525-117-1589
http://www.mcgraw-hill.com.mx
fernando_castellanos@mcgraw-hill.com

SINGAPORE (Serving Asia)
McGraw-Hill Book Company
TEL +65-863-1580
FAX +65-862-3354
http://www.mcgraw-hill.com.sg
mghasia@mcgraw-hill.com

SOUTH AFRICA
McGraw-Hill South Africa
TEL +27-11-622-7512
FAX +27-11-622-9045
robyn_swanepoel@mcgraw-hill.com

**UNITED KINGDOM & EUROPE
(Excluding Southern Europe)**
McGraw-Hill Publishing Company
TEL +44-1-628-502500
FAX +44-1-628-770224
http://www.mcgraw-hill.co.uk
computing_neurope@mcgraw-hill.com

ALL OTHER INQUIRIES Contact:
Osborne/McGraw-Hill
TEL +1-510-549-6600
FAX +1-510-883-7600
http://www.osborne.com
omg_international@mcgraw-hill.com